Kierkegaard and Philosophical Eros

Also Available at Bloomsbury

Kierkegaard: Existence and Identity in a Post-Secular World, Alastair Hannay
Kierkegaard and the Question Concerning Technology, Christopher B. Barnett
Authorship and Authority in Kierkegaard's Writings, ed. Joseph Westfall

Kierkegaard and Philosophical Eros

Between Ironic Reflection and Aesthetic Meaning

Ulrika Carlsson

BLOOMSBURY ACADEMIC
LONDON • NEW YORK • OXFORD • NEW DELHI • SYDNEY

BLOOMSBURY ACADEMIC
Bloomsbury Publishing Plc
50 Bedford Square, London, WC1B 3DP, UK
1385 Broadway, New York, NY 10018, USA
29 Earlsfort Terrace, Dublin 2, Ireland

BLOOMSBURY, BLOOMSBURY ACADEMIC and the Diana logo
are trademarks of Bloomsbury Publishing Plc

First published in Great Britain 2021
This paperback edition published in 2022

Copyright © Ulrika Carlsson, 2021

Ulrika Carlsson has asserted her right under the Copyright, Designs and Patents Act, 1988, to be identified as Author of this work.

For legal purposes the Acknowledgments on p. viii constitute an extension of this copyright page

Cover design by Charlotte Daniels
Cover image © Ludmila Carlsson

All rights reserved. No part of this publication may be reproduced or transmitted in any form or by any means, electronic or mechanical, including photocopying, recording, or any information storage or retrieval system, without prior permission in writing from the publishers.

Bloomsbury Publishing Plc does not have any control over, or responsibility for, any third-party websites referred to or in this book. All internet addresses given in this book were correct at the time of going to press. The author and publisher regret any inconvenience caused if addresses have changed or sites have ceased to exist, but can accept no responsibility for any such changes.

A catalogue record for this book is available from the British Library.

Library of Congress Cataloging-in-Publication Data

Names: Carlsson, Ulrika, author.
Title: Kierkegaard and philosophical eros: between ironic reflection and aesthetic meaning / Ulrika Carlsson.
Description: London; New York: Bloomsbury Academic, 2021. | Includes bibliographical references and index.
Identifiers: LCCN 2020034758 (print) | LCCN 2020034759 (ebook) | ISBN 9781350133716 (hb) | ISBN 9781350203938 | ISBN 9781350133723 (epdf) | ISBN 9781350133730 (ebook)
Subjects: LCSH: Kierkegaard, Søren, 1813-1855. | Erōs (The Greek word) | Kierkegaard, Søren, 1813-1855. Om begrebet ironi. | Kierkegaard, Søren, 1813-1855. Enten-eller.
Classification: LCC B4377.C3145 2021 (print) | LCC B4377 (ebook) | DDC 198/.9–dc23
LC record available at https://lccn.loc.gov/2020034758
LC ebook record available at https://lccn.loc.gov/2020034759

ISBN: HB: 978-1-3501-3371-6
PB: 978-1-3502-0393-8
ePDF: 978-1-3501-3372-3
eBook: 978-1-3501-3373-0

Typeset by Deanta Global Publishing Services, Chennai, India

To find out more about our authors and books visit www.bloomsbury.com and sign up for our newsletters.

For Daniela

Contents

Acknowledgments	viii
Note on Sources and Translation	ix
Introduction	1
1 The Temptation to Know	19
2 Unhappy Reflection	47
3 Self-Sufficient Beauty	71
4 The Philosopher Knight	89
5 The Irony of Christian Love	107
Afterword: Immediate Redemption	139
Notes	149
Bibliography	169
Index	173

Acknowledgments

This work originated in Karsten Harries' seminar on *Either/Or*, and no doubt bears the mark of my studies with Karsten more broadly, on Plato, Kant, Nietzsche, and Heidegger; on art, love, and beauty. More quietly, the book also testifies to Karsten's generosity as an adviser, giving his students the freedom required for pursuing their own lines of thought.

Conversations with David Possen, Daniela Dover, Omri Boehm, Michael Della Rocca, and Paul Franks helped advance my understanding of Kierkegaard and other subjects central to this book. Their encouragement meant a great deal to me in writing the dissertation of which the book is an expanded version. Thanks also to Verity Harte for the time she devoted to our Plato tutorial, which fortuitously coincided with my reading *Either/Or*.

I am grateful to Yale University, the institution that put me in touch with these friends and teachers and provided me with the resources required to write the dissertation. An Edna Hong Memorial Fellowship at the Hong Kierkegaard Library gave me an ideal work environment during the last few months of completing it, and I thank Gordon Marino and Cynthia Lund for welcoming me there. Three years at the Higher School of Economics in Moscow gave ample time to process my ideas further and begin to expand the dissertation into a book.

Thanks to Liza Thompson, Lisa Goodrum, and Lucy Russell at Bloomsbury for making the book happen; to Jeffrey Hanson, the series editor, for his early enthusiasm; and to Rick Furtak for his support and help, including connecting me to Jeff. Comments on the proposal and penultimate draft from three anonymous referees were helpful in improving the manuscript.

Parts of some chapters appeared previously in the following articles: "Love as a Problem of Knowledge in Kierkegaard's *Either/Or* and Plato's *Symposium*" (*Inquiry* 53:1); "Love among the post-Socratics" (*Kierkegaard Studies Yearbook*, 2013); and "Kierkegaard's Phenomenology of Spirit" (*The European Journal of Philosophy*, 24:3). I gratefully acknowledge the publishers' permission to include the material here.

Note on Sources and Translation

References to Kierkegaard's works are made by volume and page to *Søren Kierkegaards Skrifter* (1997–2013) [SKS]. Translations are the author's own except where otherwise specified, but notes also refer to the corresponding volume and page number in *Kierkegaard's Writings*, trans. Howard Hong et al. (1978–2000) [KW]. Journals, notebooks, and letters are cited by uniform designations that can be tracked in either SKS or *Søren Kierkegaards Papirer* (1909–1948) [SKP] and in *Kierkegaard's Journals and Papers* (2007–19) or *Kierkegaard's Journals and Notebooks*, ed. Bruce Kirmmse (2007–2019).

Translations of other foreign works are likewise the author's if no English edition is cited in the note.

Introduction

To engage in philosophy is to estrange oneself from the world, reflecting the familiar out of its obviousness and meaning. The philosopher has to constantly negotiate between her commitment to conceiving of the world as it is beyond its appearance—beyond secondary qualities, beyond social constructs—and an instinctive sense that that appearance is more significant than anything she might uncover beneath it, because it is her home.

What Kierkegaard identified as Socratic irony is the most extreme form of that critical reflection which, in his phrase, "negates actuality." We see it at work today most clearly in the kind of political thought that dismisses cultural institutions like ideals of femininity and masculinity, or rejects the very idea of national borders as absurd. Though ostensibly aimed at truth, what it actually achieves is negative freedom. Yet such liberation cannot be an end in itself. The value of freedom lies in what it lets us make of our lives; the ultimate value of intellectual freedom is that it allows us to know the truth. This book traces the dialectic of reconciliation between the love of freedom and the love of the world, and the different modes that "philosophical eros" takes along its path to what may properly be called the love of wisdom.

If you were asked to prove that love was the single most important issue in Kierkegaard's worldview, you might simply point to its status in his theology, and consider the task accomplished. The view developed in *Works of Love* (1847) is indeed a monism of love: God is love; the world and human beings are nothing but manifestations of this love; and the ultimate task of human life is to love God, which also means loving one's neighbor.

But love pervades all of Kierkegaard's thought. Consider *Either/Or* (1843), *Fear and Trembling* (1843), *Repetition* (1843), *Philosophical Fragments* (1844), and *Stages on Life's Way* (1845). *Either/Or* and *Stages* are about the aesthetic, ethical, and religious approaches to life. *Fear and Trembling* treats a version of the Euthyphro dilemma as it appears in Genesis 22, where God tests Abraham. *Repetition* posits a dichotomy between an intellectual, idealizing, backward-looking way of life (recollection), and an active, realistic, forward-looking one (repetition). *Fragments* is about testimony and the relation between student and teacher. There is no necessary connection between any of these topics and love—other philosophers and theologians have treated the same questions without involving love in the discussion. Yet all these works of Kierkegaard's, whatever else they are about, are also about love. Thus the difference between the aesthetic and ethical ways of life is represented through a juxtaposition between seduction and marriage. Romantic love serves as an analogy to Abraham's dilemma whether to sacrifice his beloved son to God. The life of recollection is figured by a young man who, although in love, chooses to remain uninvolved with his beloved. And the relationship between student and teacher, according to *Fragments*, is essentially a love-relation. This intermingling of love with other subject matters is remarkable—and more significant, if we are looking to understand the role love played in Kierkegaard's thought, than the fact that "love your neighbor" was his answer to the first and final existential question, "how should I live my life?" The reason he couldn't talk about anything without also talking about love is that for Kierkegaard, every approach to life is grounded in a distinct way of loving. Judge Wilhelm and the Young Man, "A" and Abraham—all, like Jesus—are who they are, and reveal that identity, by the way they love.

One book that's usually omitted in studies of Kierkegaard's view of love is his dissertation, *The Concept of Irony with Continual Reference to Socrates* (1841).[1] In this work, Kierkegaard defends the thesis that Socrates' philosophical position was "infinite absolute negativity"; that what Socrates did when he engaged others in conversation, when he laid out some thesis on the nature of virtue or justice, and also when he ended his own life, was assert his infinite negative freedom. Again, this is a topic apparently unrelated to love, and yet references to love abound in that book too. It is in the definition of love as lack, in Plato's *Symposium*, that Kierkegaard finds the clearest expression of Socratic irony. When Alcibiades, in that same dialogue, calls Socrates a seducer, Kierkegaard takes this to sum up Socrates' relation to all his students. What set Plato apart from other followers of Socrates was that he "loved Socrates in the idea"; and Kierkegaard professes, in turn, to harbor a "youthful infatuation" with Plato. That the Platonic idea of philosophy as a form of love resonated deeply with him can be gleaned from the very first page of the dissertation when, in a lyrical reflection on philosophical methodology, he asserts that the philosopher must approach the phenomenon he seeks to understand in the chivalrous manner of a man courting a woman.

The present study takes hold of these erotic references in *The Concept of Irony* and reconstructs a Kierkegaardian account of the love of wisdom. This concerns not only Socratic irony. We can discern four types of philosophical eros in the dissertation: four different approaches to knowledge, each grounded in an approach to love, and forming part of a wider existential outlook. The interpretation will proceed by drawing on Kierkegaard's next book, the first volume of *Either/Or*, where love takes center stage. As it turns out, the representatives of the varieties of philosophical eros each have a counterpart among the aesthetic lovers in *Either/Or* 1. Whereas the aesthetic approach to love is typically thought to have two poles—the immediate (Don Juan) and the reflective (Johannes the Seducer)—my reading identifies two additional approaches to love in part 1. There is the despairing, unhappy love of its female characters, Antigone and the so-called Shadowgraphs. And whereas "A" is often identified with Johannes the Seducer, his love is distinct from the latter's, and generates the philosophical approach he takes to his subject matters. The fact that these ways of loving have not caught the attention of most interpreters should be due largely to the bias exerted on part 1's readers by part 2's ethicist, Judge Wilhelm. To read *Either/Or* 1 with *Irony* rather than with part 2 is to liberate it from its usual unfavorable dialectical position, where the aesthetic is defined negatively in relation to the ethical, rather than on its own terms. Thus the joint reading of *Irony* and *Either/Or* 1 shows both works in a new light. The implications of the interpretation reach further into Kierkegaard's oeuvre, however. It gives us the key to a new reading of *Works of Love*, and it provides the basis for a reassessment of the aesthetic life.

Irony and *Either/Or* in the Kierkegaard Scholarship

The Concept of Irony has a controversial status among scholars. It stands apart from the rest of Kierkegaard's production by being a scholarly work, albeit eccentric even by the academic standards of his day. It presents a thesis and proceeds to defend it, continuously signposting where we are and how far we have left to go; and it is free of the trappings of "indirect communication" characteristic of Kierkegaard's pseudonymous works. (Nor is it concerned with Christian edification, like most subsequent books published under his own name.) Never again would Kierkegaard deign to submit a piece of writing for approval by some academic committee—or any other authority, for that matter. But it is not on the basis of these anomalies that scholars have bracketed *Irony* in Kierkegaard's oeuvre. The deciding item is that the master himself is taken to have disavowed the work by excluding it, in *The Point of View for My Work as an Author*, from a list of books comprising what he there called, with official overtones, his "authorship."[2] It is presumably in deference to this unpublished 1848 manuscript that Jamie Ferreira does not even discuss *Irony* in her introductory survey book on Kierkegaard. The dissertation is only mentioned in the biographical sketch as a notable event in Kierkegaard's life, next to his broken engagement.[3] Apparently for the same reason, William McDonald omits any mention of the dissertation in his otherwise incisive essay on agape and eros in Kierkegaard's writings—and this despite the fact that *Irony* contains a chapter devoted expressly to Plato's *Symposium*, a central text in McDonald's interpretation.[4] In fact, commentators who do refer to the dissertation often feel obliged to give a special justification for doing so. In the same vein, Kierkegaard's "wish," at the end of *Concluding Unscientific Postscript to Philosophical Fragments*, that we not attribute to him any of the claims made in the works he published under pseudonym, is almost universally fulfilled by scholars. Thus Sylvia Walsh, even as she finds that "on the whole the views set forth by Climacus are compatible with [Kierkegaard's] own views as expressed in his journals and other works published in his own name," vows in her book to attribute these views to the pseudonym by way of "respecting Kierkegaard's request."[5]

Granted, the omission in *The Point of View* is significant, and confirms most readers' own impression that Kierkegaard embarked on a fundamentally different kind of project with *Either/Or* and the simultaneously published upbuilding discourses. The dissertation's absence from that fateful list, however, does not amount to a disavowal. And even if it did, an author's retrospective dismissal of a text is hardly a reason for interpreters to disregard it. When we adopt Kierkegaard's self-interpretation and hermeneutic instructions as a matter of course, we assume that he succeeded at what he set out to do—embodying different perspectives in the fictional authors, for instance. But that is a tenuous presupposition that we take up to the detriment of incisive interpretation. There are hermeneutic-philosophical reasons for using the fictional authors' names rather than Kierkegaard's when referring to the different texts, as indeed I will, too. But such reasons are independent of Kierkegaard's own plea in that postscript to the *Postscript*, "A First and Last Explanation." To keep the pseudonyms by way of "honoring" Kierkegaard is to treat him with a disciple's piety for her prophet.

It's not a little comical, too, that while Kierkegaard's interpreters are generally so proud of the literary quality of his works, of his commitment to indirect communication, and of his claim to speak without authority, they seize hungrily upon those pieces of supposedly direct communication, like the "First and Last Explanation" or, more importantly, the signed religious writings like *Works of Love*, and rely upon them precisely as authoritative. More ironic yet is the fact that, as betrayed by the "Explanation" and *The Point of View*, Kierkegaard was actually very anxious about being understood, and disdainful of those who did not read his works in the precise way he had intended. It would have been only fair if more of his readers took his instructions as themselves indirect, made without authority, thereby putting Kierkegaard in the position of that clown "A" evokes in his aphorisms. The clown, "A" says, cried "fire!" in the middle of a performance as a fire had really broken out backstage, but was met with laughter and applause from the audience, who took it as part of his act.[6]

The "Explanation" and *The Point of View* are thus, as Joakim Garff has shown meticulously, in tension with the project of indirect communication they describe.[7] But beyond the fact that the assertion to speak without authority is self-undermining, along the lines of the liar's paradox, the "Explanation" tries to control readers' interpretation to a degree that is both illegitimate and impossible. In the pseudonymous books, Kierkegaard writes, "there is not a single word by me; I have no opinion about them except as a third party, no knowledge of their meaning except as a reader, not the remotest private relation to them."[8] Yet this is blatantly false. Every sentence in those writings is Kierkegaard's, whether or not they express his own views. He has an opinion about how they ought to be read, and without taking himself to understand their meaning better than the reader, he could not have instructed the reader on how *not* to interpret them. No one other than Kierkegaard has the natural authority to declare that his books are written without authority; to disavow a piece of writing is implicitly to claim authorship of it. Kierkegaard's relation to all his writings is an intimate one simply by virtue of the fact that they originated in his mind and reflect that mind in a myriad ways, some of which would not have been apparent to Kierkegaard himself. He renounces what he calls "feminine" ownership of his works, presumably the relation of a mother to the child she has borne.[9] But that close relation between a writer and his product can no more be canceled than a mother's biological relation to her child can. It is an organic relation which cannot be severed through an act of will. The truth is that though Kierkegaard's instructions for how to interpret his works may be helpful to us, they are themselves subject to interpretation. Like the writings they refer to, they are data points in our attempt to understand Kierkegaard's thought. In significance, they are far outweighed by the simple fact, fundamental to the reading of any of his books, that all those writings were composed by one Søren Aabye Kierkegaard, born in Copenhagen in 1813, the son of Ane and Mikael.

Although *Either/Or* stands firmly in the scholarship as one of Kierkegaard's most important works, its first part is not always given due consideration. According to the elaborate story Kierkegaard concocted for the fictional "Victor Eremita" to tell about the origin of *Either/Or* in his preface, the texts came to him as a jumble of papers. It didn't take him long, however, to sort them into two piles, the work of two authors. Eremita's most important editorial decision—to put A's manuscript ahead of B's—was based on the fact that "B" (Judge Wilhelm) seems to be addressing "A." Nonetheless, Eremita says he leaves it to the reader to decide which outlook on life—the aesthetic or the ethical—prevails; and he criticizes the kind of literary works where "specific characters are made to represent opposing views of life" and "end with one persuading the other," as though this accidental, merely "historical result" necessarily implied which view was better.[10] Despite this, the reader can hardly surmise that Kierkegaard's ordering of the texts was accidental. And so the fact that "A" doesn't respond to the Judge's criticism seems to imply that, as far as Kierkegaard was concerned, no effective retort *could* be given on behalf of the aesthetic view of life.

Still, if the Judge addresses "A," his letters are not responses to his writings, as Garff has pointed out.[11] With the exception of "The First Love," the Judge nowhere claims to have read those papers of "A" which are, of course, addressed "*ad se ipsum* [to himself]." Judge Wilhelm knows "A" privately and his criticisms are based on their interaction and what "A" has supposedly told his friend in person. In fact, there are countless topics in A's writings that

Wilhelm's letters do not touch on, and his characterization of the aesthetic is, as Garff says, "so simplified that it approaches falsification."[12] The aesthetic life he criticizes corresponds mostly with that expressed in "Crop Rotation" and "The Seducer's Diary." If we try, we can find in the letters criticisms that apply to Don Juan, Antigone, the Shadowgraphs, and the unhappiest man: that a life of sensuous pleasure lacks the right relation to time;[13] that a certain kind of grief is but covert emotional self-gratification.[14] But those criticisms appear rough and cursory when contrasted with the disproportionate richness of A's essays, which moreover contain the philosophical resources for a forceful rejoinder. The question arises why Kierkegaard bothered to make A's writings so elaborate and sophisticated if he thought the aesthetic point of view could be so easily dismissed. It might be accidental, due to the fact that the various texts comprising *Either/Or* were not written in order.[15] My own sense, however, is that it is neither accidental nor fully intentional. Rather, when the Judge fails to address tragedy and sorrow, this is a Freudian omission on Kierkegaard's part.

One might have thought that readers would dismiss as irrelevant a book that fails to address so much of the view whose refutation is its raison d'être. Instead, the Judge's neglect of many of the topics and problems "A" discusses—such as tragedy and sorrow—has resulted in their being overlooked also by Kierkegaard scholars. There is a pervasive tendency to conceive of the aesthetic through the Judge's criticism, using his terms to characterize the aesthetic life, and ignoring those aspects to which he is blind. George Pattison is typical when he defines the aesthetic life by saying that it lacks "an ethical or a religious dimension: it preoccupies itself only with what can appear on the surface of life, with what can be experienced, enjoyed, or played with, but refuses any serious commitment to anyone or anything."[16] In her survey, Ferreira summarizes the aesthetic part in one paragraph, remarking that it is "impossible to do justice here to 'A's papers.'"[17] The six pages she proceeds to devote to the Judge's letters are to serve the student as a guide to both parts of *Either/Or*.

To be sure, Wilhelm's attack is devastating insofar as it targets Johannes the Seducer. But then again, taking down a straw-man is not much of a feat. That Kierkegaard wrote the "Diary" for purposes of criticizing it is abundantly clear; he lets Johannes wear his nihilism on his sleeve. I am skeptical as to whether any people like him exist; but if they do, interpreters who criticize his aesthetic way of life would do well to give a real-life example and not content themselves with vaguely gesturing at "Romantic irony." Nor can critics condemn the aesthetic life as a whole on the basis of Johannes. There is a multiplicity of aesthetic ways of live, and these must be reconstructed from A's papers, acknowledging the positive values he espouses and exhibits. The present study will do so as part of developing the four types of philosophical eros, and that means with the help of *Irony*. Instead of reading B as a response to A, my interpretation shows that *Either/Or* 1 is a follow-up and reply to Kierkegaard's dissertation. By staging a dialogue between Socratic ethics and part 1, the variety among the aesthetic approaches will come to the fore. And by understanding what worldview it is that "A" is reacting against, we will gain a new appreciation of the aesthetic.

The Structure and Scope of *Kierkegaard and Philosophical Eros*

Rather than assume from the start that the dissertation is not essentially related to Kierkegaard's later works, we should let the texts speak for themselves. My joint reading of *Irony* and *Either/Or* invalidates the notion that the former is discontinuous with the latter. Thus I will show (in Chapter 1) that Socrates' philosophical method and stance, as Kierkegaard explicates them in *Irony*, are analogous to Don Juan's approach to love, presented by the fictional author "A" in *Either/Or*. The similarities rise to the surface when we bring a third text into view: Plato's *Symposium*, which is central to Kierkegaard's dissertation, and to which "A" makes a very significant allusion. Don Juan's seduction is deceptive, because it arouses a desire for a substantial and lasting relationship—a desire of an order he, being a pure sensualist, cannot satisfy. Socrates' questions, analogously, awaken reflection and its inherent desire for substantial knowledge. Yet reflection's function is purely negative or, in Kierkegaard's terms, ironic. It unsettles conventional wisdom, traditional values and beliefs based on experience, but it cannot arrive at new, secure beliefs, or affirm any values or worldview. When Socrates does propose some thesis (like the unity of virtue) or definition (for instance, that love is lack), these always boil down to purely formal truisms. His concepts of virtue and love are empty—that is, negative, ironic. On Kierkegaard's analysis, then, Socratic irony doesn't consist in feigning ignorance or refusing to give his students the answer, forcing them to think for themselves. Socrates really is ignorant, and he relishes in this ignorance, since it is at the same time a negative freedom: his intellect's freedom from external determination.

The idea of Socrates as a seducer invites us to look for further analogies between personas and views represented in the two works. Most obviously (as I will explain in Chapter 2), there is a kinship between Alcibiades, who claims in the *Symposium* to have been seduced and deceived by Socrates, and Donna Elvira and her fellow thwarted lovers in *Either/Or*'s "Shadowgraphs." Like the analogy between Socrates and Don Juan, the resemblance takes place on two levels: romantic love and the love of wisdom. In their relation to the beloved person and to a world that resists comprehension, Alcibiades and the Shadowgraph women manifest eros as despair. The state of aporia in which Socrates leaves his interlocutors is like that "reflective sorrow" which accompanies unhappy love according to A's analysis of the seducers' victims. Alcibiades and the Shadowgraphs do not have the willpower required to cut reflection short. Also *Either/Or*'s essay on tragedy illustrates Alcibiades' relation to Socrates. Like Alcibiades, A's modern Antigone has been awoken to the individualism that frees her from nature, family, and her cultural context. But with this freedom comes a responsibility that Antigone experiences as a heavy burden, and an alienation from all of what previously gave meaning to life. Meaning is an aesthetic phenomenon, and reflection kills it.

Next I will reconstruct Kierkegaard's view of Plato's philosophical disposition which, in *Irony*, is framed in terms of love. Like Alcibiades, Plato is in love with Socrates, but his fertile imagination allows him to suspend reflection as he dreams up myths that answer the philosophical questions which received only negative answers in the Socratic dialogue. These myths are not true but meaningful. They satisfy the mind's craving for explanation. When Plato later develops his theory of Forms, these aesthetic ideas promise insight into essences, but not being dialectical, they do not tell us by what features one essence is distinct from another. Nor can their truth be verified or their content communicated from one person to another. To that extent, Platonism remains a private dream, like Johannes the Seducer's life of recollection. Yet we will see that Plato redeems himself in a way that Johannes does not: by complementing his aesthetic method with dialogue, wherein another person puts bounds on the thinker's flights of fancy.

These first three interpretive chapters trace a development from irony/seduction through aporia/sorrow to contented intellectual/erotic solipsism. This lets us see (in Chapter 4) Kierkegaard's own philosophical approach in *Irony* as the culmination of a dialectical progression. It is an approach he himself lays out in the erotic metaphor that opens the dissertation, the same approach Victor Eremita and "A" profess to take in *Either/Or*. Enamored and inspired by the world he observes, the philosopher conceives an idea that is adequate to the phenomenon, expresses its essence, and delineates its borders in conceptual space. This philosophical eros is a procreative one: the concept is the product of the philosopher's and phenomenon's encounter in mutual desire. Thus by studying Socrates with a lover's enthusiasm, Kierkegaard promises in his dissertation to conceive the idea—irony—that expresses the meaning of the person Socrates.

These four erotic-philosophical positions move from emptiness to fullness, from negative to positive freedom, from ignorance to knowledge, and from independence through dependence to interdependence. The epistemological or metaphilosophical question that drives the interpretation is how the mind can conceive ideas that both satisfy the subject's desire to understand and respect the phenomenon's integrity. With regard to love, the question is how two individuals are to negotiate their negative freedom with their dependence on and engagement with each other.

As seen earlier, every approach to love and knowledge is represented by one or more persons in each of the two books: Socrates and Don Juan; Alcibiades, Antigone and the Shadowgraphs; Plato and Johannes the Seducer; and finally Kierkegaard himself, along with Victor Eremita and "A." This way of structuring the book follows naturally from Kierkegaard's own philosophical method. He sought to explain irony through Socrates, faith through Abraham, and self-appropriation through Judge Wilhelm. But that mode of exposition reflects a substantive metaphysical commitment, namely that there can be no rational foundation for the transition from one existential position to another. Indeed, my reconstructions contain no criteria for moving from one stage to the next. Why a person occupies one position rather than another will therefore always be a brute fact, grounded only in his or her basic disposition. To understand each position is not to grasp its reasons, but to see how a person holding that position relates to himself and to the world—it is a knowledge of identity, of essences. To transcend one's existential stance is to become an altogether different person. Perhaps what that means is that such transcendence is impossible. Alcibiades cannot become Plato without losing identity with himself: that is, by ceasing to exist.

While elaborating this extended analogy between love and philosophy, I will have occasion to discuss other works of Kierkegaard's. Against the background of my interpretation of Socratic irony, I will engage in the debate about how Kierkegaard's later view of Socrates, in the *Postscript*, compares to the early one. Despite the *Postscript*'s explicit rejection of "master Kierkegaard's" Socrates, my analysis finds Johannes Climacus' Socrates to be no more and no less of an "ethicist" than the one Kierkegaard portrays in his dissertation. In considering Alcibiades and some of the figures in the first part of *Either/Or*, I will address Judge Wilhelm's criticism of "the aesthetic life," which he lays out in that book's second part. The topic of unhappy love also invites us to look at *Fear and Trembling*, where a one-sided love serves as an analogy for resignation and faith.

The third book of Kierkegaard's to be given major consideration, however, is *Works of Love*, which promises to be his own *Symposium*, giving us his definitive view of true love. In his dissertation, Kierkegaard had contrasted Socrates' purely negative idea of love as desire with the positive love found in Christianity. God's love is not acquisitive but giving. Lacking nothing, God is an abundance that can be infinitely shared. This invites us (in Chapter 5) to read *Works of Love* together with *The Concept of Irony*. Yet rather than supply a positive idea of a love that is not lack but fullness, *Works of Love* conceives love of neighbor and God as the negative activity of self-denial. Like Socratic seduction, this is a mode of loving that does not give but takes away. Nor is the goodness of love, God, or eternity ever given content. This ethics remains as abstract and tautological as Socrates' account of virtue. Bringing Kierkegaard's own mode of analysis in *Irony* to bear on *Works of Love* allows us to elaborate points made by Adorno and Knud Ejler Løgstrup in their critical treatments of the religious work, and to phrase these more incisively yet. Only in the concrete examples *Works of Love* occasionally offers is love positive and intelligible. Yet these aesthetic ideas of love do not illustrate but contradict the general account.

After *Irony*, Kierkegaard repeatedly criticized philosophy for being dogmatic; the pursuit of objective knowledge for evading subjectivity; and reflection for staving off action. But like philosophy, his theology is bent on destroying immediacy; and subjectivity, on his conception, really consists in endless self-reflection. Just as Socratic irony volatilizes tradition, Kierkegaardian faith turns its back on ceremonies and other aesthetic religious expressions. Both aspire to access an untarnished truth through inwardness, without the interference of sensuousness, cultural constructs, and institutions. The rejection of immediacy and aesthetic meaning that Kierkegaard's Protestantism takes on jointly with Socrates is thus the one premise that goes unquestioned in the debate between philosophy and religion. In the book's Afterword, I will turn to an examination and defense of aesthetic values, particularly in their immediate form. In this way, the end of the book returns to the very beginning of the story: the paradise Alcibiades and the modern Antigone have lost, the t-1 that preceded Socrates and was destroyed by his ironic reflection. Judge Wilhelm vows that his ethics preserves all the value of aesthetic life, and that choice actually just reinforces the self's relation to its aesthetic content. But in addition to overlooking the value of immediacy as a form, Wilhelm is wrong to emphasize ethical form over aesthetic substance. It is never the commitment itself but the thing we are inclined to commit ourselves to that makes life worth living.

Kierkegaardian Pedagogy

Soon after ending his engagement, Kierkegaard embarked on a new career. He was giving up research in order to focus on teaching. Like Socrates, though, he believed that "virtue cannot be taught; that is, it is not a teaching but an ability, a practice, a way of existing, an existential reformation."[18] From this he inferred, further, that a teacher can communicate about existential matters only indirectly and without assuming authority. In fact, the student must be deceived into truth. In *Irony* he had tried to adopt the niceties of scholarship: arguing his way from one point to the next, anticipating possible objections, and addressing the reader as his equal, an academic peer. By contrast, the pedagogical presuppositions of indirect communication are such that the reader/student is an inferior, someone who needs to be enlightened and "edified"; woken up to responsibility, repentance, and faith, and yet is too deluded to be aware of this need.

The use of pseudonyms presenting views that were not necessarily Kierkegaard's own is the most prominent example of non-authoritative, indirect, and deceptive communication. Yet his reasoning about how this was sufficient and necessary for teaching the unteachable is somewhat confused. The fact that swimming is a skill does not mean that the only way for a father to teach his child how to swim is to throw her into the water where she must figure it out for herself. He can describe how she should move her arms and legs, tell her to close her mouth and not panic. It is true that grasping the meaning of his instructions does not amount to learning the skill. The instructions do not impart the ability to her. But that doesn't mean the father is not engaged in teaching. It means that his teaching, despite being theoretical and literal, is indirect. Second, theoretical knowledge, too, must be appropriated. When the slave in Plato's *Meno* learns how to draw a figure twice the size of another, he comes to understand the logic behind the method, sees for himself that a square whose side is another square's diagonal will be twice as large as the latter. It is not only virtue that is private possession. Geometry, too, is knowledge only when the student has made it his own—re-appropriated what was his already, through recollection. A teacher can only ever point at the object; the student must then see it for himself. And as for teaching without authority, finally: writing under pseudonym does not insure the reader against forming beliefs on the basis of authority. True, when an author speaks through a character or writes under an obviously made-up name, he creates an uncertainty in the reader as to whether he means what the fictional person says. But this does not preclude the reader from hypothesizing about what the true author wanted to say through the fictional mouthpiece. If she believes she discerns the hidden message, she may well accept *that* on authority, whether or not her interpretation is right. She will then not have appropriated the message even though it was conveyed indirectly.

One wonders if there has ever been a reader who was affected by the pseudonymous works in the way Kierkegaard intended. Certainly, all his scholarly readers come to the texts fully aware of the supposed deceit of indirect communication, letting it guide their interpretations, and inevitably guarding against being duped. I have already noted that we must acknowledge the possibility that the elaborate machinery of indirect communication did not succeed. But that would in no way make Kierkegaard's work a failure. His stated aims—pushing the reader toward subjectivity; showing what it means to become a Christian—hardly exhaust what he actually did in his writings. What makes *Either/Or* 1 so interesting is that, probably more than any other book of Kierkegaard's, it explodes the framework provided for its interpretation by the author himself, whether in the pseudonymous preface or in *The Point of View*. Kierkegaard had thought of writing his dissertation about Don Juan, in a study comprising two other mythical figures: Faust and the Wandering Jew.[19] He abandoned that project after discovering to his great dismay that Hans Lassen Martensen had just completed a work on Faust.[20] Instead he found a way, a few years later, to incorporate studies of them into *Either/Or*, masking them as an aesthete's inquiry into life through art. Hence the richness of "The Immediate Erotic Stages," "Shadowgraphs," and "The Unhappiest One." Kierkegaard had much more to say on the topics of sensual immediacy, tragedy, unrequited love, and alienation than was necessary for characterizing the lowly "aesthetic life" as Wilhelm would conceive it. These themes and the myths and art works he drew on had a hold on him; far from having mastered them and using them to deceive the reader into truth, we see him grappling with them. His fascination and personal involvement sings to us from those texts; they have a pathos that is altogether missing from "The Seducer's Diary."

That intense engagement is closely related to the fact that the characters who embodied those aesthetic ways of life came to him from myth, music, and literature. If *Repetition*'s Young Man is flat by comparison, and Johannes the Seducer utterly unrealistic, it's because Kierkegaard constructed those characters by himself as illustrations of approaches to life he had first conceived in the abstract. The same is true of "In vino veritas," a text I will not concern myself with in this book, despite its overt connection to the *Symposium*. As an obvious, belabored pastiche, the interpretation it begs for consists largely in deciphering a code, solving for *x*. Don Juan and Elvira's relation to the *Symposium*, by contrast, is all the more interesting for not being part of a conscious scheme on Kierkegaard's part; it is organic and alive, a spontaneous association of ideas whose full implications he has not yet worked out himself. These characters are real to the reader because they were real to Kierkegaard. Like Socrates in *Irony* they retain their substance and complexity even as Kierkegaard conceptualizes them. As Isak Winkel Holm notes, this by itself tells us something about the complicated relation between aesthetic ideas and abstract concepts in Kierkegaard's mind—the topic of Holm's book and a central concern of the present study as well.[21]

If we are interested in Kierkegaard as shrewd pedagogue, there are among his signature rhetorical devices some far more intriguing and brilliant than the use of pseudonyms. One of his favorite forms of irony is to casually and matter-of-factly make some remark that, upon reflection, turns out to be paradoxical or carry the most terrifying, radical implications. It is a maneuver Kierkegaard noticed in his study of Socrates, and then deployed himself, notably in *Works of Love*. What makes *Irony* invaluable to any study of Kierkegaard is that he there explains the irony he would go on to practice in subsequent works. Although he spoke of Socrates as his teacher and model, Socrates most likely moved Kierkegaard so much because he recognized in "that sage of Antiquity" an intellectual temperament that was already his own. In that sense, his portrayal of Socrates is a covert self-portrait.

That Kierkegaard did not learn irony from Socrates is evidenced by the fact that his repertoire of such rhetorical tricks as may loosely be categorized as ironic is actually wider than Socrates'. Consider his habit of back-tracking, apparently contradicting himself—again most casually, coyly. Thus he insists that love based on passion is selfish and ephemeral—but elsewhere, that faith is a passion, and that what is so wretched about the age is that it has no passion. An aphorism of A's, though targeting a slightly different phenomenon, makes vivid how annoying and perplexing this is for the reader:

> Just today I was getting a kick out of little Ludvig. He sat in his little chair; with apparent pleasure he looked around himself. Then Maren the nanny walked through the room. "Maren!" he cried; "yes, little Ludvig," she answered with her usual friendliness, and came up to him. He leaned his big head to one side, fixed his immense eyes on her in mischief, and said quite phlegmatically: "Not *that* Maren, I meant a different Maren." And what do we grownups do? We call to the whole world and when it comes to accommodate us we say: "I didn't mean *that* Maren."[22]

The reader is frustrated by these apparent inconsistencies, but that seems to be precisely the point: to wake her up and get her mind working. We can think of the self-contradictions as tasks for the reader, like that riddle the king in a fairy tale challenged a peasant girl to solve: she must come to him neither dressed nor undressed, neither riding nor walking, and neither on the road nor off it. As the clever girl came draped in a fishnet, dragged along the shoulder of the road by a donkey, so too Kierkegaard's readers must find the logical space that is compatible with the two claims that seem at first to exclude each other.

But that space is typically a very narrow one, which can accommodate only the thinnest, most formal ideas. How must we conceive of passion such that it can be instantiated both in the abandonment to sensuous influence whereby the individual refuses responsibility for himself, and in that devotion to a transcendent God which Kierkegaard considers a supremely free act? If the same concept—passion—is applicable to both, then sensuous passion should give us at least an initial grasp on its religious analogue, yet ultimately the two manifestations of passion are polar opposites, one being vicious, the other virtuous. In fact, Kierkegaard quietly asks us to conceive passion anew, from scratch, when we attribute it to faith. Just as everything is new in Christ, so too every action, attitude and inner disposition means something different when it has God for its object. The same goes for every quality we attribute to God. To understand him through mundane predicates would be heresy. And that means that Kierkegaard's theology is a thoroughly negative one. God is absolutely different from anything earthly. We must be ready to see Kierkegaard's irony the way he saw Socrates': not just as rhetorical device in the service of promoting a positive idea, but as a negative process of thought yielding a negative conclusion.

Of course, back-tracking and apparent self-contradiction is a natural part of dialectical arguing. You set out a view or make a claim, then point to its limits and the validity of a contrary view, finally to arrive at a third, qualified position. At every stage, the reader might be convinced by the view, until the author walks her through its problems. In fact, she *should* be convinced of it, or else she hasn't understood it and isn't entitled to moving on to a different view. To Kierkegaard's mind, any real debate should actually reach the point—at least midway—where each party abandons his initial position and adopts his opponent's view. Hence his fondness for that anecdote about an argument between a Protestant and a Catholic which ends with each convincing the other, so that the Protestant converts to Catholicism and the Catholic to Protestantism.[23] The dialectical bent of Kierkegaard's mind is also revealed in a recollection by his friend Hans Brøchner. "So long as father lived," Kierkegaard is supposed to have said,

> I was able to defend my thesis that I ought not take it [the theological examination]. But when he was dead, I had to take over his part in the debate as well as my own, and then I could no longer hold out, but had to decide to read for the examination.[24]

The contrarian's urge to defend whatever view is the opposite of the interlocutor's stems from a complex understanding of the issue. He wants the strengths of each stance to be considered, and so he takes up the position not otherwise represented in the discussion.

We should keep this in mind when we try to understand Kierkegaard's relation to the aesthetic. And if we want to be good students of his, we should not condemn aesthetic love and living until we have grasped it on its own terms and become—if only temporarily—convinced of it. Never to have known despair is nothing for a religious person to congratulate himself for. Rather, it makes his faith less profound, since it doesn't carry within itself an understanding of that which faith is not. Kierkegaard made this point toward the end of his dissertation, anticipating a major theme in his next book. "It takes courage," he writes,

> when one feels adored by sorrow, when sorrow teaches the falsification of all joy as melancholy, all longing as missing, all hope as recollection—then it takes courage to want to be happy; but it does not follow that every grownup old child with its cloying smile, its eyes drunk with joy, has more courage than the one who bowed down in sorrow and forgot to smile.[25]

All roads in Kierkegaard's philosophy lead to God, but that does not mean he didn't sympathize with those aesthetes, like Elvira, whose despair he wouldn't let Judge Wilhelm minimize. If the present study focuses on aesthetic figures, it is because what Kierkegaard has to say about aesthetic existence is in many ways richer than what he says about the religious life. This follows the familiar Tolstovian pattern of happy and unhappy families: there are many ways of failing at faith, but only one way of getting it right. From the religious perspective, pleasure, preferential love, aesthetic contemplation, depression, and despair are all ultimately versions of sin. Yet that final reductive step in the analysis is not its most interesting part. It makes his religious anthropology as abstract as his theology. Kierkegaard's greatest insights about sensuousness, love, philosophy, and psychological ailments are to be found not in his theological conclusions about them, wherein they are leveled under the category of "sin," but in the groundwork he conducts in describing them from within: Socrates' enjoyment of freedom, Elvira's reflective sorrow, A's depression, and that desire which makes Don Juan—and all the women who enter his field of attraction—feel alive.

1

The Temptation to Know

In the first proper essay of *Either/Or*'s first volume, Kierkegaard's unnamed fictional author—dubbed "A" by the fictional editor—treats of what he terms "the musical-erotic." Mozart's *Don Giovanni*, he contends, is the greatest musical work ever produced—indeed the greatest musical work *possible*, since it expresses the ultimate idea that music is capable of expressing: the idea of sensuous desire.[1] Its hero embodies this desire, which propels him forward on an endless series of seductions. His quest is not for true love in a lifelong relationship, but for momentary satisfaction.

That essay is followed by an apparently unrelated treatise on tragedy, after which "A" returns to the topic of seduction, now from the perspective of the seduced. It is with that text, "Shadowgraphs," that our joint reading of Kierkegaard's *The Concept of Irony* and *Etiher/Or* begins. As "A" closes his discussion of the three female characters who have each fallen prey to a seducer, he invokes snakebite:

> And now in parting we shall unite these three women betrothed to sorrow; we shall have them embrace one another in the harmony of sorrow [. . .] for only the person who has been bitten by snakes knows what one who has been bitten by snakes must suffer.[2]

Here the seducer is likened to a snake; his deception is understood as a painful and poisonous snakebite. The suffering that results from such deception is a particular kind or aspect of unhappy love—what "A" calls "reflective sorrow."

The figure of the snake is bound to bring to mind the serpent that tempted Eve in the Garden of Eden. The first fallen woman, the first lover of truth, is indeed a prototype for A's three Shadowgraphs. Like her, they see themselves as innocent with regard to the sin that has been committed. "The snake tempted me, and I ate," is Eve's simple answer to God's question why she tried the fruit from the tree of knowledge. As she is expelled from the Garden and cursed with the fate of bearing children in pain, and being always dependent on her husband, so too Marie, Elvira, and Gretchen suffer the terrible repercussions of being seduced: a private shameful grief as well as a loss of trust, a loss of innocence.

Yet the personage most directly referenced by A's metaphor is not Eve but Alcibiades, who mentions snakebite in his speech in Plato's *Symposium*. That, in turn, is a reference to Philoctetes, a tragic figure in Greek mythology and the protagonist of an eponymous play by Sophocles. Philoctetes found himself alone on an island during the Trojan War, abandoned by his fellow soldiers who could not bear his cries of pain and the smell of his infected snakebite wound. Speaking to a group of intimates, Alcibiades draws out what he takes to be the moral of his story:

> you know what people say about snakebite—that you'll only talk about it with your fellow victims: only they will understand the pain and forgive you for all the things it made you do. Well, something much more painful than a snake has bitten me in my most sensitive part—I mean my heart, or my soul, or whatever you want to call it, which has been struck and bitten by philosophy, whose grip on young and eager souls is much more vicious than a viper's and makes them do the most amazing things.[3]

What has bitten Alcibiades is philosophy as practiced by Socrates; Socrates who, for all the assembled amateur intellectuals, personifies the pursuit of wisdom. It follows from the epistemological principle that Alcibiades extracts from the story of Philoctetes that he considers the other symposiasts his fellow victims, fellow sufferers of a bite more painful than a snake's.

"Shadowgraphs" is one of the three texts in *Either/Or* that are ostensibly lectures delivered before the "Symparanekromenoi"—the "Fellowship of the Dead" or "Society of Buried Lives." This, we gather, is a sort of philosophical working group for the study of grief, tragedy, and unhappiness. Yet their approach to their subject matter is not disinterested scholarship, for the Symparanekromenoi are also said to sympathize with grievers. In fact, it seems that their study of grief is itself a way of grieving, since—so "A" claims—grief can be known only by acquaintance. Sympathy—co-suffering—is not a mere accompaniment to the Symparanekromenoi's inquiry, but the very method of that inquiry. For sorrow, "A" says, "sneaks about in the world in great secrecy, and only a person with sympathy for it is able to sense its presence."[4] And the

Symparanekromenoi is up to this task, being "a society that knows but one passion, namely sympathy with sorrow's secret."[5]

It follows that the Symparanekromenoi must be quite similar to the Shadowgraph women—at a minimum, they must share their capacity for grief. And although it is natural to think that the Symparanekromenoi achieve a theoretical understanding of grief unavailable to the Shadowgraphs themselves, the members of both groups live a life of the mind. The Shadowgraphs' grief leads them to study themselves. Theirs is, after all, a *reflective* sorrow: its distinctive symptoms are introversion and self-reflection. As the pain of the snake's bite calls its victim's full attention to itself, the victim turns away from the world into herself, immersing herself in her pain, burying herself in herself.

The guests in Plato's *Symposium* also form a society, a study group, even if, as far as we know, they hold only this one meeting. Friends have gathered at the home of Agathon; together they contemplate the god of love. Literally, symposiasts are people who drink together, but intellectual discussion was a central feature of any Greek symposium. Whether or not there is truth in wine, it certainly is conducive to lively conversation. In addition to their intellectual aim, ancient Greek symposia were also romantic events, occasions to flirt and seduce. This particular symposium, devoted to Eros, is then self-reflexive: it treats in theory what would normally be practiced in it. Or maybe the participants reflect theoretically on a phenomenon they at the same time practice. Rather than replace practice with theory, this particular symposium is perhaps making love by means of theoretical inquiry. For *philosophia* is a love in its own right, the love of wisdom. To philosophize about love is therefore also to philosophize about philosophy. In fact, if Alcibiades is right, the love of wisdom driving each guest's speech is at the same time a love of the person who initiated him into philosophy. They have all been bitten by the same beast, according to Alcibiades, are all haunted by the same demon: "He has deceived us all."[6] Deception is as much a preoccupation of Alcibiades' speech as it is of "Shadowgraphs." Reflective sorrow is a response to deception, and seducers like Don Juan are always also deceivers, "A" says, even as they are not reflective enough to be able to lie or intentionally mislead anyone. Don Juan's seduction is aesthetic, and therefore deceptive by its very nature.

By way of pursuing this comparison between Plato's and A's symposia, suggested by the snakebite reference in "Shadowgraphs," I will begin with an exposition and analysis of Don Juan's seduction, and then explain how Socrates' philosophy can be understood as an endeavor very much like that seduction. According to Kierkegaard's treatment of Socrates in *The Concept of Irony*, Socrates' philosophical stance is irony, which is an entirely negative stance. That it is negative does not mean only that it prohibits Socrates from making any positive claims about the nature of phenomena or the ideals that must bind us. On Kierkegaard's view, Socrates negates the phenomenal world, but without putting in its place some heaven of ideas. His irony evacuates all the contents of the world, and leaves his interlocutors as empty-handed and disappointed as Don Juan's women.

Many scholars have found the analysis of Socrates in Kierkegaard's first book problematic. In light of Kierkegaard's religious doctrine, they insist, the Socrates of the 1841 dissertation must either be dismissed as a youthful mistake of Kierkegaard's or else reinterpreted as a more positive thinker. Another commentator yet has proposed that Kierkegaard's dissertation on Socrates was really a critique of Hegel. But, as we will see, Kierkegaard comes very close to Hegel in his understanding of Socrates. Their differences, though important, arise from subtle disagreements about easily overlooked points. Rather than turn Kierkegaard's Socrates into a positive thinker, and rather than despair about Socratic irony's dead end, we should look to Kierkegaard's portrayal of Socrates' disciples—Alcibiades and Plato—if what we want are models of a positive approach to knowledge.

The Feminine Universal

Don Juan's servant Leporello is an amateur statistician who doubles as the book-keeper of his master's romantic life. He has a record of each conquest, and in his second aria in Mozart's opera, he starts throwing out numbers. He tells Donna Elvira how many French girls Don Juan has enjoyed, how many Italian. In Spain alone, Leporello knows, Don Juan has seduced 1,003 women.

Don Juan's love life does lend itself to a mathematical treatment, because his seductive endeavor is an exercise in abstraction. As "A" puts it, "it is not the extraordinary that Don Juan desires" in a woman "but the ordinary—that which she shares with every woman."[7] What Don Juan loves is a universal; something that admits of being shared and indeed cannot be claimed as private property. Although very numerous, these Many women fall conveniently under One. They are many of a kind and can be counted with the same basic unit. This also means that the number of the seduced could "just as well be any number whatever, a much larger number," "A" points out. The significance of the number, 1,003, is purely aesthetic: being "uneven and random," it "gives the impression that the list is not at all complete, that Don Juan is still on the move."[8]

From Christianity and on, universality has been a mark of morality. In Kant's ethics, for instance, each person shares in a universal humanity through the faculty of reason. Persons should be treated according to universal principles, and not in response to their particular qualities. But for Kierkegaard—and, as we see, also for "A"—morality is about the individual, not the universal. And the universal at issue in A's interpretation of Mozart's *Don Giovanni* is not reason or freedom but a shareable quality instantiated in individuals *qua* natural beings. Far from endowing them with dignity—which Kant glossed as "pricelessness"—this universal makes them fungible, exchangeable for one another. Thus the women that have crossed Don Juan's path are of no concern as individuals insofar as we are studying the aesthetic approach to love from this seducer's perspective, because women are not unique individuals to him. Sensuous love, "A" says, "is not faithful but absolutely faithless; it loves not one but all."[9] Don Juan has not just been faithless to 1,003 women: his love is *essentially* unfaithful. According to "A," Don Juan's seduction lacks the consciousness required to single out one individual over another. He responds to a genus because he is himself generic. He is not a particular man of a particular age, with particular facial features.[10] He is more like a force of nature:[11] the very force of sensuousness, which like every other force operates equally on all of nature. It targets kinds and acts on particulars only in virtue of their generic features. When Elvira takes the stage to hear Leporello's enumeration, she is "a witness *instar omnium* [worth them all]," "A" says, though "not because of any accidental privilege on her part but because, the [seductive] method remaining essentially the same, one represents everyone."[12]

This is why, according to "A," opera is the appropriate medium for representing Don Juan. Music, he says, "articulates not the particular but the general in all its generality, and yet it articulates this generality not in the abstraction of reflection but in the concretion of immediacy."[13] Although music is sometimes called a language, it is immediate whereas verbal language is reflective. Music lacks reflective distance: it cannot describe or name a feeling, let alone a person or an event. It communicates without the intermediaries of concept and symbol. It does not designate moods and feelings but evokes them, making them present not *to* our minds through concepts, but *in* our minds as phenomena. That makes Mozart's *Don Giovanni* a classical work: one in which subject matter and form—inside and outside—cannot be separated but are reflected into one another.[14] For just as Don Juan recognizes and loves not individual women but femininity in general, so music can express only the general. Having no distance to what it evokes, music is as immediate as a bodily impulse; it is the artistic corollary of sensuality itself. For the sensuous, too, is immediate, and that means—following the Hegelian metaphysics operative here—abstract.[15] Indeed, the idea of sensuousness, "A" says, is the most abstract one conceivable.[16] In music, "the sensuous-erotic" receives an expression that does not corrupt its immediacy, does not mediate it out of immediacy.[17] And this relation is reciprocal: sensuous desire is music's "absolute subject matter."[18]

By contrast, a representation of Don Juan in epic form—as a narrative unfolding in time—could not do justice to him, according to "A."[19] That is because Don Juan's existence is ahistorical. There is no progression in his seductive endeavor. If we have to think of him in temporal terms, then we can think of him as existing in a single moment, yet one with an eternal recurrence. If Don Juan would have to be assigned an age, "A" would have him be thirty-three—an impersonal age or, as he terms it, "the age of a generation."[20] It is the generic age of man *qua* sensual, natural being; the basic temporal unit of the ever-recurring generation and decay of human life. Don Juan desires and "enjoys the satisfaction of desire," but "as soon as he has enjoyed it, he seeks a new object and so on infinitely."[21] Thus he draws women into his own, sensuous realm, has his way with them, and moves on. He goes from one aesthetic experience to the next, from one instance of femininity to another. He sees, he desires, he conquers, and moves on. There is no external telos governing the series of his seductions; if it comes to an end, this will not be dictated by the nature of Don Juan's endeavor. His seductive enterprise could only ever come to an arbitrary halt—never to a conclusion. His seduction, his momentary aesthetic enjoyment of femininity, is an end in itself.

That Don Juan is a force of nature means that the hero of Mozart's opera is more of an aesthetic personification than a person. A demon, as "A" calls him, he hovers between individuality and ideality.[22] He appears as a character onstage, in situations with other characters, and he expresses himself in words—in this sense, he is represented as an individual. But his words are sung and the music represents him as idea. In discussing Elvira's first aria, "A" remarks that it is quite proper for her seducer to be kept in the background,[23] because the spectator should not see him "together with Elvira in the unity of the situation; he should hear him inside of Elvira, out of Elvira."[24] For Don Juan is not so much a man who desires as desire itself, and to say that *he seduces* is almost to attribute too much agency to him. "A" would rather spell out the mechanics of Don Juan's seduction like this: "He desires, this desire acts seductively; thus he seduces."[25] "A" knows that the glow of desire in a man has a visceral effect on the woman who feels his gaze upon herself. It can frighten or disgust, but it can also give her a tingle of excitement, arouse her curiosity about that man for the first time, and make her long to enjoy in the most intense way possible that desire of his, through which she feels her whole being affirmed. As "A" sees it, sensuous desire is contagious, it transports itself from one person to another like a shock wave. As sensuality asserts itself in Don Juan, he arouses the sensuous in the desired woman. It is as though all of nature were akin: her nature answers when Don Juan calls. Sensuality overpowers her from within; when Donna Elvira is "in the vicinity of Don Juan, she is beside herself."[26] Thus Don Juan's desire is one with his seduction: one, almost, with its satisfaction. No sooner has he presented himself as a woman's lover than she is in love with him herself.

But the love Don Juan arouses is not mere sensuous desire; as his women understand things, the seduction is just the beginning of a relationship. That much is apparent from the sorrow Don Juan leaves them with. The sensuous is personal for them: it belongs in the *ethical* realm, albeit not as Kierkegaard conceives it. In that sense, Don Juan's seduction is deceptive, though "A" would caution us about using morally charged language about him. As a force of nature, Don Juan operates without conscious intention: he does not make false promises, does not deceive by calculation. He is not reflective enough to be capable of lying, does not seduce with words.[27] Describing him in moral terms is therefore an inappropriate anthropomorphism; calling his seduction evil is committing a category mistake.[28] Don Juan cannot establish relationships with women *qua* persons because personality is an ethical entity that Don Juan's cognitive apparatus is not equipped to perceive. Being sensuous through and through, he can only detect sensual, or aesthetic, qualities. Once he has seduced a woman, he has nothing more to do with her, and so he rushes on to new ventures.

To the women, however, the sensuous is ripe with a promise of a deeper love. Don Juan himself does not make false promises; he neither lies nor intends to deceive. It is "the power of the sensuous itself that deceives the seduced."[29] Don Juan's seduction is deceptive in a purely epistemological, not yet moral, sense: the sense in which we say that appearances can deceive. Don Juan's deception is a natural ill, like an earthquake, but it is not evil. Aesthetic categories are more appropriate than moral ones when we look at natural phenomena: the beholder can take pleasure in the playfulness of a butterfly appearing like a leaf, deceiving thereby its predator as well as the human eye. An observer with a sense of irony is amused by such phenomena—indeed, in *The Concept of Irony*, Kierkegaard writes that we can "regard all sensory illusions as irony on the part of nature."[30]

Philosophical Seduction

Like Don Juan in Spain, Socrates moves in his Athens from one to the next. He meets a person, asks him philosophical questions, brings him to a state of aporia, and then moves on, leaving the other hanging. The dynamic of the Socratic philosophical encounter is analogous to that of the seductive encounter, and like Don Juan, Socrates operates in monotonous repetition. Alcibiades already compares Socrates' philosophical art to seductive music in the *Symposium*. You are "quite the flute-player," he says to Socrates—"aren't you? In fact, you're much more marvelous than Marsyas, who needed instruments to cast spells on people."[31] But the medium by which they operate is the only difference between Socrates and Marsyas, according to Alcibiades: "you do exactly what he does," he tells Socrates,

> but with words alone. You know, people hardly ever take a speaker seriously, even if he's the greatest orator; but let anyone—man, woman, or child—listen to you or even to a poor account of what you say—and we are all transported, completely possessed.[32]

As a character in Plato's dialogues, Socrates indeed seduces his interlocutor into the love of knowledge. In one dialogue after another, the same process is repeated. Socrates' legacy is not a doctrine but a particular way of asking questions, one that can be applied to any person, on any subject matter, and that acts subversively on that person. If we think of Don Juan as a force of nature, we might think of Socrates as a force of thought. This is true, at least, of Kierkegaard's Socrates in *The Concept of Irony*. That Socrates is not a man in the ordinary sense. Certainly, he is not an essentially historical figure for Kierkegaard. "For the observer," he writes, "Socrates' life is like a magnificent pause in the course of history."[33]

A testament to the generality, the abstractness, of Socrates' irony is its indifference to the particular qualities of the interlocutor. If Don Juan seduces French and German girls just well as Italian and Spanish ones—"as long as she wears a skirt"—Socrates, similarly, "spoke just as well with hide tanners, tailors, sophists, statesmen, poets, with young and old, spoke with them equally well about everything, since he found everywhere a task for his irony."[34] This task, moreover, is an end in itself. For "irony has no purpose," Kierkegaard writes; or its purpose "is immanent to itself, it is a metaphysical purpose"—the attainment of negative freedom.[35] Irony is often considered roguish, and insofar as it involves a dissonance between the inner and the outer, it might be compared to dissimulation and hypocrisy.[36] The ironist never speaks earnestly: what he says he does not really mean. Yet in distinction with dishonesty, irony is not intended to mislead. It is not an instrument of vice, and falls not under moral, but metaphysical categories.[37]

Reading Plato, the midwife image of Socrates often strikes us as inapt. He doesn't assist so much in the birth of true ideas as in the killing of false ones. Yet this is actually how Socrates himself explains the meaning of that metaphor, in the *Theaetetus*. The opportunity he is offering, he says to Theaetetus, is to

> come to me as to one who is both the son of a midwife and himself skilled in the art; and try to answer the questions I shall ask you as well as you can. And when I examine what you say, I may perhaps think it is a phantom and not truth, and proceed to take it quietly from you and abandon it. Now if this happens, you mustn't get savage with me, like a mother over her first-born child. Do you know, people have often before now got into such a state with me as to be literally ready to bite when I take away some nonsense or other from them.[38]

But if Socrates leaves his interlocutors disappointed and frustrated, it's because a promise seems to inhere in the very structure of the Socratic philosophical practice, consisting as it does in asking questions. Questions seem to promise answers. Falsity, too, seems to presuppose truth: if Socrates can bring his interlocutors to see that their beliefs about virtue are false or at least disputable, must he not be able to lead them to the truth? But Socrates is not, strictly speaking, a deceiver, for he makes no explicit promises of knowledge. Indeed, he is always happy to point out that he himself knows nothing. Socrates is a deceiver in the same passive sense as Don Juan. It is the maieutic method itself that deceives.

Abstraction as Negativity

For "A," Don Juan embodies the idea of sensuous desire; for Kierkegaard, Socrates is the personification of irony. As a linguistic phenomenon, irony is usually defined as a use of words where the pragmatic, or actual, meaning is the opposite of the literal meaning. For Kierkegaard, irony is an individual's assertion of his negative freedom. Irony as a figure of speech is like a riddle whose solution is instantly apparent.[39] This is the most innocuous expression of a practice that, at its most radical, is the foundation of human dignity.[40] "When I am aware as I speak that what I am saying is what I mean," Kierkegaard writes, "then I am bound in what I've said; that is, I am positively free therein."[41] A sincere speaker enjoys a positive freedom, but this freedom is bought at the expense of his negative freedom. For when "what I say is not my meaning or the opposite of my meaning, then I am free in relation to others and to myself"—free from the kind of commitment that is normally entailed by an assertion.[42] Socratic irony doesn't merely upset that connection between utterance and assertion that is the foundation of linguistic communication. It unsettles the very institutions of belief and value. By exercising his ability to question anything and to refuse to make any positive claims, the ironist demonstrates his infinite negative freedom. What the ironist has discovered is that no belief can force itself on him against his will. The multitude of virtuous phenomena in the world does not hold the key to the concept of virtue, that by which instances of virtue are what they are. What is left when the individual has said "no" to the pretense of every phenomenon is his pure subjectivity and freedom. Only on the premise of such freedom can we have knowledge of the nature of things like virtue, though Kierkegaard repeats again and again that

Socrates only arrives at the condition for the possibility of *a priori* concepts, not at any actual concepts. In Kierkegaard's estimation, this is why Socrates rightly called himself ignorant. To objections like Friedrich Schleiermacher's that, in Kierkegaard's words, "it's not possible that Socrates knew only that he didn't know anything, because that necessarily presupposes that he knew what knowledge is,"[43] Kierkegaard responds by quoting Heinrich Theodor Rötscher. Socrates' knowledge that he knew nothing, Rötscher writes,

> is not at all the pure empty nothing it is usually taken to be, but the nothingness of the determinate content of the existent world. The knowledge of the negativity of all finite content is his wisdom, through which he is driven into himself and asserts the inquiry into his own inwardness as his absolute goal, as the beginning of infinite knowledge, yet no more than the beginning, since this consciousness has no fullness but is only the negation of everything finite and existing.[44]

Phenomena have no reality for the subject until he conceptualizes them.[45]

Insofar as Socrates' infinite negativity is a philosophical stance, it is an entirely practical one, in two senses of the term. First, Socrates' primary concern is with value. Time and again he returns to virtue: Can it be taught; are there several virtues or just one; what exactly is its nature? Second, his philosophy is a practice, a craft of sorts, and cannot be summed up in theoretical terms. Irony is action more than doctrine. It is therefore appropriate that Plato's early dialogues, as Kierkegaard reads them, do not propound irony as a theoretical credo but rather present it dramatically. We must understand irony dynamically—as a movement from something to nothing and the principle, or force, that drives this movement. As "a qualification of personality,"[46] irony is not just a method but showmanship—a charismatic teacher's employment of a method.

Questioning, Kierkegaard writes, is "the abstract relation between the subjective and the objective" and this very relation "ultimately became the primary issue" for Socrates.[47] Much of Kierkegaard's discussion of Plato comes under the heading "The Abstract, in the Earliest Platonic Dialogues, Rounds Itself Off in Irony," and the idea of abstraction as a form of negativity is crucial to Kierkegaard's argument.[48] It allows him to defend his thesis from the objection that Socrates certainly seems to have affirmed a number of philosophical views and that not all of the Socratic dialogues end in aporia. In a moment we will see how, exactly, Kierkegaard understands abstraction, and this will clarify how he understands negativity and positivity. As it will turn out, the *Symposium* is the key dialogue in Kierkegaard's discussion of abstraction: there we get not merely abstract ideas and arguments but a definition of the abstract itself. But first, a few words more about the nature of questions and the irony that inheres in dialogue.

To ask a question is not to "negate" something in the sense of denying it, yet a question is the negative to which answers are the corresponding positive. By demanding grounds and justifications, moreover, questions undermine naïve beliefs or the uncritical manner in which a person has accepted certain ideas and values. Questions thus pave the way for denials. As such, Kierkegaard writes, Socratic questioning is

> analogous to the negative in Hegel, except that the negative according to Hegel is a necessary moment in thought itself, a determination *ad intra*; in Plato, the negative is made visible [*anskueliggjøres*] and placed outside the object in the inquiring individual.[49]

The question plays in a conversation the same role that the negative plays in Hegelian dialectic: it is the "propelling element in thought," says Kierkegaard: thought's unrest.[50] Nonetheless Kierkegaard won't call Socrates a dialectician in Hegel's sense. Such a dialectic is too impersonal for Socrates. In Hegel, the dialectic "spreads out infinitely and flows into the extremities," whereas irony leads the dialectic "back into personality, rounds it off in personality."[51] Furthermore, Socratic questioning, far from helpfully driving thought toward the answer, often results in aporia. Although questions usually express a desire for answers, one can ask a question "not out of any interest in the answer, but in order to suck out an apparent content by means of the question, and leave an emptiness behind."[52] This form of interrogation, which assumes that there is such an emptiness to be uncovered, is the ironic one.

In fact, the entire trajectory of the Socratic questioning in the early dialogues is negative, in Kierkegaard's view: the conversation ends with a negative conclusion and every seemingly positive statement Socrates makes is only seemingly so. As an example, he refers to Socrates' argument that every craft is done for its own sake. "Tell me," he asks Thrasymachus, "doesn't every craft differ from every other in having a different function?" For example, he continues, "medicine gives us health, navigation gives us safety while sailing" and we would not consider "medicine wage-earning, even if someone becomes wealthy while healing." Making money comes from the "practice of some additional craft"—a meta-craft—"the craft of wage-earning."[53] From this purely formal argument, Socrates infers that no craftsman looks first of all for personal gain, but "provides and orders for its subject and aims at its advantage."[54] The conclusion relies on an equivocation between the craft's inherent aims and the motives of the craftsman, and what according to Kierkegaard makes it ironic is the fact that the general idea by which Socrates suffocates Thrasymachus' account of certain phenomena, far from being more substantial than those phenomena, is so abstract as to be empty. What Socrates says about craft is really about the nature of concepts. The apparent positivity of restoring to each craft the dignity and integrity of possessing its own essential function, distinct from its contingent benefits, turns out, ironically, to deprive it of any content. "To lift every craft up into an ideal sphere," Kierkegaard writes,

> where it is only performed for its own sake, without regard for any earthly debasement, is a very positive thought in and by itself, but also so abstract that in relation to every particular craft it is a negative qualification. The positive thought, the actual πληρωμα [fullness], would be given only if we caught sight of that wherein it desires itself. The negative qualification that it does not desire anything else would follow the positive qualification like a shadow, as the perpetually cancelled possibility of such a desire.[55]

Socrates speaks of the crafts' purposes as that in virtue of which they are what they are. Making money is the essence of wage-earning; healing is the essence of medicine. At least when we are dealing with crafts, essence is constituted by purpose. To say of some craft x that it is its own purpose is then to say that the essence of x is x. Such a determination is not informative unless we already have a grasp of x's nature. When we say, in Kierkegaard's expression, that "x desires itself"—where desire figures purposiveness—we predicate a purely formal relation of an unknown entity. Only if we could replace the indexical in "desires itself" with a descriptive term would we have a grasp of x's nature in a positive sense. In the case of medicine, for instance, a conception of health independent of our understanding of medicine could provide a conceptual anchor for this craft. Kierkegaard does find such a conception in the later books of the *Republic*. There justice is equated with mental health, and health is in turn understood positively, he writes, as abundant flourishing, as "the rich fullness of a blissful life."⁵⁶ But this major thesis of the *Republic* is decidedly Platonic, according to Kierkegaard—not Socratic.

Similarly, the process in the *Protagoras* which "is intended to annihilate the relative dissimilarity between the different virtues in order to save the unity" has a semblance of positivity.⁵⁷ "Wisdom, temperance, courage, justice, and piety—are these five names for the same thing," Socrates asks, "or is there underlying each of these names a unique thing, a thing with its own power or function, each one unlike any of the others?"⁵⁸ As Protagoras understands this question, for virtue to be one is for each virtuous person to be wise *and* temperate *and* brave *and* just *and* pious. When he rejects the unity of virtue, it is on the grounds that "you will find many people who are extremely unjust, impious, intemperate, and ignorant, and yet exceptionally courageous."⁵⁹ Protagoras then thinks quite concretely about virtue as a power or function inside the person, like an organ of the soul. This view does not require that the disparate virtues resemble each other, only that they have a common source, evidenced by their co-presence in individuals. The unity of virtue could be a completely contingent fact of human psychology—at any rate, establishing the fact of its unity or disunity is an empirical matter.

For Socrates, however, the question is not an empirical one and could not be settled by appeal to actual virtuous individuals in the world. He supports the unity of virtue with the law of excluded middle—that everything has exactly one opposite—so that wisdom and temperance must deep down be identical since both have as their opposite "folly, which is a single thing."⁶⁰ It is then not by articulating a common feature of all the virtues—"that wherein all the virtues, so to speak, love one another"—that Socrates seeks to prove their unity.⁶¹ Socrates merely suggests that there must be such a common feature. Like the crafts in the *Republic*, virtue loves itself, but what it means to love virtue—what it is about virtue that virtue narcissistically loves—we are not told. Virtue is "egotistically concluded in itself," Kierkegaard writes, and does not become "audible," does not resound in the individual virtues.⁶² Without articulating the essence that grounds the kinship of the different virtues, the claim that virtue is one becomes "the most weakly inspired articulation possible of its existence,"⁶³ a statement of its conformity to the law of identity or, as Kierkegaard puts it elsewhere, of "the ideal's infinite consistency in itself."⁶⁴

In an aphorism about tautology, "A" mentions statements of precisely the kind Kierkegaard here ascribes to Socrates, but also divides them according to two types:

> Tautology is and remains the highest principle, the highest axiom of thought. No wonder, then, that most people use it. Nor is it all that impoverished but can very well fill up a whole life. It has a jesting, witty, entertaining form—the infinite judgment. This kind of tautology is paradoxical and transcendental. Then it takes the serious, scientific, and upbuilding form. Its formula is as follows: when two quantities are equal in size to one and the same third quantity, the first two are also equal in size. This is a quantitative conclusion. This kind of tautology is particularly useful on podiums and in pulpits, where one must say a great deal.[65]

The second type is phrased as a hypothetical conditional, and is easily recognized as the law of the transitivity of identity. In *Irony*, Kierkegaard doesn't give any example of a Socratic thesis that takes this precise form, but the idea that *if* something is a craft then it serves its own purpose, and that if a cobbler and a carpenter both make money then at least in that respect, their crafts are the same, comes very close to it. The unity of virtue, insofar as it relies simply on the law of contradiction, can be classified at the same level of complete abstraction or formality.

The first kind of tautology, however, is not a law but a judgment. Hegel defines an "infinite judgment" as the judgment that "the individual is individual" or "the universal is universal."[66] Such a judgment has a "positive moment" which, Hegel writes, is "the reflection of individuality into itself."[67] It takes hold of the individual's or universal's "return into itself."[68] When Kierkegaard says that the thesis of the unity of virtue amounts to a statement of virtue's existence—a judgment about virtue that it is a kind, a universal—this is a more substantial claim than the iteration of a law. It is the judgment about a particular thing that it is an individual or a kind. It is positive in the weak sense that it posits the existence of such a universal; it is negative to the extent that it has yet to be given a definition that would allow us to apply it to a phenomenon. We shall encounter a fully positive variety of tautology in Chapter 4. For now, let us return to the *Protagoras*.

Socrates eventually concludes that all virtue depends on knowledge, so that the other four virtues are subsumed under wisdom, a conclusion that—again—seems to contradict Kierkegaard's thesis about the vacuity of all Socratic doctrines. After all, it appears to rule out the most promising theoretical contender—that virtue should be a natural disposition—and as such, the thesis is not trivial. The claim that virtue is the skill of measurement, so that being virtuous is just another craft next to shoe-making and medicine, seems if anything to make of virtue something very concrete and accessible, an appropriate complement to the vulgar conception of the good as pleasure. But when virtue is thus reduced to the problem of weighing different pleasures against one another and correcting for perspectival distortions, it doesn't thereby become a problem with a practical solution. The measurement presupposes knowledge of future events and the consequences of all actions, most of which information is inaccessible to us. Socrates' definition of virtue as knowledge has at once made it mundane and brought us further from virtuous living.

But the truly vacuous concept of knowledge is not to be found in the *Protagoras*' conception of virtue as craft but in the *Phaedo*, where Socrates stipulates death as a condition for knowledge. His disciples concur when he suggests that the Just, the Beautiful and the Good are never seen with the eyes but only grasped through reasoning. And the soul, Socrates continues,

> reasons best when none of these senses trouble it, neither hearing nor sight, nor pain nor pleasure, but when it is most by itself, taking leave of the body and as far as possible having no contact or association with it in its search for reality.[69]

In Kierkegaard's estimation, the Socratic theory that we stand to regain a long-lost knowledge upon our death does not amount to much of an epistemology, because knowledge is here understood only negatively as that which sense-perception *prevents* us from having. However hard philosophy tries "to scare this pure essence of things out of its hiding places," Kierkegaard writes, "a considerable doubt remains as to whether anything will turn up other than the purely abstract (health, magnitude, etc.), which as such, by contrast with the concrete, is nothing."[70]

The process of abstraction is said to yield "nothing" because it consists in *taking away* something from a concrete particular. Virtue in itself, health in itself—these are derived by stripping particulars (or less general ideas) of their inessential elements. But Socrates does not expound on the essences that remain at the end of this process.[71] He conceives the abstract ideal simply as that which is *imperfectly* instantiated in the concrete, and the soul is said to be involved in a permanent conflict with the body. Knowledge is impossible in earthly life, and that also means we can know nothing about any other life. The philosopher must depart from the world with which he is acquainted, must become nothing, in order to obtain knowledge. Socrates' invitation into the fellowship of the knowing dead is really an invitation to make a leap into the unknown. His enthusiasm notwithstanding, the annihilation of the body does not appear as the return to a blissful eternity. Ironically, the philosopher's death wish, which Socrates states so casually, turns out to be absolutely subversive, and just as morbid as it initially sounded.

The doctrine of recollection promises to be much more substantial a theory of knowledge, for whereas the idea of enlightenment in the afterlife remains a hypothesis for which the living participants of the *Phaedo* have no real evidence, recollection can be observed in this life. Is it not the case, Socrates asks, that whenever someone, "on seeing something, realizes that that which he now sees wants to be like some other reality but falls short," the person in question "must have prior knowledge of that to which he says it is like?"[72] This transcendental argument certainly seems to be a substantial, positive claim: the argument posits the existence of universal essences.[73] And indeed the idea of recollection is a source of great epistemic optimism in Plato's philosophy and contributes to securing his metaphysical realism.

But there is a second way of understanding the theory of recollection that is actually cynical about our prospects for knowledge. It is typically Platonic, Kierkegaard writes,

> to fortify existence with the upbuilding thought that man is not driven empty-handed out into the world, to call to mind one's abundant equipment through recollection. It is Socratic to dismiss all reality and refer people to a recollection that retreats further and further toward a pre-historic era, just like that noble family's origin which no one could remember.[74]

Socrates' theory of recollection is like the platitudinous answer "Knowledge is knowledge" to which a frustrated inquirer must repeat the question. To say that if ever I come to know some x, I must have known it all along—or that if I judge an account of x to be true, I must already know what x is—is to say that coming to know presupposes knowing already. On the cynical interpretation, the transcendental argument for recollection means first of all that the origin or foundation of my knowledge is unknown. But just as aristocracy, founded as it is upon the inheritance of past greatness, would be undermined if that original greatness were forgotten, so knowledge would seem to cease being knowledge (reverting to mere opinion) if its origin—understood as its justification and foundation—can no longer be recalled. In Socrates' understanding of recollection, the origin of knowledge appears to ever recede into the past—in effect, to have been forgotten. The ironic ear should hear in Socrates' claims that virtue is knowledge and that knowledge cannot be taught the utterly negative conclusion that no account of virtue can in fact be given. On Kierkegaard's interpretation, Socrates' view of recollection is as formal as the qualification that each craft is done for its own sake. Just as the proposition "x is the essence of x" presupposes prior knowledge of x, so too the notion of virtue as knowledge ends up in the circular thesis that knowledge is had through knowledge.

Thus whereas Hegel lauds Socratic irony for "showing how to make abstract ideas concrete,"[75] Kierkegaard's Socrates cannot bridge the gap between the concrete and the abstract. "His abstract," he writes, "is a completely empty designation. He starts out from the concrete and arrives at the most abstract and there, where the investigation should begin, he stops."[76] Socratic abstraction constitutes a failure to provide an answer to a philosophical question. Socrates stops short of real inquiry; when he stops speaking, the question remains. At best, his answers clarify what the question really is. One might say that he analyzes the question and that, as such, the answers he gives are analytic. Just as we must already know the answer to the question "What is x?" in order for the answer "$x = x$" to be informative, so all Socrates ever offers by way of answer or theory are merely reformulations of the question. Together, question and answer make a tautology.

On Kierkegaard's interpretation of Socrates, he comes out as at once a cognitivist about morality and a doxastic voluntarist. His philosophical inquiry into the nature of virtue implies that we can think our way to the answer: virtue is knowledge. At the same time, Kierkegaard's Socrates regards knowledge as something for which the subject is responsible, because in assenting to a proposition he exercises his freedom. When Socrates explores the nature of virtue—which pertains to the realm of action and freedom—he is then necessarily also exploring the nature of knowledge and thought. His thinking is about thinking itself; his inquiry into virtue is itself virtuous. If

Socrates' practice of philosophy is an art, it is a classical one: in it, form and content are reflected into one another. Just as Mozart found in sensuality the subject matter that inheres in music, so virtue inheres already in the approach to philosophy with which Socrates inquires into virtue's nature.

The *Symposium* is the key text in Kierkegaard's treatment of Socratic irony. Here Socrates professes to have learnt the art of love from Diotima, and to have knowledge about nothing except love. Plato scholars are sometimes troubled by this claim to knowledge, which contradicts Socrates' usual line about being ignorant. Yet on Kierkegaard's interpretation, the Socratic art of love is not some theoretical knowledge but a practice—and a negative one. The Greek "ta erotika"—"matters of love"—sounds related to the word for "question" ("erotisi"). In the *Cratylus*, Plato explicitly suggests a connection between the meanings of these terms:

> The name hero (*heros*) is only a slightly altered form of the word love (*eros*)— the very thing from which heroes sprang. And either this is the reason they were called heroes or else because they were sophists, clever speech-makers and dialecticians, skilled at questioning (erotan).[77]

As for negativity in the form of abstraction, Socrates offers in the *Symposium* not just the usual abstract qualifications of virtue or craft or knowledge but tells us about the very nature of the abstract itself. Beginning with one of his signature questions, whether love is the love of nothing or of something ("Of something, surely!"), and invoking as a necessary truth the impossibility of desiring what one already possesses, Socrates concludes that love is lack.[78] This is not only a negative definition but a definition wherein love is determined as negativity itself. "Love, you see, is desire, craving, etc.," Kierkegaard explains. "But desire, craving, etc. are nothing. Now we see the method."[79] Through this line of reasoning, love is

> continually disengaged more and more from the contingent concretion in which it appeared in the previous speeches and is taken back to its *most abstract definitions*, wherein it appears not as this or that love or as love for this or that, but as love for a something which it does not have, that is, as desire, longing.[80]

A particular kind of love, like the love of wisdom, is on Socrates' account defined as the lack of that thing—here, the lack of wisdom. Love in general must then be lack pure and simple, the fact of lacking some x, where x could be anything and has yet to be determined. The love thus described is "irony's love," Kierkegaard writes; "but irony is *the negative in love*, it is love's incitement,"[81] its "immanent negativity."[82] The result Socrates arrives at, Kierkegaard writes, "is actually the indeterminable determination of pure being: 'Love *is*,' because the addendum that it is longing, desire, is no determination, since it is merely a relation to a something, which is not given."[83] This definition is "the most abstract one, or more correctly, it is the abstract itself, not in the sense of ontology, but in the sense of that which lacks its content."[84] Eros is pure desire, pure negativity, for Socrates, and therefore the most abstract idea conceivable—indeed, abstraction itself. Socrates' idea of love is then the kind of idea that, according to "A," only music can express.

Irony as the Foundation of Ethics

Socrates' conceptual analysis of love is briefly stated, and soon Plato lets Diotima take over, albeit through Socrates' mouth. Like Socrates, she conceives love as lack—but not as mere lack. She presents Eros as the spirit that presides over all human striving, calling the individual to a quest for something truer and better, the precise nature of which as yet eludes him. According to Jacob Howland, the Socrates of Kierkegaard's *Philosophical Fragments* (signed "Johannes Climacus") is an eroticist in precisely this way. "Philosophy has two roots," Howland writes: "it is answerable to, and authorized by, the god" to whom Socrates refers in the *Apology*, "but also by what Socrates calls eros," which "is a daimonic or intermediate passion that binds the human with the divine and the self with that which transcends it."[85]

In *Concluding Unscientific Postscript*, Climacus in fact proposes to equate existence with eros. Like eros in the *Symposium*, he writes, existence is a continual striving, and life is a synthesis of infinite and finite.[86] As the inducer of such receptivity and striving, Howland continues, "eros is also a ground of faith"—faith that the desired object exists or that it is possible to achieve some aim.[87] Climacus' Socrates is, according to Howland, "confident that the philosophical quest is meaningful because he is confident that there is some truth to be uncovered."[88] Kierkegaard would seem to agree with this in his discussion of the condemnation of Socrates in *The Concept of Irony* when he writes that "the foundation of everything, the eternal, the divine—of this

[Socrates] was ignorant; that is to say, he knew that it was, but he did not know what it was."[89]

Thinking along similar lines, Jonathan Lear contests the idea that irony, for Kierkegaard, is purely negative. His argument echoes Socrates' claim in the *Phaedo* that judgments about the imperfections of concrete particulars presuppose knowledge of the essences they deficiently instantiate.[90] Lear's ironist senses that actuality is deficient—that it is mere "pretense"—and this experience prompts him to search for the ideal.[91] A teacher, for example, may become disillusioned about his teaching and begin reflecting on what is the good of teaching, what makes a good teacher. Such an experience gave Descartes a proof for God's existence—"For how could I understand that I doubted or desired—that is, lacked something," he asks, "unless there were in me some idea of a more perfect being which enabled me to recognize my own defects by comparison?"[92] Although the precise content of that idea may not be apparent at the moment of crisis, Lear seems, like Descartes, to have faith that it is accessible through something like a process of recollection.

Notwithstanding Kierkegaard's remark about Socrates' certainty of the ground of all being, the Socrates of his dissertation is more negative than the one Howland finds in *Fragments* and the irony Lear locates in all human aspiration. This points us to a slip in Socrates' argument about love in the *Symposium*. Socrates equates lack with desire, but a lack by itself does not necessarily give rise to a desire. One can resign to a lack, or welcome it as a liberation. In his definition of love, Socrates adequately describes his irony's effect on his disciples—it does stir up longing in them—but not, ironically, his own enjoyment of lack as freedom. In his dissertation, Kierkegaard conceived of Socratic irony as a destructive force that cleared the way for autonomous thought and action, for morality and ideality. But this absolute negativity neither presupposes nor entails the positive—it only clears the way. "Socrates had *the idea as boundary*," Kierkegaard writes.[93] And if what sustains the conceivability of a perfect ideal on Lear's picture is simply that human beings always aim for what they take to be good, it does not entail any positive, thick, ideals—that we ought to cultivate our intellect, for example, or always be forgiving of others' flaws. The idea that the good is whatever anyone strives for—Socrates' initial characterization of the good in the *Protagoras*—is a completely abstract and empty idea. Such a conception of the good is characteristically Socratic, according to Kierkegaard: "even the good he had only as infinite negativity."[94]

Christine Habbard, too, thinks Socratic irony yields something positive, though in a slightly different way than Howland and Lear. She understands Socratic irony as Kierkegaard's alternative answer to Hegel's question, in the beginning of the first book of the *Science of Logic*, "With what must the science begin?"[95] Habbard suggests that irony makes a good philosophical beginning because it is the beginning of ethics. *The Concept of Irony*, she writes, "gives the impetus to one of Kierkegaard's most important moves: the shift from metaphysics to ethics as *Prima Philosophia*, the decision to take existence seriously."[96] Socrates, she continues, "inaugurates philosophy by dislodging ontology to establish the original move of ethics as the only source of absoluity."[97] The ironist, "in his absolute negativity, becomes aware of himself as a principle of self-determination; he creates the objective void in which the self can then deploy itself in its independence to all givenness, in its irreducibility to all phenomena."[98] But it's not clear how anything within the ironic standpoint—the assertion of negative freedom—allows the ironist to move beyond it. Habbard talks about "self-determination" and it is certainly true that what the ironist has discovered is that nothing other than he can determine his thought and will. Yet this negative freedom does not issue any principles according to which the ironist can reach positive judgments or volitions. It doesn't follow from his negative freedom that, for instance, he should always treat the other as an end and never merely as a means. Nor does negative freedom supply him with epistemological criteria according to which he can decide such things as whether his sense impressions are veridical. Although Kierkegaard does repeatedly call Socrates "the beginning," Socratic irony as he conceives it is in fact better thought of as an ending. He concedes as much when he writes that irony

> is the *beginning*, and yet no more than the beginning; it is and it is not, and its polemic is a beginning that is just as much a conclusion, for the destruction of the earlier development is just as much its ending as it is the beginning of the new development, since the destruction is possible only because the new principle is already present as possibility.[99]

The ironist is capable only of denying and undermining: of alienating the phenomenal world from ideality. In the rest of her discussion, Habbard finds a solution to this problem only by conflating Socrates and Judge Wilhelm, the fictional author of *Either/Or 2*. "Socrates' lesson," Habbard now says, is that "relating to oneself is *not* about knowing oneself, but about the acceptance, the recognition, of something that I can neither know, nor master, in me, but of which I nonetheless must take responsibility."[100] Nowhere in Kierkegaard's exposition of Socratic irony do we find such a lesson, such a call to an affirmation of the given. The Judge's imperative about the appropriation of one's own past, one's cultural context, and all the contingent features of one's finite embodied self is the diametrical opposite of Socrates' resistance to all external determination.

Troubled by the pure negativity of the dissertation's Socrates, John Lippitt looks to yet another model of ethics in Kierkegaard's scholarship—the *Postscript*—as a corrective. "Socrates is used by Kierkegaard in *The Concept of Irony* as the exemplar of 'total' irony," Lippitt writes, "yet later, by Climacus in the *Postscript*, as an exemplary subjective thinker. In order to play the latter role, there needs to be a degree of stability to Socrates' irony"[101]—it cannot be infinite negative freedom. The appropriate place for irony, according to Lippitt, is as a teacher's "incognito" in speaking to a pupil without directly conveying the truth. This irony may not be that riddle "to which one at the same time has the solution," but it is a riddle that in principle admits of a solution, a riddle that hides a positive claim. To speak ironically is not to assert nothing but to speak ambiguously such that, for example, the speech admits of an exoteric and an esoteric interpretation. The pupil is to figure out the meaning for himself, and in so doing rely on his own intellectual capacity rather than the authority of the teacher. Arguing along similar lines, Martin Andic writes that "*The Concept of Irony* is itself an ironic work" because it "means something different and more than what it seems to mean."[102] Socrates' irony, he explains, "seems entirely negative but that is an appearance to a viewpoint outside it. Irony is meant to be understood and from within it is seen to be positive in its orientation to the ethical."[103] In other words, infinite negative freedom is thought to square badly with Socrates' pedagogical aspirations and with his role as "ethicist." Lippitt and Andic thus conceive Socratic irony the way Hegel does: as a form of pretense that can be used maieutically.[104] It "does *not* follow from the fact that an author uses irony and humour that all he says thereby descends into undecidability," Lippitt insists. In order to escape "Kierkegaard's powerful charge" in the last chapters of the dissertation against "total" irony, Lippitt writes, "it is important that the ironist has a position."[105]

These readings both presuppose that Kierkegaard presented his Socrates as a model for emulation. As such, it is easy to see why these interpreters should be anxious to temper Socrates' negativity. But Kierkegaard does not urge his readers to become ironists, and for all his insistence that Socrates' position was irony, it is doubtful whether anyone other than God—or the devil—could be a perfect ironist. Rather, Socrates is for Kierkegaard the embodiment of a certain point in the development of consciousness, philosophy, morality, and world history, and the dissertation is very much a dialogue with Hegel regarding these issues. Louis Mackey reads *The Concept of Irony* as a critique of Hegel, and far from wanting to temper Socrates' negative freedom, Mackey thinks that it is precisely in the utter negativity of irony that the challenge to Hegel lies. The "purpose of Kierkegaard's analysis of irony," Mackey writes,

> is to mount an attack on two important Hegelian concepts. The concept of the *nothing* (=bare being) from which the Hegelian system is alleged to begin; and the *negation* that is alleged to move the dialectic and thereby provide the Idea with the repeated new beginnings essential to its unfolding and fulfillment in history.[106]

Kierkegaard's "anti-Hegelian point," Mackey continues, is that "negation is really negation. From nothing—real nothing—nothing can begin. Certainly not *das absolut Wissen*."[107] Although Mackey doesn't cite Hegel's writings, he seems, like Habbard, to have in mind the *Science of Logic*, where Hegel discusses the question of how philosophy begins.

Mackey is right to identify Kierkegaard's insistence that Socratic irony is the nothing from which nothing comes as a criticism of what he takes to be Hegel's view; but he seems to miss that Kierkegaard is just as adamant in making the apparently contradictory claim that Socratic irony itself came out of nothing. At any rate, it is with Hegel's *Lectures on the History of Philosophy* rather than with the *Science of Logic* that Kierkegaard is debating. What he objects to is Hegel's view, as he takes it, that world history is a process whose every stage is logically related to what preceded it. There are no radically new beginnings within the world thus conceived; no philosophical outlook begins from nothing. In his lectures, Hegel says that Socrates "stands in continuity with his time"[108] and that Plato's philosophy is in turn a continuation of Socrates'.[109] Because "Philosophy in its ultimate essence is one and the same," Hegel writes; through history, "Philosophy has one thought," not many.[110] To further develop the philosophy that preceded him is the philosopher's task. Every philosopher "will and must take up into his own, all philosophies that went before."[111] Kierkegaard summarizes this by saying that "the world process" for Hegel is "not a revolution but an evolution."[112] Contrary to Hegel, Kierkegaard claims that Socrates is "the nothing with which we must nonetheless begin"[113] and that despite Socrates' apparent continuity with this past,

> one must remember that he cannot be absolutely explained by what preceded him, that if in one sense he may be regarded as the logical conclusion to the premises of the past, there is [nonetheless] more in him than what was present in the premises: the *Ursprüngliche* [the primordial thing] that is necessary for him to be truly a turning point.[114]

Mackey might be right that Kierkegaard does not "offer a new solution to Hegel's problem"—the problem of beginning in philosophy.[115] Socrates' discovery and assertion of his infinite negative freedom is an original movement, according to Kierkegaard, and it is true that Kierkegaard seems more fascinated than Hegel by the mystery of how such original movements occur in the midst of history. But even if Kierkegaard, as Mackey puts it, takes "Hegel's problem (infinitely) more seriously than he himself did,"[116] Kierkegaard is less skeptical than Mackey about the possibility of new beginnings. What the modal claim that nothing comes from nothing means for Kierkegaard is that no post-Socratic philosophy developed inevitably out of Socratic irony. Plato's philosophy, for example, is an original beginning.

This disagreement between Kierkegaard and Hegel takes place against the background of their very similar accounts of Socrates' stance. Hegel calls Socrates "the founder of morality":

> Socrates expresses real existence as the universal "I," as the consciousness which rests in itself; but that is the good as such, which is free from existent reality, free from individual sensuous consciousness of feeling and desire, free finally from the theoretically speculative thought about nature.[117]

Like Kierkegaard, Hegel thinks that Socrates discovered the "I" in its negative freedom and that, as such, he was also the first person to achieve self-consciousness. But Hegel goes on to identify that negative freedom with the good. Kierkegaard agrees to this identification only insofar as this good is conceived in the thinnest possible way. If the ironist were constrained by the categorical imperative or specific moral principles involving thicker moral concepts such as brutality and compassion, his negative freedom would not be infinite.

In other words, Kierkegaard thinks that one can be both free and evil and he knows that Hegel concedes this in *Philosophy of Right*. Even though Hegel "wants to reclaim a positivity" for Socrates, "it nevertheless turns out that the individual is arbitrarily self-determining in relation to the good, and that the good as such"—in a thicker sense—"has no absolutely obligating power."[118] It may be suspended, as Kierkegaard thinks it was for Abraham, in favor of some other telos. In his more elaborate discussion of the origin of morality, Hegel indeed considers indifference to be a stage in the development of conscience. "Once self-consciousness has reduced all otherwise valid duties to emptiness and itself to the sheer inwardness of the will," he writes,

> it has become the potentiality of either making the absolutely universal its principle, or equally well of elevating above the universal the self-will of private particularity, taking that as its principle and realizing it through its actions, i.e. it has become potentially evil.[119]

The self at this stage is mere "formal subjectivity" and it is a stage that according to Hegel ought to be surpassed.[120] Yet whereas he said that Socrates was continuous with his time, Hegel doesn't think that "the sheer inwardness of the will" necessarily yields a more substantial morality. In principle, the individual may dwell indefinitely at that point before good and evil. The only good that binds such a person is the bare, thin good of the *Protagoras*: the good presupposed by any telos, the good in relation to which the will is always strong. No one, Socrates says there, "goes willingly toward the bad or what he believes to be bad"; nor is it "in human nature, so it seems, to want to go toward what one believes to be bad instead of to the good."[121] But this good is a formal idea that can take as its content—can attach value to—anything. Rather than have binding power upon the individual, it applies by default to any desire. It is unclear how different Kierkegaard's and Hegel's views ultimately are. Their most significant difference might be, as I suggested earlier, that Kierkegaard relishes in the idea that negative freedom leaves everything open. Hegel, like Lippitt and Andic and, perhaps, Climacus, is anxious to hurry humanity across the abyss between infinite negative freedom and the state where we are bound by universal morality and know the difference between good and evil.

Hegel admits that the subject is at one point indifferent between good and evil, and yet as he tells the story, the good somehow prevails.

Liberation and Privation

To ask how Kierkegaard's Socrates can be saved from the pure negativity of his irony or turned into a positive thinker is to ask the wrong question. We encounter in his dissertation characters who do go beyond negative freedom—or, at least, fail at irony. *The Concept of Irony* invites us to study what distinguishes Socrates' negative philosophy from a philosophy with positive aspirations by addressing the question of what it is that keeps Socrates' disciples from taking up the ironic position. Kierkegaard gives us the beginning of an answer when he writes that the disciples at first felt "liberated and expanded by the ironist's touch,"[122] but that

> the freedom [Socrates] himself enjoyed in ironic satisfaction the others could not enjoy, and so it developed longing and yearning in them. Therefore, while his own position rounds itself off in itself, this position becomes only the condition for a new position when absorbed by the consciousness of others. The reason Socrates could be satisfied in this ignorance was that he had no deeper speculative craving.[123]

The disciples are freed like Socrates is free; but unlike Socrates, they take no pleasure in this freedom. The latter, moreover, are hurt that Socrates pushes them away: as Socrates retreated, leaving the disciples alone with their freedom, "they felt the deep pain of unhappy love," Kierkegaard writes; felt "that they were betrayed, that it was not Socrates who loved them but they who loved Socrates, and yet that they were not able to tear themselves away from him."[124] Studying how these figures differ from Socrates will highlight the gap between irony and substantial morality or positive knowledge.

If Kierkegaard is right, Socrates reveals the truth not only about the nature of his abstraction but also of his own philosophical practice when he defines love as lack. For insofar as Socrates' philosophy is an exercise in that kind of abstraction, it serves to create a lack. Socrates, Kierkegaard writes,

> placed people under his dialectical air-pump, deprived them of the atmospheric air in which they were accustomed to breathing, and left them

standing. For them everything was now lost, unless they could breathe pure ether. Socrates, however, had nothing more to do with them but rushed on to new ventures.[125]

In creating such a vacuum, such a lack, Socrates is according to his own definition arousing a desire. That is why the charge that Socrates "seduced" the youth was fair, in Kierkegaard's view, for undoubtedly Socrates was an "eroticist" who awakened in the Athenian youths a love that he did not reciprocate. He "had all the seductive gifts of the mind," Kierkegaard writes,

> but share, fulfill, enrich—this he could not do. In this sense, one might call him *a seducer*, he infatuated the young, *awakened longings* in them but *did not satisfy* them, let them flare up in the thrilling joy of being touched but never gave them strong and nourishing food. He deceived them all just as he deceived Alcibiades, who himself says, as was mentioned earlier, that instead of being the lover Socrates became the beloved.[126]

Socrates undermines his interlocutor's beliefs by showing them to be inconsistent or otherwise inadequate. That is, he creates in his interlocutors—or makes them for the first time aware of—a lack of knowledge. And out of this lack of knowledge springs a desire, a love of knowledge, which love is therefore from the beginning an unhappy, unrequited love. The new position for which irony creates the condition is Diotima's eros, which Howland and Lear attribute to Socrates: love as longing and, as we will see in the next chapter, despair.

2

Unhappy Reflection

Though he's never mentioned in it, Socrates haunts *Either/Or*. Most obviously, the Socratic revolution is the backdrop of A's essay on tragedy. The tragic comfort of ancient Greece is not available to modern man, "A" writes, because

> Our age has lost all the substantial determinations of family, state, kindred; it must turn every individual over to himself completely such that, in the strictest sense, he becomes his own creator.[1]

The modern individual has discovered in himself an infinite negative freedom that affords him autonomy of thought and action. He is answerable for himself, for his own beliefs and deeds, and only for them. He can neither hide behind tradition and attachments to cultures or states when called upon to justify what he thinks and does, nor be held accountable for those institutions, which are external to him.

It would be natural to assume that in this characterization of modernity, "A" has in mind a worldview shaped by Enlightenment thinkers—Descartes, Spinoza, Kant—except that it follows to a T the account of Socratic irony Kierkegaard gives in his dissertation. Socrates, Kierkegaard wrote there, "cut the umbilical cord of substantiality"[2]—"tipped one individual after the other out of the substantial actuality of the state."[3] And anyway, what is the common denominator of those seventeenth- and eighteenth-century rationalists if not a Socratic bulldozing of common sense and received opinions? What must take the place of conventional wisdom is rational thought, whose locus is not the culture as a whole, nor the sovereign state, but each individual mind. Thus in the *Republic*, Socrates argues that justice cannot be whatever powerful men stipulate it to be; in the *Euthyphro*, that the good is not whatever pleases the gods. Any appeal to such authorities are invalid, because the good and the just are ideals knowable to everyone through reflection, and far from deciding what is good and just, the rulers and the gods are subject to others' assessment as to how well they live up to that ideal. Regarding Socrates' reaction to the jury's verdict, in the *Apology*, Kierkegaard remarks in his dissertation that Socrates "begins by expressing his amazement at being convicted by such a small majority; by this he indicates that he does not see in the state's sentence an objectively valid view in contrast to the particular subject."[4] Whether Socrates is guilty as charged is hardly a matter that can be decided by a vote, by the greater power of the majority. The credo "know yourself" is not a call to any theoretical pursuit, according to Kierkegaard, but a practical and entirely negative command: separate yourself from all other things.[5] And just as by way of irony, Socrates "went beyond the validity of the substantial life of the state, so too *family life* had *no validity* for him. For him the state and the family were a sum of individuals."[6] He "dissolved that law of nature by which the individual member of a family rested in the whole family—i.e. piety."[7]

Yet Socrates did not go beyond the subjectivity achieved by ironic reflection. In this chapter, we will see what effect Socratic irony has on a typical student, Alcibiades, who like the modern Antigone and the Shadowgraphs does not want to live in perfect independence. I will begin by explaining how the difference between ancient and modern tragedy illustrates the difference between Antiquity and Modernity more generally, according to "A." Dissatisfied with modern tragedies, he suggests how the ambiguous guilt essential to tragedy might be recovered even in a modern storyline. In his rewriting of *Antigone*, what must take center stage is love, a rare vestige of ancient "substantiality." But because this modern love is separated from its object, it gives rise to an anxious reflection. "A" elaborates on this in "Shadowgraphs," whose heroines are caught up in endless reflection, trying to ascertain whether their lovers deceived them. This symptom of unrequited love resembles aporia, the effect a contradiction has on the intellect, and the predicament Alcibiades complains of suffering from in the *Symposium*.

The Tragic Loss of Tragedy

As we saw earlier, "A" characterizes Modernity exactly as Kierkegaard described the world Socrates left in his wake. He departs from Candidate Kierkegaard only when it comes to assessing this world. Although the author of *Irony* keeps a certain distance from his subject, his private admiration for Socrates sometimes erupts through the surface of disinterested scholarship:

> My reviewer! Please permit me but one point, one innocent parenthesis, in order to vent my thanks, my gratitude for the relief I found in reading Plato. For where is bliss to be found if not in the infinite tranquility with which, in the still night, the idea soundlessly, solemnly, gently, and yet so powerfully unfurls itself in the rhythm of dialogue, as if nothing else existed in the world.[8]

Also when speaking in a measured scholarly tone, Kierkegaard proclaims Socrates to be the absolute. For he brought irony into the world, and every dignified human life begins with irony, begins with an assertion of negative freedom. "A," on the other hand, is very critical of modernity's emphasis on the individual and negative freedom. At times, he questions the truth or coherence of this worldview, other times he points to its damaging results. Because we moderns believe ourselves to enjoy freedom of action, we also "know that there is something called responsibility and that this means something."[9] This is the root of our depression, "A" says[10]—it is a heavy thought that weighs our minds down, inflects our temperament with a seriousness that holds us back from carefree abandon to joy. We cannot blame our crimes or misfortunes on fate, in the way of Oedipus. But if Oedipus' self-mutilation upon realizing that he has killed his own father and married his mother testifies to an overwhelming pain—how existing in this revolting world has become unbearable to him—"A" thinks our predicament worse yet.

In *The Birth of Tragedy*, Nietzsche advanced an argument similar to Kierkegaard's by asking his reader to consider "the consequences of the Socratic maxims: 'Virtue is knowledge; man sins only from ignorance; he who is virtuous is happy.' In these three basic forms of optimism lies the death of tragedy."[11] Whereas Kierkegaard emphasizes in *The Concept of Irony* that Socrates' philosophical stance is entirely practical, and "A" too thinks modernity is characterized by our ethical self-conception, Nietzsche's Socrates is an exemplary "theoretical man" whose optimism derives not from the discovery of freedom but from a faith in knowledge and a conviction that "thought, using the thread of causality, can penetrate to the deepest abysses of being."[12] In other words, Nietzsche attributes the death of tragedy to Socrates' insistence on the world's intelligibility. A tragedy like *Oedipus Rex* is undermined by this Socrates, too. Its hero sinned in ignorance. By the logic of the "Socratic maxims," Oedipus has nothing to be sorry about.

But for "A" as for Kierkegaard, the difference between the modern and ancient worldviews lies first of all in the metaphysics of morality. Ancient tragedy, according to "A," is played out on the middle ground between Pelagianism—which affirms human freedom and denies original, "hereditary," sin—and substance monism, in which there is no individuality, no negative freedom whatsoever. If the individual is completely isolated and "absolutely the creator of his own fate," as per Pelagius, "there is nothing tragic anymore, but only evil."[13] But if, on the other hand, "individuals are just modifications of the eternal substance of life"[14]—as in Parmenides—then there is no distinction between activity and passive suffering. Any collision between different forces or principles—the obligations of citizenship and the love of kin, for example— is then merely apparent, the tragic view of the world doesn't cut to the bone of life, and tragic drama peddles an illusion. Tragedy requires a kind of agency that doesn't originate inside the agent. He feels responsible for his actions even as he knows himself not to be fully in control of them or the intentions which they execute. His guilt, when he does wrong or at least does harm to others or himself, is a soft guilt. The tragic hero must be both responsible and not responsible. Oedipus is both guilty and not guilty. He married Jocasta, married her voluntarily—but that she was his mother, he did not know. Incest was not his intention. Throughout his life, he learns, his actions have followed that preordained fate his parents sought to avoid when they threw him down the hill in infancy. His retrospective knowledge that he acted in ignorance and indeed could not have done otherwise—could not have escaped his destiny— does not dissolve his horror, his disgust with himself. It is he, after all, who has engaged in incest, who has killed his own father. As Bernard Williams puts it, insisting like "A" on the ambiguity of Oedipus' agency, responsibility and guilt: "the terrible thing that *happened* to him, through no fault of his own, was that he *did* those things."[15]

Love and Substantiality

The last part of the Oedipus trilogy, *Antigone*, may seem to be fundamentally different as its heroine commits her crime with eyes wide open. When

Antigone defies King Creon by burying her brother, she is fully aware that this is a transgression against the state. Her intention is to honor her brother, but she knows that this action is at the same time a breach of her civic duty. It certainly seems that she could have done otherwise—Sophocles makes this clear when he presents us with Antigone's sister, Ismene, who refuses to disobey Creon's decree. Nonetheless the claims of piety and blood are forces compelling Antigone's will from a larger sphere of influence. Moreover, her action is a *re*action to a state of affairs she had no hand in bringing about, and may even be seen as reflexive, not the outcome of deliberation. And to the spectator, Antigone's predicament will seem to be a continuation of Oedipus' misfortune. Antigone's sad fate, "A" says, "is like a reverberation of the father's," and when she decides to bury her brother despite the new king's prohibition, "we see in this not so much a free act as a fateful necessity, which visits the iniquities of the fathers upon the children."[16] In this way, there is both freedom and compulsion in Antigone's action: her action is at the same time a suffering, something the gods do to her, something she does not as an individual but as part of a family.

Quite aside from the question of what she should have done, Kierkegaard's Socrates would say that Antigone is responsible for her action and cannot blame it on anyone else. There is no direct causal link between the divine command to honor one's family and the action by which Antigone carries it out. Between the two stands a free individual who can subject that command to her own rational scrutiny rather than be subject to it. If she is caught between two conflicting duties then she must figure out which takes precedence. And if Socrates is right that a family is just a number of individuals, Antigone's selfless loyalty to her brother is utterly irrational. By sacrificing herself to save her brother Polyneices' honor, it is as though Antigone took upon herself the responsibility for his crime, which crime is Creon's reason for prohibiting that traitor's burial. But one person cannot be responsible for what another does: there is no metaphysical connection between persons to allow such a transference of guilt. In the light of Socratic individualism and libertarianism, Antigone's tragedy evaporates. She is either guilty or innocent, and there is no middle between them.

Why, then, should we be worse off with this autonomy, this morality that sees a clear cut between right and wrong, innocence and guilt, action and suffering? "A" explains it through an exposition of the different emotions that attend suffering and doing harm. He proposes to use the term "pain" to designate an acute displeasure. The worst pain is remorse, an agent's regret about an action of his, and a distinctly moral feeling. By contrast, "sorrow" denotes by A's stipulation an immediate awareness of some ill. It pertains to what one undergoes or witnesses. In ancient tragedy, where the hero's actions are also understood as events that happen to him, "the sorrow is deeper, the pain lesser," "A" says.[17] And sorrow, unlike pain, is soothing; in sorrow, we are resigned to our fate, and this allows us rest. To know that one can do nothing to change one's fate can break one's spirit, but it also bars the regret that so easily turns into self-loathing. To regret is to pick at the wound by reflecting on what one ought to have done, what could have been done differently. As we recall the critical moment, the will charges again and again as if to act, and yet this agitation cannot be discharged in action, because the moment for intervention is forever past.

The element of innocence in tragic guilt also allowed the spectator of an ancient tragedy to abandon himself to cathartic compassion, a compassion that wished to further redeem the hero by sharing his sorrow. But the modern tragic hero, fully responsible for his crime, must bear his pain alone. The modern spectator shouts at the tragic hero: "help yourself, and heaven will help you!"—in other words, "A" says, "the spectator has lost compassion."[18] Not only is freedom a burden, according to "A," but modern individualism has lost sight of what a person really is. Our generation, he says, thinks of itself as "a kingdom of gods."[19] But negative freedom does not amount to omnipotence, and despite our freedom we cannot design our own fate. Every individual, "however original, is still a child of God, of his age, of his nation, of his family, of his friends, and only in them does he have his truth."[20] There is always an element of "substantiality" in a person: we are all determined partly from without. Our attachments to persons and our culture are part of our identities, as is our history. Yet in modern tragedy, all of this has been abstracted away. It is not concerned with narrating the hero's entire life, finding the roots of his transgression in his past, but only with the particular situation in which he commits it. "Modern tragedy has no epic foreground, no epic remainder," "A" says. "The hero stands and falls entirely on his own deeds."[21] It treats the hero as a criminal, and is as impatient as the harshest judge with stories about extenuating circumstances. "When a criminal before a judge wants to be excused with reference to the fact that his mother had a habit of stealing, and particularly during the time she was pregnant with him," then the judge will point out that "he is dealing with the thief, and not the thief's mother."[22]

To "A," it is tragic that modern man finds himself so alone; and as he points out, it is precisely in the anxiety that inevitably haunts freedom that writers have found stuff for modern tragic dramas. The focal point of such tragedies is the hero's psyche rather than the objective facts of his situation; *Hamlet*, for example, portrays the agony of reflection as the protagonist tries, first, to determine whether his uncle killed his father, and second, to decide on a course of action of his own. Still, "A" wants modern tragedy to recover the substantiality of human beings, and he proceeds to sketch a modern drama where the tragedy does not lie in ceaseless reflection but in the struggle between reflection and passion, subjectivity and substantiality, inside the person. He finds it best to cast a woman in the leading role of such a tragedy. "As a woman," he explains, "she will have enough substantiality for the sorrow to appear but as one belonging to a reflective world she will have reflection enough to feel pain."[23] Her guilt will be tragic—not of her own doing—so that if reflection were "present in its infinitude" it would "reflect her out of her guilt."[24] But when reflection constantly runs up against her ties to the external world which refuse to be severed, it will "not reflect her out of her sorrow but into it; at every moment it will transform sorrow into pain for her."[25]

"A" decides to create a modern version of *Antigone*, illustrating by contrast with Sophocles' original work the difference between Antiquity and Modernity. The ancient Antigone's kinship with Oedipus is an objective relation and, "A" says, "the father's guilt and suffering are an external fact" in which Antigone participates with "childlike piety."[26] She shares his sorrow, but his misfortune is "an unshakable fact, which her sorrow does not move (*quod non volvit in pectore* [which she does not turn over in her heart])."[27] She doesn't ruminate over what could have been done to prevent Oedipus from committing his crimes. It is a fixture of her world. But in A's modern version, nobody knows what Oedipus has done—nobody except Antigone. Her father is dead, and she does not know whether he himself knew. This, "A" says, is an occasion for anxiety.[28] If she knew that he knew, then the pain he must have felt would be crystallized into an unchangeable fact, something to sorrow over. But with the uncertainty—with the room for hope—she constantly returns to it in thought, trying to ascertain whether he knew, now surging with hope that he didn't, now crashing in pain and despair with the thought that he did. Until a fact has been established, there is a task for reflection, and this reflection is a nagging anxiety that holds Antigone hostage inside her own mind, preventing her from enjoying her life, her youth, the romantic love of another man. Whereas the ancient Antigone was sentenced to live burial, the modern Antigone's love for her father is its own punishment. In attending to her reflective project, she buries herself alive. Thus whereas Sophocles' *Antigone* concludes with the heroine's lamenting the cruel punishment whereby she is neither among the living nor among the dead, "our Antigone can say that about her whole life."[29]

If she could assert herself as a fully independent individual then she would shake off the whole gruesome business of Oedipus' crimes—then she could say, as Socrates would have her say, that what he did is not *her* problem. But as it is, "A" says, she "loves her father with all her soul, and this love pulls her away from herself into her father's guilt."[30] Reality, Kierkegaard writes in his dissertation, "stands in a twofold relation to the subject: partly as a gift that refuses to be rejected, partly as a task that wants to be fulfilled."[31] Oedipus is a gift offered to the modern Antigone; her love for him becomes a lifelong project of protecting his honor and agonizing in his stead. Her father is part of her identity; in loving him, she becomes herself. But whereas "choose yourself" is something Judge Wilhelm *commands* "A" to do, the modern Antigone is not moved by duties or principles but by inclination, and by an intuitive sense of the meaning of family. Her loving attachment is the substantial element in an otherwise modern girl. She had no share in committing those crimes, yet by virtue of loving him, she regrets his actions on his behalf. Her regret would make of her, retroactively, his accomplice. She does not repent but *regret* her way into family. In this way, her love exhibits the ambiguity between deed and suffering that for "A" is essential to tragedy.[32] At the same time, her approach to love is decidedly modern. The ancient worldview had blood and name and gods and did not need subjective, reflectively endorsed and willfully reinforced love to bind family members together. A love like the modern Antigone's is a distinctly post-Socratic phenomenon.

It is worth pausing here to remark upon how different this Antigone's approach to life is from that of *Either/Or*'s seducers. Whereas an aesthetic lover like Don Juan is constituted entirely by his desire and is completely immediate, the modern Antigone also has a sense of responsibility—so strong is this sense that it extends beyond the realm of her own agency. She doesn't act out all her impulses but knows to hide some things; through the power of her will, her outside is separate from her inside. And whereas Johannes the Seducer takes an aesthetic distance to Cordelia, enjoying his flirtation with her as a spectacle of which he is also the director, Antigone's love wants nothing other than to sustain a bond with her father, however painful that bond is. And her reflection is driven by a desire to know—her love is also a love of truth—whereas Johannes is happy to create his own reality.

Endless Reflection

Among Sophocles' works is one that—even in its ancient form—tends toward modern tragedy, according to "A." This is *Philoctetes*.[33] The insult added to Philoctetes' snakebite injury was that he did not enjoy his comrades' compassion. Annoyed by his cries and disgusted by his reeking wound, they abandoned him. This is the premise of the play. Alcibiades had offered as the moral of the story that we can only sympathize with the kind of suffering we ourselves have endured—that like is known by like. For "A," what is remarkable in this tragedy is how misfortune arouses the hero's reflection. Philoctetes does not just suffer but ventures to ask questions about his suffering. Pain begins when a certain kind of doubt enters the hero's mind. "The first doubt with which pain really begins," "A" writes, is "Why has this befallen me; can it not be otherwise?"[34] With this urge to find explanations, the individual's consciousness enters a higher level. Though Schopenhauer considered *Philoctetes* a failed and repugnant tragedy, its hero would actually serve him as a good example when he writes that the world poses a theoretical problem only because it is a practical, or moral, problem.[35] The first philosophical question, on this view, is "Why are things this way when they ought to be another way?" The problem of evil is the fundamental philosophical problem. It is the incomprehensibility of suffering and the seeming incongruence between *is* and *ought* that sparks Philoctetes' thinking. "No evil thing has been known to perish," he says bitterly;

> no, the gods take a tender care of such [things], and have a strange joy in turning back from Hades all things villainous and knavish, while they are ever sending the just and the good out of life. How am I to imagine these things or wherein shall I praise them when, praising the ways of the gods, I find that the gods are evil?[36]

Philoctetes' suffering seems unjust to him: he cannot see what he's done to deserve it. The encounter with evil prompts him to question the grounds of the piety expected of humans.

In reflection the mind turns inward and tries to find sufficient reasons and establish relations between ideas. The awakening of reflection is also the awakening of self-consciousness and subjectivity and it effects an estrangement from the external world to which naïve, immediate consciousness was subservient. In asking why he has to suffer, Philoctetes marks a distance between himself and the world. Just by raising the question, he rebels against the givenness of the world and implies that actuality is not necessary, that things could have been otherwise. At the same time, he opens himself to the possibility of hearing an answer that he won't like. For it might be that his suffering is a just punishment for some wrongdoing of his. By asking for a justification he thus sets himself up for the deep pain of remorse. If, on the other hand, his question remains unanswered, reflection will continue to ponder the matter, and for as long as no answer is found, Philoctetes will be in limbo. For he can neither be sent to the hell of remorse nor go back to the soothing sorrow that presupposes unreflective fatalism. The question "why" ushers us across a point of no return.

Caught up in such barren reflection, the tragic individual vacillates between sorrow and pain. "A" calls this intermediate state "reflective sorrow" and devotes the next essay, "Shadowgraphs," to the living dead who populate that no man's land between the aesthetic and the ethical: a world of shadows whose inhabitants can neither be portrayed in painting nor express themselves in the universal terms of language. We have already been introduced to the three characters in whom "A" detects this kind of sorrow: Marie from Goethe's *Clavigo*, Elvira from Mozart's *Don Giovanni*, and Gretchen from Goethe's *Faust*. Each suffers from unrequited love: they have all been seduced and abandoned. That is what is significant for "A." "Her story is brief," he says of Marie: "Clavigo became engaged to her; Clavigo left her. This information is enough" to give an idea of her predicament, just as it is sufficient to know of Sisyphus that he "rolls a stone up the mountain."[37] In Elvira's case it is not a question of a broken engagement but the vow of chastity she broke in order to be with Don Juan. For as "A" points out, Elvira used to be a nun: "it is from the peacefulness of a convent that Don Juan has torn her."[38] Regarding Margaret, finally, suffice it to recall the image Goethe evokes for us of this young girl, herself a flower, picking the petals off a daisy one by one.

If Philoctetes' philosophical rite of passage was an encounter with injustice, the Shadowgraphs are first initiated into philosophy by a rift between appearance and reality. Elvira confronts evidence that Don Juan's love might have been *merely apparent*, a false impression created by his seduction. Taking sensuality to be infused with personal love—something ethical—Elvira is not only heartbroken when Don Juan abandons her. She is also quite simply perplexed. His deception is not just an ethical problem but becomes, for her, a theoretical one. In that sense her experience is an example of the experiences that Plato, in the *Republic*, calls "summoners": contradictory perceptions that prompt reflection and *summon reason* to come to the senses' aid.[39] Some illusions can be dispelled by simple explanations: if a deception is proven, "A" says, "and the person concerned has realized that it is a deception, then the sorrow does not cease, but it becomes an immediate sorrow, not a reflective sorrow."[40] Yet "that a deception really is a deception is often very difficult to determine clearly."[41] For all that could be brought in as evidence of a man's true feelings and intentions are outward signs: what he said, what he did, how he looked and sounded. But such signs are themselves sensory, are themselves appearances, and since what's in question is the relation between sensory appearance and reality, these signs cannot yield any conclusive verdict.

As long as there are doubts about the deception, "A" says, the sorrow "will find no repose but must continue pacing back and forth in reflection."[42] What's special about reflective sorrow is precisely "that the sorrow is continually seeking its object."[43] For the Shadowgraphs, the theoretical question whether the beloved was a deceiver remains open and is plagued by particular dialectical difficulties. Marie's grief is uncertain of its object and indeed, as those around her ask impatiently,

> what is she sorrowing over? If he was a deceiver, then it's a good thing that he left her, the earlier the better; she should rejoice instead, and only be sorry that she ever loved him. And yet it is a deep sorrow that he was a deceiver.[44]

The reason it is easy for others to believe that Clavigo was a deceiver is that they never loved him.[45] But for Marie the very idea that her lover was a deceiver seems unfathomable. For love, "A" says, deception is a paradox—"an absolute paradox, and therein lies the necessity of a reflective grief."[46] Love requires transparency: a lover neither deceives nor accepts deception from the beloved. This condition is inherent in love: it is inconceivable to the Shadowgraphs that the seducer deceived them. A contrapositive formulation of this conditional—that if he deceived then he did not love—cannot help them. For they have solid evidence that he did love. What was his seduction, after all, if not a sensuous manifestation of love? What motivated his proposal, if not love? Nor are the Shadowgraphs capable of ceasing to love the beloved. The love he has aroused persists in spite of them. And so the Shadowgraphs' sorrow does not have an object, for the fact of deception is never established.

Deceptive appearances served as the Shadowgraphs' philosophical initiation but we can understand that which keeps them in the hamster wheel of reflection as an incongruence between the empirical reality of a seduction or a promise and their *a priori* ideal of love. The possibility that what a man says out loud does not manifest what he feels inside is a possibility to which the Shadowgraphs have an instinctive resistance, a resistance "A" presents as an intellectual, logical one. Marie fumbles for a causal principle that would let her deduce her beloved's innermost feelings from his speech, deed and outward appearance. His voice, she notes to herself,

> was so calm and yet so inspired, it sounded from an inwardness, the depth of which I could scarcely suspect, as if it were breaking a path through masses of rock. Can that voice deceive? What is the voice, then—is it a tap of the tongue, a noise that one can bring forth as one wishes? Somewhere in the soul it must surely have a home; it must have a birthplace.[47]

Something in Marie revolts against the very idea that a person might project a false exterior and, more generally, that what appears in the world might just be show. Yet even if intention could be infallibly inferred from speech, the result of this inquiry would be at odds with the painfully obvious fact that her beloved has broken off with her.

As long as she cannot abandon either the principle of transparency or her love, she will run up against the paradox. "The paradox is unthinkable," "A" says, "and yet love wants to think it, and depending on which factor stands out at the moment"—the different bits of evidence supporting one side or the other—"it approaches the thought, in different, contradictory ways, but it does not manage to think it."[48] This "path of thinking," he continues, "is infinite."[49] "Like the pendulum in a clock," reflective sorrow "swings back and forth and cannot find rest. It keeps starting over, deliberating anew: it interrogates the witnesses, comparing and scrutinizing the various statements."[50] It is really a trial that takes place in the minds of these women. The aim of the process is a judgment, a verdict regarding the seducer's guilt or innocence. But a young girl, like Marie Beaumarchais, "is not a lawyer."[51] She can pass a judgment, but not a conclusive one. This girl's judgment, "A" says,

> will always be such that although at first glance it is a judgment, it also contains something more that shows that it is no judgment, and also that at the very next moment a completely contradictory judgment may be passed.[52]

Marie is seeking to arrive at a judgment through reflection. Judgments, however, are not products of thought but acts of will: and will and thought are distinct mental faculties between which there can be no mediation.[53] This is the ethics of belief with which "A" seems to operate—a form of doxastic voluntarism. Although judgment may be construed as a collaborative effort between thought and will on this picture, "A" emphasizes that thought cannot provide the will with anything that would constitute sufficient conditions for a particular judgment. Every path of thinking is infinite: it cannot bring itself to an end. A real judgment is always an interruption, never a conclusion, of thought. By analogy, the evidence provided by a prosecutor does not mandate a jury or judge in a court of law to give a particular verdict. The evidence is subject to judgment. This is what allows a judge to arrive at a single verdict even when presented with opposing views from defense and prosecution. The unity of this judgment is not a synthetic unity: his task is not to make the two sides agree with one another, or to find a middle point between guilt and innocence. Therefore he is not prevented from making a judgment just because the two sides persistently contradict one another. He makes a verdict that cuts their argument short. Though a judge must be sensitive to the evidence presented by both the defense and the prosecution, he is not bound by a prior allegiance to either party. Similarly an effective will "must remain altogether indifferent," "A" says; "must begin in the power of its own willing."[54] But Marie's will does not have the courage to stand on its own; it wants to rely on reflection and always works, as "A" puts it, "in the service of reflection."[55]

Aporia as Despair

It is no wonder that Kierkegaard lets "A" compare the Shadowgraph women to Alcibiades by means of a reference to Philoctetes, for in his dissertation,

Kierkegaard seized upon Alcibiades' unhappy love, and the struggle of making sense of his situation which he relates in the *Symposium*, as evidence for Socrates' irony. Addressing a company of fellow-grievers, Alcibiades tells of his seduction into philosophy, his awakening from a naïve slumber, the slumber of immediacy. His heart and soul have been bitten by philosophy.[56] As befits a good *eromenos*—the younger part in an erotic-intellectual relationship—Alcibiades' account does not distinguish between Socrates as lover and as philosopher. This young man's infatuation with an older man is at the same time a longing for wisdom. The moment Socrates begins to speak, Alcibiades says, "my heart starts leaping in my chest."[57] With his words and arguments, Socrates "cast[s] spells on people"; indeed, Socrates' words have an intoxicating effect on Alcibiades, much like wine or snake venom, and therefore, "If I were to describe to you what an extraordinary effect his words have always had on me," he says, "you might actually suspect that I'm drunk!"[58]

Alcibiades envisions entering into both a romantic and an educational relationship with Socrates, as custom prescribes. When they first met, Alcibiades says,

> I thought [...] that what he really wanted was *me*, and that seemed to me the luckiest coincidence: all I had to do was to let him have his way with me, and he would teach me everything he knew.[59]

But Socrates did not pursue Alcibiades. He "presents himself as your lover," Alcibiades says, "and, before you know it, you're in love with him yourself!"[60] Once that happens—once the would-be beloved falls for the temptation—Socrates retreats, leaving his victim "deeply humiliated."[61] In Kierkegaard's words, Alcibiades "felt inseparably bound"[62] to Socrates and his sorrow reveals his lack of self-sufficiency—his inability to be happy without Socrates, which is also his inability to *be like* Socrates, a man who is sufficient unto himself. In the *Symposium*, Alcibiades despairs over Socrates' withdrawal from him: "I can't live without him!" he cries.[63] Just as Elvira cannot return to the convent once she has tasted romantic love, so Alcibiades cannot return to his former life and self, for he, too, lost his innocence when Socrates made him see that his "political career is a waste of time, while all that matters is just what I most neglect."[64] But although he claims that Socrates' arguments are "of great—no, of the greatest—importance for anyone who wants to become a truly good man,"[65] he also admits to having failed to adopt a new way of life. This is to be expected if Kierkegaard is right when he says that Socrates' teachings are wholly negative. He advised Alcibiades against a military career without proposing an alternative. Indeed, Alcibiades says, "he makes it seem that my life isn't worth living!"[66] According to Kierkegaard, Alcibiades' relation to Socrates is not exceptional; on the contrary, he fully grants Alcibiades' claim to be speaking for all the symposiasts (except, of course, Socrates himself). Indeed, if we are looking to understand Socrates' relation to his disciples, his relation to Alcibiades can serve us as "an example *instar omnium*."[67]

With his questions Socrates tempts his interlocutors to adopt a critical stance toward their own beliefs and ideas. Infinite negative freedom is achieved when the individual refuses to assert anything and refuses to let the empirical world determine his concepts. But to Socrates' disciples, this loss of belief does not feel like a liberation but a privation; what Socrates leaves behind is a vacuum that pulls on the world, wants only to be filled again. The state the disciples are left in is described in the first person not only in the *Symposium* but also in the *Meno*. Addressing Socrates, Meno says:

> you are bewitching and beguiling me, simply putting me under a spell, so that I am quite perplexed. Indeed, if a joke is in order, you seem, in appearance and in every other way, to be like the broad torpedo fish, for it too makes anyone who comes close and touches it feel numb, and you now seem to have had that kind of effect on me, for both my mind and my tongue are numb, and I have no answer to give you.[68]

Descartes, too, reaches this limbo state somewhere between the first and second meditations. Having faced the possibility, at the end of the first meditation, that all his beliefs might be false, that "the sky, the air, the earth, colors, shapes, sounds and all external things are merely the delusions of dreams" by means of which a malicious demon deceives him, and having tried to think of himself "as not having hands or eyes, or flesh, or blood, or senses,"[69] he finds, upon beginning his second meditation, that his thought is unable to progress, unable to move in any direction. "So serious are the doubts into which I have been thrown as a result of yesterday's meditation," Descartes reports upon waking up on the second day,

> that I can neither put them out of my mind nor see any way of resolving them. It feels as if I have fallen unexpectedly into a deep whirlpool which tumbles me around so that I can neither stand on the bottom nor swim up to the top.[70]

He does eventually find a way out of his aporia. His own existence is not subject to doubt, he finds; it is immune to doubt much as Socrates' freedom is immune to ironic negation. But this kind of self-assertion is not available to the Shadowgraphs—they cannot exorcise their malicious demon by declaring, with Descartes, *Let him deceive me as much as he can, he will never bring it about that I am nothing, so long as I think that I am something.* For, as we will see, the independence achieved by taking that stance toward the world also precludes the kind of love these women long for. In fact, asserting the contrary of Descartes—that she is nothing—would be a more appealing solution to aporia for Gretchen. If, "A" says,

> she could hold onto the thought that in the strictest sense she was simply nothing, then reflection would be precluded, and then she would not have been deceived, either; for if one is nothing, then there are no relations, and where there are no relations, we cannot speak of deception, either.[71]

The Shadowgraphs indeed tend toward self-denial rather than self-assertion. This tendency has defined their approach to the beloved from the very beginning. Gretchen's first impression of Faust "is completely overwhelming," "A" says; "she becomes nothing next to him."[72] Eventually she "completely disappears in him," and

> imperceptibly, without the slightest reflection, he becomes everything to her. But just as from the beginning she is nothing, so she becomes, if I daresay, less and less, the more she ascertains his almost divine superiority; she is nothing, and exists only through him.[73]

Marie, likewise, doesn't have "the strength to stand" when her Clavigo "pushes her away; she collapses powerless into the arms of those around her."[74] Donna Elvira, lastly, gave up her world—religion—for Don Juan. Now she needs him to be her world:

> In him she has everything, and the past is nothing; if she leaves him, she loses everything, also the past. She had renounced the world; then there appeared a figure she cannot renounce and this is Don Juan. From now on, she renounces everything in order to live with him. The more significant that was which she abandons, the more firmly must she cling to him; the more firmly she has embraced him, the more terrible becomes her despair when he leaves her. From the very outset, her love is despair; nothing has significance for her, neither in heaven nor on earth, except Don Juan.[75]

In *The Sickness unto Death*, Anti-Climacus diagnoses such resistance to self-sufficiency as a form of despair which typically afflicts women. For woman's nature is devotedness: "In devotion she loses herself, and only then is she happy, only then is she herself." If you take this devotion away, "then her self is also gone."[76] When a young girl despairs, he writes, it is usually over love—over "the loss of her beloved, over his death or his unfaithfulness to her." In fact, she wants to be only in being loved by him: "This self of hers, which she would have been rid of or would have lost in the most blissful manner had it become 'his' beloved, this self becomes a torment to her if it has to be a self without 'him.'"[77] But when despair is occasioned by a loss, it becomes evident that the person was in despair all along. For to depend on something that can be lost—something contingent and external to the individual—is to be in despair, whether one knows it or not.[78] A human being is "a synthesis of the infinite and the finite" and to try to give oneself over to something contingent and external is to deny one's own infinity.[79] Such devotion is doomed to failure, because what is infinite, eternal, and necessary cannot be grounded in the finite and contingent. The Shadowgraphs' self-effacing devotion is a hopeless project; this is part of their tragedy. Says Anti-Climacus, if one were to tell such a girl who despairs over a beloved, "'You are destroying yourself,'" she would answer that what destroys her is precisely that she cannot destroy herself.[80]

The Beloved's Freedom

One fundamental way in which each of these women is dependent on her beloved is that she wants him to love her back. This feminine love is not all giving but contains a need: the need to be requited. Jean-Paul Sartre, who gives love a central role in his discussion of interpersonal relations in *Being and Nothingness*, considers the desire for reciprocity constitutive of loving. But this reciprocity could not be achieved through coercion, not is it a duty on the beloved's part. If he were an automaton that could be programmed to love, that love would be worthless.[81] The beloved must be independent of the lover, must be free *not* to love. His love must originate inside him in such a way that in loving, he is autonomous, is himself. As such, personal love has an interest in the beloved's independence and self-determination, and in this regard it is fundamentally different from any attitude we can take to inanimate objects.

In *Kierkegaard on Faith and Love*, Sharon Krishek, too, notes that the beloved must be someone who potentially does *not* love, someone who cannot be possessed as private property and whom the lover always risks losing. As she puts it, the beloved is always "essentially lost" to his lover, because she could in principle lose him.[82] The threat of loss, she states, "may express itself in many ways, but all are essentially connected to the passage of time."[83] We live in the world of becoming where things come to be and pass away, and everything in that temporal realm, because it will some day wither, is essentially lost.[84] True love, she argues, must begin with a sober recognition of this fact.

All is essentially lost—yes, but Krishek is too quick to attribute all loss to time. The loss that threatens Abraham on Mount Moriah is not due to natural, inevitable decay, but to an action he can choose to perform or not. It is not the distance between t_1 and t_2 that threatens Abraham with loss: it is God's command, and his own decision whether, between t_1 and t_2, to obey it or not. Nor can time account for the loss, in the form of privation, involved in unrequited love. The Shadowgraphs' loss occurred in time but is not therefore due to the passage of time. It is due to the beloved's independence from the lover. When Margaret falls for Faust, it is obvious to her that whether he loves her or not is not for her to decide. That Goethe lets her pick the petals off a flower, repeating "He loves me; he loves me not," is not supposed to illustrate her curiosity, "A" says, but humility before love and her beloved, whom she cannot control.[85]

The desire to be loved distinguishes the Shadowgraph women from *Either/Or*'s seducers. These women have not asserted their freedom and independence as Socrates has, and their despair can very well be characterized as a refusal to be oneself. But they do recognize the beloved as an autonomous person—not an instance of an enjoyable universal, nor a plaything. Their desire to be loved contains indirectly a recognition and appraisal of that in the beloved which is infinite and raises him above mere earthly things. It is not quite true to say that when she despairs over her beloved, a young girl despairs over something finite and mundane. Because a person, a self, is not a proper part of the earthly realm of contingency where things come to be and pass away. He is also something beyond that realm, something superior to nature. Anti-Climacus says himself that aside from God, "there is nothing as eternal as a self."[86] But he doesn't note that this view of persons is in tension with his account of feminine despair.

Fear and Trembling's fictional author Johannes de Silentio might have a way of dispelling this tension. What is earthly in the Shadowgraphs' despair, he could say, is not the beloved himself but the fact of his requiting or not requiting their love. The "knight of infinite resignation" takes an approach to love not unlike the Shadowgraphs': his love, too, is complete devotion. A young man "falls in love with a princess," de Silentio writes, "and the entire content of his life lies in this love."[87] But although this love "cannot possibly be realized" in a relationship, the knight does not stop loving.[88] He makes a movement of infinite resignation whereby "the princess is lost."[89] He gives up his desire to be with the princess and in fact makes himself immune to anything his beloved does. If she were to marry, for example, this would be an earthly fact that could affect the knight's love only if he had not resigned from being loved and if his love for her were not the substance of his life.[90] Although according to de Silentio the knight still loves the princess, he has grasped "the deep secret that also in loving another person one should be sufficient unto oneself."[91] Any person who understands this, "whether man or woman, can never be deceived."[92]

What Johannes de Silentio wants to emphasize is that the knight stands in different modal relations to his own love for the princess and her attitude toward him. Loving her is up to him, but whether she loves him is not for him to decide. Yet from the fact that something is beyond a person's control, it does not follow that he should refrain from wanting it. De Silentio wants to block the possibility that the knight love the princess only insofar as she loves him, as though love were a kind of economic exchange. (Extorting love as the repayment of a debt is a privilege reserved for God, in Kierkegaard's philosophy.) But such a vulgar approach to love is not implied in the desire to be loved in return. As Sartre understood, love is not conditioned upon its actually being returned, only on the *possibility* of reciprocity. By making his knight immune to the princess's desires, de Silentio actually makes him indifferent to the fact that his beloved is not a thing but a person capable of loving—of seeing, recognizing, being moved by and caring for others.

Of course, Johannes de Silentio's story doesn't end with resignation. There is a second movement: the movement of faith. The knight, he writes, "makes another movement more wondrous than everything, for he says: still, I believe that I will get her—by virtue of the absurd, by virtue of the fact that for God all things are possible."[93] Resignation is something a person can achieve on his own; being loved, on the other hand, is a gift bestowed from without. That the princess love him is now an object of religious faith for the knight. It is up to God to bestow this gift upon him. The direct object of the knight's faith is thus God and God's power; his faith is only indirectly about the princess. He prays for it the way a farmer can pray for rain. But this is to deny the fact that loving, though not freely chosen, must have its source in the lover; the princess's love must be an expression of her soul. Yet in *Fear and Trembling*, the princess's inclinations and attitudes are made irrelevant in the first movement and brought back into the picture in the second movement only through the mediation of God and as objects of God's infinite power, dissociated from her. Loving a person, according to Johannes, consists in achieving a certain relation to oneself—sufficiency—and, subsequently, a certain relation to God.

The word "resignation" suggests weakness—insofar as an act of resignation merely preempts an impending defeat, it may be considered equivalent to defeat. But Johannes de Silentio presents the achievement of infinite resignation not as a tragic, sorrowful acceptance of one's fate but as a victory. Purged of vain desires, the knight achieves self-sufficiency. Nor is he a rebel like Philoctetes, who cannot make peace with his loneliness. Although the knight stands alone, he is not lonely: stoically, he triumphs in solitude. Johannes calls the knight's love "complete devotion," but his position is actually more akin to Socratic irony than to the love that gives substance to the Shadowgraphs' lives. It is also strangely reminiscent of that aesthetic approach to love which is practiced by both Johannes the Seducer in *Either/Or* and Quidam of *Stages on Life's Way*. This is love by way of recollection—that is, imaginary love. By loving idealized memories or figments of their imagination, these men make themselves immune to loss. As Pattison writes, the aesthete "is from the beginning confined to the magic circle of his own self-projection."[94] He cannot be part of a relationship, he knows "no 'Thou.'"[95]

Krishek proposes that the seducers must make a movement of resignation like the one Johannes de Silentio describes in *Fear and Trembling*. But actually such a move makes no sense for the solipsistic lover, who has never known the need to be loved in return. He is from the start as self-sufficient as the knight of infinite resignation; he is alone but not lonely. Cordelia is not a "thou" for Johannes, but neither is the princess, for the knight. The princess is a third person about whom the knight talks to God. But to be truly open to the princess would mean for the knight to acknowledge his dependence on her— to resign to this dependence rather than from his desire. Only then would it be true to say that this love is the entire content of his life.

The distinction between being alone and being lonely gives us a hold on the difference between Socrates and Alcibiades—both in their relation to one another and in their approaches to philosophy. To Alcibiades, irony must seem like solipsism; the refutation of solipsism becomes philosophy's first task for him. Although Socratic irony doesn't deny the existence of an external world, it refuses to grant *reality* to phenomena, and distances itself from the concrete world. The separation from the world thus achieved is at the same time an assertion of the thinking subject's self-sufficiency. Knowledge of phenomena, of concrete existing things, is in tension with self-sufficiency. To know anything at all outside one's own mind requires being open to the external world. To seek knowledge is to willfully adopt the receptivity—passivity—that will allow one's beliefs to be determined from without, by the object of knowledge. Socrates insisted that concepts cannot be derived from experience, but even as we grant the *a priori* component of knowledge, we must also reckon with Alcibiades' insight: that concepts by themselves do not yield knowledge of the world. Concepts must refer to phenomena, must have instances. In his pursuit of knowledge, the philosopher must relinquish his infinite negative freedom and make himself dependent on something external. This love of knowledge may properly be described as the devotion in feminine despair. The philosopher wants external reality to determine his beliefs: he wants his worldview to be constituted by the world. Johannes Climacus' assertion in *Concluding Unscientific Postscript* that the objective thinker, so-called, abstracts from his own existence and "forgets" that he himself exists does call to mind the despairing woman who would be blissfully rid of her self if she could devote herself to a man.[96] And indeed Alcibiades' philosophical eros has yet to recognize the need to construct or discover concepts that allow him to grasp phenomena through their essences. But in his turn, Alcibiades could accuse Climacus of making his subjective thinker a solipsist.

Socrates tries to assure his interlocutor in the *Meno* that "I am more perplexed than anyone when I cause perplexity in others. So now I do not know what virtue is; perhaps you knew before you contacted me, but now you are certainly like one who does not know."[97] But of course Meno experiences this perplexity very differently: not as a pleasant liberation but as aporia, alienation, and even sorrow. Socrates' negative arguments make doubters rather than ironists of his interlocutors. Irony and doubt, Kierkegaard writes, initially seem quite similar. We must consider these states dynamically and dialectically in order to notice their differences. In doubt, "the subject constantly wants to enter the object, and his misfortune is that the object keeps escaping him. In irony, the subject constantly wants to get out from the object."[98] In doubt as in irony, subject and world are separated from one another. The crucial difference lies in the opposite pull of the eros in each philosophical approach. The ironist's estrangement is his salvation. He may be alone, but he is not lonely. The doubter, by contrast, is an unhappy lover who wants to be in and with the world.

Feminine Virtues

There is in one of Kierkegaard's journals an entry, from 1843, titled "My Opinion of *Either/Or*." Despite that headline, it does not mention aesthetics and ethics, "A," the seducers, or the Judge; nor does it contain the word "I" in any of its grammatical cases. Instead, Kierkegaard speaks of himself by way of two persons whom *Either/Or* does not mention: Alcibiades and Socrates. "There was a young man as fortunately gifted as an Alcibiades," he writes,

> He lost his way in the world. In his distress he looked around for a Socrates, but among his contemporaries he could find none. Then he asked the gods that he himself be transformed into one. And behold! He who had been so proud of being an Alcibiades, he felt so ashamed and humbled by the gods' grace, that when he had finally received what he could be proud of, he felt lesser than everyone.[99]

Socrates was Kierkegaard's model, but precisely for that reason he also saw himself in Alcibiades. If I am right in placing Alcibiades among the Shadowgraphs and Antigone, then there is a kinship between this remark and Kierkegaard's haunted confession after a night at the opera in 1839:

> In some ways I can say of *Don Giovanni* what Elvira says to him: "You *murderer* of my happiness"; for truly, this is the piece that has gotten such a diabolical grip on me that I will never be able to forget it; it was this piece that drove me like Elvira out of the convent's quiet night.[100]

His modern Antigone, too, was partly a self-projection. In giving up on her romantic love for Haemon, she mirrors Kierkegaard's own broken engagement with Regine Olsen. The autobiographical origin of his modern Antigone is confirmed in a journal entry where Kierkegaard explains wherein the collision would lie if his tragedy had a male protagonist:

> He abandoned the beloved because he couldn't keep her along with his own pain. In order to do it right, he had to turn his whole love into a deception of her; otherwise she would share in his suffering in a completely indefensible way.[101]

Kierkegaard didn't want to weigh his betrothed down with his depression, destroy her as Faust destroyed Gretchen. But like Faust, he loved Regine's innocence and immediacy: "To her and my late father," he wrote, "all my books shall be dedicated: my two teachers, the wisdom of an elderly, and the dear ignorance of a woman."[102] In her feminist critique of Kierkegaard, Céline Léon seizes upon similar remarks in Judge Wilhelm's musings on feminine simplicity,[103] and when read into the treatment of "young girls" and their despair, the praise for Regine does bring out a condescending undertone in those published thoughts. But we should also take account of this remark, just a few entries below the one just quoted:

> In a certain sense a woman is a terrifying creature. There is a kind of devotion that terrifies my being, because it is so contrary to my essence: womanly devotion, so womanly unscrupulous, terrifying precisely because femininity in one sense is so powerfully bound to scruples.[104]

Perhaps part of what so gripped Kierkegaard about *Don Giovanni* was its display of such devotion. Certainly, it is Kierkegaard's own voice we hear, when "A" confesses in "The Immediate Erotic Stages," that

> although I otherwise thank the gods that I was born a man and not a woman, Mozart's music has taught me that it is beautiful and refreshing and rich to love as a woman loves.[105]

3

Self-Sufficient Beauty

The problem of Socrates is one that all interpretations of Plato must face, so also Kierkegaard's dissertation. He reminds us that not only the truthfulness of Plato's portrayal of Socrates is in question; the fact that Plato populated his dialogues with an array of different speakers and never wrote in the first person raises the question of how he stands with regard to the views represented in his texts, including those he expresses in Socrates' voice. "And now we approach the important problem," Kierkegaard writes in the introduction to his treatment of Plato in *Irony*: "*what* in the Platonic philosophy belongs to Socrates, and *what* belongs to Plato, a question we cannot dismiss, however painful it is to separate these two, who are so intensely united."[1] This chapter begins and ends with the problem of Socrates. For Kierkegaard, the very existence of the problem is a clue to its solution.

In *The Concept of Irony*, Plato and Socrates are presented as polar opposites, yet their different inclinations do not so much wage war as complement each other. The most characteristically Platonic elements of the early dialogues are the myths, according to Kierkegaard, where the origin of the world, the possibility of knowledge, and the nature of love are made intelligible through narrative and personification. Kierkegaard's attention to Plato's myths must be understood in the context of the Romantic adoration for folklore, its appraisal of the imagination, and its faith in art and extrasensory perception as sources of knowledge. Though during his student days, his sensibility was uninhibitedly Romantic, many of his published writings deride that movement, and we must ask whether Plato is vulnerable to the same criticism. Certainly, Kierkegaard's notion of aesthetic recollection would seem to be modeled on Plato's epistemology. But if we look closely at Plato as he appears in *Irony*, we will see that his philosophical eros sets him apart from Johannes the Seducer and his fellow Romantic ironists in other books.

Separating Plato and Socrates

The thesis that Socrates was an ironist is compatible, Kierkegaard thinks, with Xenophon's and Aristophanes' portrayals of him. In fact, it *explains* why Socrates should appear so meek in Xenophon's writings and why Aristophanes should have found him comical. Yet Kierkegaard's view of Socrates is based chiefly on Plato's works, even though their portrayal is more complex and even contradictory. Like others before him, Kierkegaard detects a set of "duplexities" in Plato's work: two parallel lines of thought and methods that are fundamentally alien to one another. The most plausible explanation for their co-presence, he suggests, is that they originated in two different minds. If we are interested in understanding Plato in the deepest way, we should neither bracket that in his work which is properly Socrates' nor avail ourselves of some "charitable" hermeneutic maneuver that would harmonize the two philosophical approaches. The fact that Plato harbored these duplexities is not an awkward fact to be explained away but a clue to understanding, at the most fundamental level, his approach to knowledge and love.

Kierkegaard groups the two tendencies in Plato into "negative" and "positive," and in the early dialogues, he says, the positive complement to Socrates' negative abstraction takes the form of myth. "The dialectical," he explains, "clears the terrain of everything irrelevant"—this is the negative, Socratic work—"and now tries to climb up to the idea, but since this fails, the imagination reacts. Tired from the dialectical work, the imagination lies down to dream, and from this comes the mythical."[2] This affords a contemplative pleasure which "restless reflection might reach [only] by a long detour."[3] Consider the *Meno*, which stalls in aporia as Socrates brings his interlocutor to see that one cannot find the nature of virtue without first knowing what virtue is. Theoretical inquiry more generally should therefore be impossible. It is at this point of despair that the myth of the soul's preexistence is introduced. "As the soul is immortal, has been born often, and has seen all things here and in the underworld," Socrates explains, "there is nothing which it has not learned."[4] This myth is not a continuation of the conversation that preceded it: the positive is not a product or conclusion of the negative. The immortal and knowledgeable soul is not inferred from painstaking reasoning but simply posited, on the authority of "priests and priestesses."[5] Plato lets Socrates promote the idea not on epistemic grounds but for practical, pragmatic reasons.

We must not believe "that debater's argument," Socrates says, referring to the negative conclusion which has since become known as "Meno's paradox," "for it would make us idle, and fainthearted men like to hear it, whereas my [new] argument makes them energetic and keen on the search."[6]

The idea of recollection is, then, a useful assumption. With the myth, the dialogue makes a fresh start and the new propositions brought in to aid the investigation are not subjected to the rigorous scrutiny with which Socrates earlier made Meno's every answer implode. True, the subsequent mathematical demonstration, wherein a completely uneducated person manages to draw a square exactly twice the size of another, serves as a transcendental argument for innate ideas and thereby constitutes evidence for the soul's preexistence. But what made the idea of innate ideas initially plausible was the myth, which explains the soul's possession of knowledge in an intuitively compelling way: it has learned through experience. The preceding conversation's assault on empiricism is completely overrun by the myth—it is Plato speaking now, through the character Socrates.

In the *Symposium*, too, Plato puts two wildly different discourses into Socrates' mouth. In the first part of his speech, Socrates analyzes the concept of love until he arrives at a completely formal idea of desire as lack. Kierkegaard grants that desire is one component of love. But, he says,

> love is also infinite love. When we say that God is love, we are saying that he is infinitely self-communicating; when we speak of abiding in love, we speak of sharing in a fullness. This is what's substantial in love. The desire and the longing are the negative in love, that is, the immanent negativity.[7]

The substance of love is communion. Plato has to enter the conversation and give his own speech, disguised as Diotima. "Now I'll let you go," Socrates tells Agathon, thus suspending the interrogation in favor of a freer, less rigorous form of theorizing: the retelling of "the speech about Love I once heard from a woman of Mantinea."[8] In this second, mythical speech, Kierkegaard writes, "Plato the poet daydreams and visualizes everything that Socrates the dialectician was looking for"; and in this "world of dreams, irony's unhappy love finds its object."[9] Eros is tough, says Diotima,

> and shriveled and shoeless and homeless, always lying on the dirt without a bed, sleeping at people's doorsteps and in roadsides under the sky, having his mother's nature, always living with Need. But on his father's side he is

a schemer after the beautiful and the good; he is brave, impetuous, and intense, an awesome hunter, always weaving snares, resourceful in his pursuit of intelligence, a lover of wisdom through all his life.[10]

The idea of love or desire is here given "under the qualification of time and space," through narrative and anthropomorphism, in the figure of conscious, active beings who have an origin, a history and an aim.[11] Even the negative element, so elusive in the abstract, is here made intuitable as poverty. We picture a hobo with all his privations: no shoes, no home, nowhere to bathe. The restoration of Eros as a person gives the otherwise completely abstract idea of an indeterminate lack a concrete guise: "What the mythical presentation adds to the dialectical movement," Kierkegaard writes, "is that it lets the negative *be seen*."[12] In this way, Diotima's account of love offers an instant gratification for Plato's speculative craving. Moreover, the dynamic element, the energy we know to be part of desire, is rehabilitated in the myth as that resourcefulness and power of initiative which is Eros' inheritance from his father, Plenty.

In the world myths present, the inside is the outside and the outside is the inside. Persons, objects, and events have *meaning*: they are endowed with metaphysical or ideal significance. The Garden of Eden is a place that figures a human state of being, a blissful plenitude. Eve's temptation is taken to represent some universal feature of the feminine character and fate. Our sense that life is too harsh for us, that the human condition at its most fundamental is a condition of exile, is presented as a punishment for disobedience and hubristic ambition: for the weakness of will that gave in to a love of knowledge. Even birth pangs are in this story absolved of mere bodily facticity, of contingency, and assigned a place in a cosmos of meaning. If myths give the mind rest, it is because they provide explanatory closure. Eros' life is teleological: it plays out his fate, which is determined by his parentage and thus constitutive of who he is.

It is tempting to view the positive and the negative in Plato as but "two languages," Kierkegaard writes; "of which one is less articulated, more childlike and soft; the other more developed, more sharp-edged and hard."[13] In this vein, Hegel says that myth "belongs to the pedagogic stage of the human race" and that in Plato, the myths "belong entirely to the manner of presentation,"[14] so that their content could be rendered in a different form, translated into a more advanced, distinct discourse. Although Kierkegaard agrees with much of what Hegel has to say about myth, he holds that Plato's own thought was inextricably bound up with these sensuous representations. "Every attempt to interpret the myth historically"—as literal statements of fact to be verified empirically—"already indicates that reflection has awoken and is killing myth. Like fairy tales, myth reigns only in the imagination's dusky darkness."[15] It is "reserved for a later, a more truthful moment of time" to perceive that a myth is false or accommodate it as allegory.[16] From within what we might call "mythical consciousness," these stories are taken neither metaphorically nor literally. This consciousness is immediate; it doesn't operate with the notions of literal and transferred truth.

What Kierkegaard considers the most important piece of evidence that the aesthetic in the early dialogues is not just an alternative mode of presentation, nor the sign of a primitive, preliminary form of thinking, is that "the mythical in Plato has a history."[17] Plato's thought remained aesthetic—it developed, but not toward abstraction. "Plato's element is not thought," Kierkegaard writes, "but representation [*Forestilling*]."[18] His epistemology is modeled on perception: intellectual insight is for him analogous to the sense of sight. If we recall that "it was from a productive life as a poet that Socrates called the twenty-year-old Plato back to abstract self-knowledge, then it seems quite natural," Kierkegaard writes, that there should be an aesthetic element to his philosophical work.[19] Plato did not really renounce poetry; his poetic spirit found a task in philosophy, as a complement to the "famished Socratic dialectic."[20]

The Forms are the culmination of this aesthetic development—apprehended instantaneously, they are like condensed myths. The teleology which in myth unfolds in time, as a narrative, now becomes a visible purposiveness. The Form of beauty "loves itself," as Kierkegaard would say; and the many beautiful things love themselves in the Form, have their telos in it. Yet while the myths could of course be recounted in the text, a Form can only be beheld, not articulated. In the *Symposium*, the Form of beauty is instead baked into a myth: because it cannot be conjured forth before the reader, he is made to imagine someone else beholding beauty-in-itself. What is fascinating to Kierkegaard about the Forms is the tension between their abstractness and their visibility. Thus Diotima insists on abstracting all contingent elements from beauty. One "goes always upwards for the sake of this Beauty," she says, "from one body to two and from two to all beautiful bodies, then from beautiful bodies to beautiful customs, and from customs to learning beautiful things" so that "in the end he comes to know just what it is to be beautiful."[21] But even when the beautiful is stripped in this way of all perceptible qualities, the lover "is turned to the great sea of beauty," and "gazing upon it" he gives birth to beautiful ideas.[22] Thus Plato stubbornly insists, Kierkegaard notes, "that the in-and-by-itself beautiful is supposed to be *beheld*."[23] "That's how things always go with '*das Ding an sich*' if one cannot cast it away and consign it to oblivion," he remarks. Having excluded it from thinking, "one now lets the imagination pay the debt and compensate for the loss."[24] If knowledge for Plato was indeed vision or acquaintance, as Kierkegaard thinks, this would explain Plato's preoccupation with beauty and his claim in the *Symposium* that beauty is the object of love. For the beautiful may be thought of as visible perfection—even perfect visibility—and thereby also as the supreme object of visual perception. Beauty is aesthetic plenitude; it is to Plato's philosophy what emptiness is to Socrates'. And with his yearning for knowledge combined with an artistic creativity, a virile imagination, Plato is just like Diotima's Eros in his approach to philosophy: poor but creative.

Romantic Platonism

In his early twenties Kierkegaard was smitten with the Romantic notion of mythology as a history of human consciousness or an aesthetic recollection of history. "What I call the mythological-poetical element in history," he wrote in 1836,

> is the aura that hovers over every genuine historical endeavor. This is not an abstraction, nor prosaic actuality, but a transfiguration [*Forklarelse*], and each genuine historical trend will give birth to such a mythological idea.[25]

Myth is neither a myopic recounting of facts nor a distant summary in general terms, but an imagistic representation that reveals the spirit of a time. As he noted elsewhere, the term *Forklarelse* is ambiguous between "transfiguration" and "clarification" (it is also related to the verb "to explain," *at forklare*). Poetry, he remarks, is *Forklarelse* in both senses;[26] and we must say the same about myth. The mythical representation makes an epoch intelligible aesthetically, intuitively. Jørgen Bukdahl identifies Henrik Steffens as one of Kierkegaard's influences in this area. In his dissertation, Kierkegaard refers to a book of

Steffens' which, he says, begins by painting one of those truly big mythical pictures, where "natural existence becomes a myth about spirit's existence."[27] In the notes for his 1803 Copenhagen lectures, Steffens writes about a kind of *Ahnelse*—meaning a hunch, suspicion, divination, intuition—that connects us to history and all of nature. Through such extrasensory perception, Steffens writes, "nature's eternal life speaks to our spirit, as if through a mystical cipher" so that we come to understand nature from within ourselves.[28]

As Pattison tells the story, Kierkegaard's attack on Romanticism in his writings began as he woke up to the naiveté and dogmatism of its monistic worldview. If everything in nature is not akin, and if the soul has not seen all things here and in the underworld over the course of its many lives, then it has no direct access to transcendent reality. Whereas the Romantics raised the imagination's status by attributing to it the capacity for divination, Kierkegaard now demoted the imagination, dismissing the epistemology of extrasensory perception.[29] He embarked instead on a career as a cultural critic and Christian pedagogue, making pseudo-religious Romanticism, with its "pantheism of the imagination,"[30] the target of a fierce philosophical assault. He had once called divination "the homesickness of earthly life for the higher, for the perspicuity [*Anskuelighed*] which man must have enjoyed in his paradisic life";[31] now, Pattison writes, he denied it any religious significance and instead relegated it to the department of theological psychiatry, as a symptom of anxiety or melancholy.[32] Instead of "homesickness," he now preferred speaking of man's relation to his long-lost Eden in terms of sin.

The Concept of Irony doesn't quite represent either of these two attitudes. Kierkegaard is clearly intrigued by myth, keen to understand its psychology. When he writes that myth is "the enthusiasm of *imagination* in the service of speculation," this is a psychologistic characterization that a true believer would not make.[33] Even his earlier characterization of *Ahnelse* as homesickness for a lost paradise implies that divination is not possible, and that the *appeal* to such inexplicable hunches is a reflection of our psyche and our basic existential condition—alienation. As for the 1836 notes about the mythological idea presiding over every historical endeavor, that idea does not entail metaphysical commitments on the order of animism and divination. It concerns human culture and its development over time—not its relation to nature. And as Bukdahl points out, Kierkegaard's own appeal to "semi-mythical, ideal figures" such as Faust, Don Juan, and Ahasverus in his writings testifies to the endurance of his belief in myth as a source of insight about the spirit and psyche of an era.[34] Holm sees Kierkegaard taking up a position in between the Romantic view according to which "boundless intuition contains more significant meaning than do concepts," and "a rationalist and 'Hegelian' theory, which regards intuition as the handmaiden of abstract concepts."[35] When Kierkegaard identifies a "misrelation between myth and dialectic" in Plato's works, this is, according to Holm, a reflection of Kierkegaard's own view—inadvertently, a comment on the incongruity of aesthetic figures and abstract concepts in Kierkegaard's own writings.[36]

Pattison is of course right that Kierkegaard's writings from *Either/Or* and onward are very critical of Romanticism and "the Romantic ironist." When he makes recollection a centerpiece of the aesthetic life, that appears to reflect a particular attitude to Plato, too; and in the *Postscript*, Plato is criticized directly. The proposition that all knowledge is recollection, Climacus writes,

> suggests the beginning of speculation, but for that reason Socrates did not pursue it, and it became essentially Platonic. This is where the road forks and Socrates essentially emphasizes existence, while Plato, forgetting this, loses himself in speculation.[37]

In a footnote, he adds that recollection is "immanence."[38] According to Gordon Marino, this speculative thinker is really an aesthete.[39] If Socrates is analogous to Don Juan, and Alcibiades a brother to Marie, Elvira, and Gretchen, then Johannes the Seducer would seem to be the best candidate, in *Either/Or*, for a counterpart to Plato. Granted, it is in A's "Diapsalmata" and "Crop Rotation" that we first encounter recollection as a way of life. From the fortified castle of his sorrow, "A" writes,

> I swoop down into reality and snatch my prey, but I don't stay down there, I bring my booty home, and this booty is a picture I weave into the tapestry at my castle. Then I live as one already dead. Everything I have experienced I immerse in the baptism of oblivion unto an eternity of recollection. Everything finite and fortuitous is forgotten and blotted out. Then I sit pensively like an old gray-haired man and explain the pictures in a soft voice, almost whispering, and beside me sits a child, listening, although he remembers everything before I tell it.[40]

Whereas memory brings back the past in abundant detail, recollection is a retrospective consecration of experiences, a crystallizing of their essence. Such stylization can be described as a distortion as becomes clear when "A" satirizes a bit of marriage counseling wisdom: that a temporary separation can rekindle the love in a relationship gone stale. This advice, "A" says, expresses his own credo that "recollection is more abundantly filling than all reality."[41] For the hearts of the separated couple "grow fonder," he writes, in "a purely poetic way."[42] Free from the distraction of the actual partner with his or her irritating idiosyncrasies, and from the need to engage with the other, the individual is able to form an idealized image of the spouse more lovable than the actual person. In "Crop Rotation," "A" urges his reader never to enter into close relationships in the first place.[43] The implied criticism concerns the content of recollection— it is inevitably distorted—but also its very form. Recollection reduces other people to ideas, and relationships to objects of solitary contemplation. Also the recollector's self-relation is skewed. One should not relate to one's past as to a poem, a beautiful, meaningful whole enjoyed from an aesthetic distance.

In Johannes the Seducer's writings, "A" finds this way of life raised to a new level. Not only does he narrate his life poetically in his diary, so that it relates events in the subjunctive mode, but his life itself "has been an attempt to realize the task of living poetically."[44] His experience is conditioned by his poetic nature, "A" writes: "it was the poetic that he enjoyed in reality's poetic situation, and this he later reclaimed in the form of poetic reflection."[45] One day Johannes notices a girl about town; intrigued, he begins to imagine this Cordelia's thoughts and feelings, and soon starts insinuating himself into her life so as to make his subsequent voyeuristic musings all the more exciting. His engagement with the world and his recollection thus feed each other. The present supplies him with ideas for a creative endeavor whose result is an elaborate semi-fictional world in which Johannes dwells alone. The evaluative criteria he applies to his own life are those of the art critic: they presuppose a distance from their object like the one that separates a stage from the spectator. "How beautiful it is to be in love," he writes; "how interesting it is to know that one is in love."[46] He distances himself further and further from the original object of his experiences so that eventually it is not Cordelia he admires or loves, but his own feelings for her. To live through recollection is thus to live in a dream world and just as these are private, so too, William Afham says in *Stages on Life's Way*, "each one must tread the wine press of recollection alone."[47] That means that "every recollection is a secret. Even if others are interested in the object the recollector is recollecting [. . .], this apparent publicity is an illusion."[48] There can be no such thing as a "fellowship of recollection,"[49] then; recollection is solipsistic.

Johannes the Seducer's recollection is not oriented toward understanding ultimate reality. Its ostensible epistemic object is Cordelia and himself. Still, this life of recollection has clear analogies to Plato's philosophical method. Platonic recollection is solitary, and Kierkegaard had compared the myths to pleasant dreams giving respite from a more strenuous pursuit of knowledge. Like Johannes's poetic transfiguration of life, the deliverances of recollection can always be suspected of reflecting the nature of the thinker's mind more than the external object he seeks to know. But Plato's myths are not complete fancies. In the early dialogues, Kierkegaard remarks, the mythical "is not so much Plato's free composition, tractable and obedient to him, as it is instead something that overwhelms him."[50] Not being of his own making, Plato takes this inspiration to be a missive from transcendent reality. Whatever the shortcomings of this method, there is no active manipulation and instrumentalization of reality in Plato's thought. Kierkegaard emphasizes that immersion in myth is pleasant, and Holm detects a tinge of moral condemnation in the way he speaks about myth's shortcut to gratification, as though it were intellectual masturbation.[51] Yet the fact that myth gives pleasure does not mean that it aims exclusively at pleasure. It aims to grasp the truth, only Plato happens to think that understanding is pleasant, as indeed it is. When it presents the foundation of knowledge itself, or as we behold in it the essence of virtue, the aesthetic idea provides a fullness of intelligibility that also manifests itself as beauty. Kierkegaard's parody of recollection in "The Seducer's Diary" does identify the limits of Plato's aesthetic philosophical method. But in his innocent earnestness and reverence before truth, Plato's character and motives are the opposite of Johannes's.

Narrative Self-knowledge

Given its focus on his own life rather than metaphysics, Johannes's diary resembles more closely a caricature at narrative self-knowledge. When John Davenport tries to impute a view of personal identity as narrative to Kierkegaard, though, he bases this largely on *Either/Or*'s second part. As Judge Wilhelm writes, the self "contains an infinite multiplicity inasmuch as it has a history," and in this history, the individual "recognizes his identity with himself."[52] Through this history, the individual also "stands in relation to other individuals in the race and to the whole race, and this history contains painful things, and yet he is the person he is only through this history."[53] To become a self—that is, to choose oneself—requires taking responsibility for this history both in the sense of appropriating it into one's self-conception and repenting for it.

To identify oneself with one's history, however, is not yet to see that history as a narrative. Like recollection, narrative is selective and interpretive. It leaves out the noise of history, drawing out what is taken to be essential from a series of events, and represents their meaning. It also relates these events to one another, placing them on one trajectory—the Aristotelian line with beginning, middle and end. In order to be integral parts of the narrative, the individual events must have their meaning in the whole, in relation to each other. In Alastair MacIntyre's account of narrative identity, an individual's life should have a "ground project"—an overarching life project—and it is with reference to this project that she understands and assesses her past and plans her future.[54] For someone with a ground project, retrospect and prospect are closely related and inform one another.

To Davenport, narrative self-understanding is a mark of the ethical life.[55] Aimed at pleasure, aesthetes' lives depend more on circumstance and less on the individual's own agency, and thus lack coherence over time.[56] This might be true of "A" as the Judge describes him, but as Lippitt points out, the pursuit of pleasure could very well count as a ground project.[57] Moreover, the aesthete Johannes *excels* at narrative. His prospect and retrospect live in a flourishing symbiosis. If the Judge's talk of appropriating one's history provides a basis for attributing a narrative identity view to Kierkegaard, the critique of recollection marks the limit of such an interpretation. Kierkegaard could not accept the blurring of retrospect and prospect: they differ as contemplation does from action or, indeed, as recollection does from repetition. One of his most famous journal entries insists on this distinction and infers from it the impossibility of grasping the definitive meaning of one's own life:

> It is quite true, what Philosophy says, that life must be understood backwards. But they forget that other premise, that it must *be lived forwards*. Which premise, the more we think it through, concludes in the fact that life in temporality never becomes fully comprehensible, precisely because no

moment allows me the complete rest from which I might occupy the stance of "backwards."[58]

One cannot live life in the narrative mode, and we must all be prepared to find, when we look back upon life, that it will appear quite different from how we saw it when we were in its midst.

That said, Kierkegaard's criticisms can be called into question. There is a logical space to be claimed between narrative living as it appears in "The Seducer's Diary," and the appropriation of one's history through repentance for which Judge Wilhelm advocates. To see how narrowly Kierkegaard conceives of recollection, let us look again at the way Afham contrasts it with memory. In remembrance, a past experience is immediately before the mind, and it is "perfectly possible to remember an event without recollecting it," that is, without making it an object of reflection.[59] Children have plenty of memories but do not recollect much; in old age we lose our memory but retain our recollections.[60] As we interpret and recount our past over the course of our lives, the multitude of experiences comes to be fixed into stories.

This distinction between raw and processed memories is valid conceptually. But in reality, memories are shaped by our reflections on them as well as by our subsequent experiences. They vary in the *degree* to which they have been interpreted and edited, and the pristine memory in which an experience is perfectly preserved is a very elusive ideal—and uninteresting perhaps, if we consider the fact that experiences are themselves conditioned by circumstances and our faculties. Moreover, interpretation can aid memory. Just as it is easier to recall a poem that rhymes, so too we remember events better insofar as we can fit them into a pattern—a lifelong narrative with a tragic slant, for example. Those of Kierkegaard's readers who want to defend a narrative identity view must reconsider the oversimplified notion of recollection he attributed to his "reflective aesthetes," and those of his portrayals of the aesthetic life that are but facile caricatures.

Dialogue and Dialectic

It is tempting to define the dichotomy of the negative abstract and the positive mythical or ideal in Plato as one between question and answer. This would yield the view that in some profound sense, if not literally, in the Platonic philosophy it is Socrates who asks and Plato who answers. There is some truth to this but Plato's relation to dialogue is in fact more complex, according to Kierkegaard. He detects two kinds of dialogue in Plato's works and two ways of asking questions. Socrates, recall, asks questions that serve to show the inadequacy or inconsistency of the interlocutor's beliefs; the purpose of a Socratic question is to extract the apparent content and leave an emptiness behind. The speculative mindset, by contrast, asks questions in earnest, out of an interest in positive knowledge and "with the intention of receiving an answer containing the desired fullness," so that "the more one asks, the deeper and more significant becomes the answer."[61] None of this yet tells us to prefer one form of interrogation to another, for the two are based on different assumptions. The Socratic interrogation presupposes that there is in the interlocutor's mind an emptiness; the Platonic, that there is a plenitude.[62] And, Kierkegaard adds, if the speculative question "may be characterized as desire, craving, as the glance that looks at the idea desiringly, then the mythical is the idea's fertile embrace."[63]

But the mythical is only a preexistence of the ideal, and even the Forms of Plato's mature philosophy are not full-fledged ideas, according to Kierkegaard. Plato's dialectic is not "the Idea's own dialectic,"[64] the Hegelian dialectic whereby, in the example discussed in Chapter 1, self-consciousness is first pure inwardness of the will, but then binds itself by the universal to achieve a truer freedom, the positive freedom of rationality and morality. When the lover in the *Symposium* comes to behold a distillate of beauty by climbing the ladder of abstraction, this is not the dialectical thought process by which the notion of beauty is separated from ugliness, sublimity, goodness, and pleasure. Beauty-in-itself is there to be beheld once the contingencies of its spatiotemporal manifestations have been cleared away. Borrowing Baumgarten's characterization of aesthetic ideas, we can think of Plato's Forms as "clear and confused" ideas.[65] They are clear in the sense of immediately comprehensible: through our senses, or the imagination, we understand what is presented. But they are not yet delineated in logical space, do not present themselves through distinction with that which they are not. That is what a dialectically developed idea would do. As for Socrates' ideas, they could be called distinct but obscure. All he tells us about virtue is that it is a distinct thing, a concept. But no clear content appears to us on either side of those delineated borders. Socrates' thought process is also not dialectical in Hegel's sense, then. Still, Kierkegaard concedes, Socratic questioning is "distantly yet unambiguously analogous to the negative in Hegel,"[66] the propelling force in thought. Crucially, though,

> the negative according to Hegel is a necessary moment in thought itself, a determination *ad intra*, in Plato the negative is made visible and placed outside the object in the inquiring individual. In Hegel thought does not need to be questioned from the outside; for it asks and answers itself in itself.[67]

In Hegel's system, thought has an internal drive to confront ideas with each other, resolve their contradictions and thereby make them more and more determinate. Contradiction "is the root of all movement and vitality," Hegel writes; it is "in so far as something has a contradiction within it that it moves, has an urge and activity."[68]

In *The Life of the Mind*, Hannah Arendt pays Socrates the superlative compliment of being the only philosopher to perfectly exemplify what it is to think.[69] For although thought is a solitary activity in Arendt's view, it nonetheless consists in conversing: to think is to carry on a conversation with oneself. "It is this duality of myself with myself," she writes, "that makes thinking a true activity, in which I am both the one who asks and the one who answers."[70] The aim or success criterion of this activity is not truth but consistency, she writes. To think inconsistently is to be out of joint with oneself; it is to become one's own adversary. This seems to be the important sense in which the thinking subject is one rather than two: although the process of thinking consists in this back and forth, its aim is unification, the elimination of duality. We can bear to disagree with others, but not with ourselves.

This makes it tempting to regard the Platonic dialogues as the illustration of a thought process that normally takes place within a single person. But to Kierkegaard it makes a great difference whether thought advances through interpersonal dialogue or through the kind of dialectic that is moved from within. The two presuppose different modal relations between successive dialectical steps. On the Hegelian view, which Arendt echoes, thought is bound to evolve toward greater consistency. The negative is a necessary moment in Hegelian thought, Kierkegaard said; the propelling element is intrinsic to it. Thus thought cannot but advance until all questions have been answered: that is, until the positive has usurped the negative. But Plato's dialogues give a different view of the progress of thought; there, thought does not prompt itself. Instead, Kierkegaard writes, "it answers only insofar as it is being asked, but this—its being asked—is accidental."[71] A thinker needs a midwife—it takes two to think. That makes philosophy on the Socrato-Platonic conception an inherently social practice: the dialogue form relates a person not only to a subject matter but also to another person.[72] As a contrast to his own interactive method, Socrates liked to point out the essentially asocial nature of sophistry. Whereas Socrates' art was that of asking questions, the Sophists, Kierkegaard writes, excelled only at the art of answering. In other words, Socrates charged that although the Sophists were well *versed* on all kinds of topics, they did not know how to *converse*.[73]

In Plato's dialogues, individuals don't bring about their own philosophical enlightenment. Meno would not have recognized the diaspora of virtue as a problem but for Socrates' questions. The fact that he ran into Socrates and that Socrates probed him with those particular questions are, however, contingent and external matters of fact. He could have lived a whole life without becoming aware of harboring contradictory beliefs. Even if all knowledge is *a priori* knowledge, the process of recollection must be activated—inconsistency does not by itself make thought move. Therefore, although the interlocutor does not accept his insights on Socrates' authority, he is indebted to him. Without Socrates he would not have learnt what he already knew.

Knowing Together

The contingency of intellectual progress is thus for Kierkegaard intimately connected to the interactive method of Platonic philosophy. Perplexing perceptions are not what prompts philosophical reflection. In Plato's works, it is Socrates and only ever Socrates who summons us to philosophy. Understood as a personal interaction, Kierkegaard writes, the Platonic dialogue is "an account to be settled between the one asking and the one answering, and the thought development consummates itself through this rocking (*alterno pede*) gait, in this hobbling between the two sides."[74]

It is true, Kierkegaard writes, that the dialogue form is a mere formality in Plato's later works, as though it were a stage he surpassed. In the *Republic*, *Timaeus*, and *Critias*, he says, "the one who answers functions more as an attesting or a parish clerk with his 'yes' and 'amen'—in short, there is no conversation anymore."[75] But even as his metaphysical doctrines became more and more elaborate, Plato could never give up writing in dialogue, a form that uses agreement between persons as a criterion of truth. In his negative capacity, Socrates points out flaws with his interlocutor's ideas and reasoning he had not thought of himself. Conversation partners force each other to "stick to the subject" and be consistent—this is for Kierkegaard the crucial distinction between dialogue and monologue.[76] The partner functions as the thinker's self-consciousness, his intellectual conscience. What Plato's use of dialogue shows is that even theoretical philosophy had for him a practical, ethical foundation. For Plato, Kierkegaard suggests, philosophy is driven not only by a speculative craving but also by a longing for communion with another person. "Just as Socrates so beautifully ties human beings to the divine by showing that all knowledge is recollection," he writes, "so Plato feels inseparably fused with Socrates in the unity of spirit to the point that all knowledge is for him co-knowledge with Socrates."[77] What ultimately checks the speculative craving, keeping the thinker from conjuring up and losing himself in a beautiful illusion in the vein of Johannes the Seducer, is the love of another person, the longing to know a reality beyond one's own mind, which can be shared with others.

According to Kierkegaard, Socrates merely cleared the way for ideality, for concepts and norms that are independent of material and historical actuality. Conceiving such ideas presupposes intellectual autonomy, and Socrates tried to make others discover in themselves the freedom required for such an assertion of mind over matter, individual over tradition. But the Socrates of Plato's dialogues goes further than this negative freedom and has "gained ideality": Plato, Kierkegaard writes, "provides him with the idea"[78] and "loved him in the idea."[79] Plato's Socrates has "conquered those vast regions that hitherto"—and for Kierkegaard's ironic Socrates—"were a *terra incognita*."[80] It is not only in an assertion of negative freedom but also from a positive position that Plato's Socrates "disdains usefulness, is indifferent to what is established, is a decided enemy of the mediocrity that to empiricism is the highest, is the object of pious worship, but to speculation is a troll changeling."[81]

By letting Socrates access the contents of ideas, not only see their shells far away on the horizon, Plato sought in his dialogues to "fill up" the "secretive nothingness that was really the whole point of Socrates' life."[82] Although the dialectical and the ideal in Plato—and more generally the negative and the positive—are not continuous and even in the latest dialogues do not constitute a synthetic unity, Plato wants to stick them together. It was understandably difficult, Kierkegaard remarks, for Plato to "reproduce irony in its totality, and in this reproduction refrain from adding any positive content."[83] Eventually, Socrates' irony becomes in Plato's work "a negative power in the service of a positive idea."[84] When irony

> cuts the ropes that hold speculation back, helps it to shove off from the merely empirical sandbanks and venture out on the sea, this is a negatively liberating activity. Irony is *in no sense* a partner on this expedition. But insofar as the speculating individual feels liberated and an abundance spreads out before his observing eye, he may *readily believe* that he owes all this to irony, his gratitude may wish to owe everything to it.[85]

Plato saw in Socrates nothing less than an "*immediate possessor* of the divine": that is, "a primitive personality," a person with an "absolute status," who stands apart from the rest of mankind.[86] "Such an original personality's momentous impact on and relationship to the human race," Kierkegaard writes,

> is consummated partly through his sharing with it his life and spirit (as when Christ breathes upon the disciples and says: Receive the Holy Spirit), partly by his liberating the individual's locked-up powers (as when Christ says to the paralytic: Stand up and walk).[87]

Plato "saw the unity of these two elements in Socrates," or rather, "illustrated their unity in Socrates."[88]

That this kind of personal relationship "is a relation of love," Kierkegaard remarks, "you will surely grant me."[89] And after Socrates' death, Plato's "desire to hear his own professions from the mouth of Socrates" must have become even more urgent; "Plato needed Socrates to rise transfigured from his grave to an even more intimate co-habitation" and "the confusion between mine and thine had to increase now."[90] But even though Plato's "poetic picture" of Socrates might be incongruent with "the historical reality," the conflation represents the truth of *philosophy* as Plato understood it. Socrates "flows through the whole fertile territory of Platonic philosophy" and Plato wanted to owe everything to Socrates, Kierkegaard explains,

> because nothing was dear to him unless it came from Socrates, unless the latter was at least co-owner and co-knower of these love-secrets of knowledge, because there is for the likeminded a self-expression that is

not constricted by the other's limitations but is expanded and is endowed with a preternatural magnitude in the other's conception, since thought understands itself and loves itself only when it is absorbed by the other's being, and for such harmonious beings it becomes not only irrelevant but also impossible to determine what belongs to each, because each one always owns nothing but owns everything through the other.[91]

The question about what in the Platonic philosophy belongs to Socrates and what belongs to Plato is misguided insofar as it assumes that a relationship between two persons is the sum of its parts whereas in Plato's approach to philosophy, the boundary between two persons is transcended in love.

4

The Philosopher Knight

Adorno writes in his study of Kierkegaard that the "pathos of his philosophy" from "the very first sentence of his pseudonymous works" is directed against "the assertion of the identity of the external and the internal."[1] And he quotes from Victor Eremita's preface to *Either/Or*:

> It may at times have occurred to you, dear reader, to doubt somewhat the accuracy of that familiar philosophical thesis that the outer is the inner and the inner is the outer. Perhaps you yourself have concealed a secret that was too dear to you, in its joy or in its pain, for you to initiate others into it. Perhaps your life has put you in touch with people about whom you suspected something of this kind, although neither through power nor through cunning could you make the hidden thing appear.[2]

The theme indeed recurs throughout Kierkegaard's work. We find it, for example, in *Fear and Trembling*, in Abraham's inability to speak.[3] On the mountain in the land of Moriah, all but alone in the world, the Abraham who decides to sacrifice his son cannot articulate what he's doing. There can be no description of that act, no external expression of the inner decision in general terms, with predicates involving universals. But Kierkegaard's preoccupation with this issue began before *Fear and Trembling* and *Either/Or*. He engaged with it already in his dissertation. There Kierkegaard writes, for example, that one feature common to all irony is that "the phenomenon is not the Being [*Væsenet*] but the opposite of the Being."[4] Irony "maintains the contradiction between Being and phenomenon, between the interior and the exterior,"[5] and Socrates was the kind of person "with whom one cannot stop at the exterior. His exterior always indicated something else and opposite."[6]

The fact that even his own contemporaries had such different views of him—so that there is such a problem as the problem of Socrates—is according to

Kierkegaard a consequence of Socrates' inside-outside discord. Yet if we cannot observe Socrates more directly, that need not impede our understanding of him. On the contrary, Kierkegaard ventures audaciously, it serves to isolate our understanding of Socrates from the disturbances of historical-phenomenal noise, and is an occasion to "conjure him forth with the aid of the idea, to make him visible in his ideal form—in other words, to become conscious of the idea that is the meaning of his existence in the world."[7] The confusion to which Socrates gave rise need not dismay us in our quest for the truth about Socrates: we should seize upon it as another clue in our investigation. In Socrates, the outer "was not in harmonious unity with the inner," Kierkegaard writes, and only "under this angle of refraction is he to be understood."[8] His thesis that Socrates' stance was irony is not only compatible with all the facts and conflicting views, he thinks, but explains why Socrates should have given rise to such confusion and been the object of such different interpretations. Indeed, by interpreting Socrates as an ironist, Kierkegaard thinks he shows why Socrates was such an enigma to his contemporaries and also how so many disparate philosophical descendants "claim his legacy as their birthright."[9]

Kierkegaard, as we saw in the previous chapter, is undaunted by the problem of Socrates and it is anyway part of his thesis that Socrates is not an essentially historical figure, not a product of his time. Kierkegaard's Socrates is more of a mythical personage; we could understand the story Kierkegaard tells of Socrates as a recollection that is truer than empirically accurate accounts. But his idea of Socrates does not unfold as a mythical narrative. If Kierkegaard saw in Plato's epistemology a progression from myth to Forms and interpreted the Forms as aesthetic entities that are "beheld" by the mind's eye, he proposes similarly that his own inquiry will yield an "image." He vows to help us "see" the concept of irony in and with its phenomenological manifestation, the person Socrates. This seeing, to be sure, is a "higher," "internal" form of seeing; the image Kierkegaard wants to project is one arrived at by ignoring not only actual sight but also the kind of empirical data that amounts to no more than shallow appearances. It is by "listening" to Socrates rather than "looking" at him that Kierkegaard hopes to grasp the truth about Socratic irony, a truth he then promises to transfigure into—or use to "conjure forth"—an ideal, intellectual image.

Kierkegaard's strategy for arriving at the truth about irony implies an entire philosophical methodology. It is this metaphilosophy that we will pursue in the present chapter, using as our guide the views of love and art in which it is grounded. I will begin by sorting out the meaning of Kierkegaard's metaphors of outer and inner as well as seeing and hearing in his account of knowledge and history. We find in *Either/Or* metaphors very similar to those Kierkegaard uses when talking about inside and outside in his dissertation and as it will turn out, Kierkegaard's philosophical project is akin to those of Eremita and "A." This calls for a close examination of the erotic metaphor in the dissertation's introduction. We will then be in a position to see how Kierkegaard draws on, and improves upon, the philosophical methodologies of Plato and Socrates. Kierkegaard construes philosophical truth as a positive analogue to Socrates' negative, empty, tautologies. Yet in order to achieve not only truth but actuality, Kierkegaard's approach must assimilate also Alcibiades' philosophical eros.

Hearing and Seeing, Inner and Outer

In a postscript to his discussion of Plato in *The Concept of Irony*, Kierkegaard cites "results of scientific research" which suggest that the *Apology* is a reliable document on the historical person Socrates.[10] "Most scholars agree in assigning historical significance in the stricter sense to the *Apology*," he writes, "and consequently I must, as I have done, lay primary stress upon it."[11] As for his own contribution to these research findings, Kierkegaard claims to merely have "endeavored to ascertain their correctness by an unbiased examination of a large portion of Plato."[12] Encouraged by this passage, Paul Muench proclaims that the *Apology* is Kierkegaard's most important source on Socrates in the dissertation.[13] But the remark is a red herring. Titled "Justifying Retrospection," the postscript is at once arrogant and defensive. By invoking "scientific results" and a scholarly consensus, Kierkegaard was trying to preempt an objection from his dissertation committee. The "form of the whole treatise," he writes elsewhere, "has come to depart somewhat from what is now the common and in so many ways meritorious scholarly method."[14] But even as he tries to appease his prospective critics, his invocation of scholars and their findings implies that he himself is not a scholar. His aspiration was never to ascertain historical truth "in the stricter sense"; and it is not clear what it would even mean for a project such as his to be "an unbiased examination." The *Apology* may be historically accurate, but even in his treatment of that dialogue,

Kierkegaard goes on to say, "I have had to conjure forth the spirit of irony, so to speak, let it gather itself and show itself in its complete totality."[15] Only thus can the real Socrates be made to appear.

To say that Socrates embodied an idea is to say that his life had a distinct meaning. But this meaning cannot simply be read off the historical facts of his life. There is a truth about Socrates that is not merely factual and that cannot be accessed through historical scholarship but only through philosophy. It cannot be remembered but must be recollected. Kierkegaard likens the dissertation's task to that of a priest who hears confession. For philosophy, he writes,

> really relates to history as a father confessor to a penitent and, like him, ought to have a sensitive, alert ear for the penitent's secrets; but after having heard the whole sequence of confessions, he is also in a position to make them appear before the penitent as something else.[16]

The visible world is, in this metaphor, deceptive; and it can distract us from the underlying reality we seek to know. Kierkegaard is then proposing that the philosopher join Victor Eremita in making hearing his "dearest sense" for, as Eremita puts it in *Either/Or*, just as "the voice is the appearance of an inwardness incommensurable with the exterior," so "the ear is the instrument that apprehends this inwardness, hearing the sense by which it is appropriated."[17] And Eremita continues:

> A father confessor is separated from the penitent by a grille; he does not see, he only hears. As he listens, he forms [the image of] an exterior that corresponds to what he hears; thus he encounters no contradiction. It is different, however, when one sees and hears simultaneously, but sees a grille between oneself and the speaker.[18]

In this capacity, a priest must be a good listener but also something of an artist who conjures forth images that capture the essences of things, revealing their inside.

A number of features of sight and hearing motivate Eremita's choice of metaphor. A look at Hegel's philosophy of art can help us to sort it out. Hegel calls both sight and hearing "theoretical" senses, yet hearing is more "ideal" than sight, he says, and conveys subjective inwardness rather than external objects.[19] In music, he continues, the ear "listens to the result of the inner vibration of the body through which what comes before us is no longer the peaceful and material shape" of painting and sculpture, "but the first and more ideal breath of the soul."[20] Also language is apprehended through hearing but while music consists entirely of sounds and relations between them and does not point to some absent object beyond itself, language is not inherently audible. Sound is a wholly accidental medium for language—sign language relies on gestures instead. But also in spoken language, we disregard the sounds of the words spoken in order to attend to their meaning. Although there is a poetic and rhetorical use of language that tries to revive the audible medium by calling attention to the sound of words using rhyme and alliteration, such regress toward musicality, as we might call it, is an exception to the rule. The tendency of language is to strip its medium of the sensuality of sound; in grasping a word's meaning we become deaf to its sound. As "A" notes in his essay on the musical-erotic, the sensuous in language

> is reduced to a mere instrument and is thus annulled. If a person spoke in such a way that we heard the flapping of his tongue etc., he would be speaking poorly; if he heard in such a way that he heard the vibrations of the air instead of words, he would be hearing poorly.[21]

Curiously then, sound mediates both what "A" considers to be the most and the least sensual forms of expression. For "A," recall, music expresses sensuality itself—something Hegel would contest.[22] But hearing perceives, in addition to music, what both Hegel and "A" regard as the most spiritual of all forms of expression—language. Yet both music and language are "inner" media in the basic sense that they are not spatial. Whereas visual perception presents surfaces and rays of light located outside us in space, sounds are relatively difficult to place. When an orchestra plays a concert, the music appears to fill the whole room. True, when a person speaks, sight assists hearing in determining that his voice comes from inside his body. Yet what his words represent is not the vibrations of his vocal cords but his thoughts—his spirit, which though it appears to be emanating from his body through his voice does not in fact have a definite spatial location, since it is not an extended object.

To say that Socrates should be understood through hearing does not mean that we can understand him simply by taking account of the things he says in Plato's dialogues. Socrates' words were not transparent to his spirit, according to Kierkegaard; his speech was not a direct transmission of his thoughts. Socrates "was not like a philosopher laying out his views in such a way that the idea is present therein," Kierkegaard writes; "what Socrates said meant something else."²³ As part of his insensitivity to the dramatic aspect of dialogue, Xenophon lacks a sense of how Socrates' way of delivering his lines pointed inward, to his personality. But whereas speech is usually "the propagation of thought by way of sound," Socrates' speech "was not an immediate unity with what was said, not a flowing out but a continual flowing back."²⁴ Speaking about Socrates as a theater performer, Kierkegaard says that "what one misses in Xenophon is an ear for the infinitely resonant reverse echo of the lines"—the actor's discourse—"in the persona."²⁵ "We trust that the readers will agree with our statement," Kierkegaard writes, "that the empirical determinant is the polygon, that the intuition [*Anskuelsen*] is the circle, and that a qualitative difference will separate them for all eternity."²⁶ Xenophon's observation, myopically hung up on details and with no ear in Socrates' heart, "is always wandering about in the polygon" and instead of arriving at an *Anskuelse*—the higher seeing that apprehends a full aesthetic idea—only ever finds new angles.²⁷ Xenophon everywhere trivializes Socrates. Whereas in Plato's dialogues, Socrates is ever soaring toward the conceptual, Xenophon brings Socrates' discussions down to the empirical. Thus the notion of the good Xenophon attributes to Socrates is that of being useful,²⁸ and the investigation's "enchanting infinity" is deflated and replaced with the "bad infinity" of the empirical.²⁹

It is hearing that allows the philosopher to square the circle; but just as this hearing is a metaphor, so too the disregard for a person's exterior for which the confession metaphor calls should not be taken in its most literal sense as, in the case of Socrates, a call to disregard his alleged ugliness in our assessment of his philosophy. Or rather, it should not be taken *merely* literally, for Socrates' appearance should not be considered a mere contingent fact. The meaning of Socrates' appearance is irony, because it is not indicative of his personality. It is a phenomenon that is not identical to Being. Alcibiades already makes this claim when he compares Socrates to a Silenus statue in the *Symposium*, the kind of statue that is hollow and "split right down the middle, and inside it's full of tiny statues of the gods."³⁰ The disparity between Socrates' outside and his inside is a manifestation of his irony, according to Alcibiades, and Kierkegaard agrees that the significance of Socrates' outward appearance is precisely its insignificance. The truth of his appearance is conjured forth with the help of an idea—irony—and Kierkegaard's metaphors promise a vision of Socrates based on a recollection that supplants his actual appearance. Hearing can yield a higher form of seeing; a good listener is able to visualize the speaker before his intellectual eye. It is in this sense that Kierkegaard wants to say to Socrates what the latter had said to a prospective disciple: Speak, so that I may see you.[31]

Like Kierkegaard, like Eremita, "A" concerns himself with persons whose insides are out of joint with their outsides. The three Shadowgraph women are terminally preoccupied with a grief that doesn't manifest itself outwardly. Like irony, sorrow "seeks to return into itself."[32] The face is usually a mirror of the soul, "A" says, and there are people "whose make-up is such that when their emotions are stirred, the blood rushes out to the cutaneous system, so that the interior motion becomes visible in the exterior."[33] But then there are persons "so constituted that the blood recedes, withdraws into the heart chamber and the inner parts of the organism."[34] The first constitution described, he continues,

> is much easier to observe than the second. In the first, one sees the expression; the interior motion is visible in the exterior. In the second, one divines the interior motion. The exterior pallor is like the interior's farewell, and thought and imagination hurry after the fugitive, which hides in the secret recesses.[35]

In their quest for sorrow's secret, the Symparanekromenoi do not rely on spoken confessions but rather on external cues which are not transparent to their sources in the soul but nonetheless indicate them. The exterior is "the object of our observation," "A" says, "but not of our interest."[36] The emotional lives of the three women neither reveal themselves in the natural world nor lend themselves to representation in painting. Rather, "A" proposes to describe them in words. He wants us to understand these portraits by analogy with shadowgraphs, which, he says,

> are not immediately visible. If I pick up a shadowgraph, I get no real impression, cannot form an image of it. Only when I hold it up toward the wall and do not look at the figure directly but at what appears on the wall, only then do I see it. In the same way, the image I want to show here is an inner picture that becomes perceptible only once I see through the exterior.[37]

These shadows are not unlike the two trees in Kierkegaard's analogy, in his dissertation, which do not themselves represent anything other than trees, but jointly produce a negative image of a person's silhouette in the empty space between them:

> There is a picture that represents Napoleon's grave. Two tall trees shade the grave. There is nothing further to see in the picture, and the immediate observer sees nothing else. Between the two trees there is an empty space; as the eye traces along the outline, suddenly Napoleon himself emerges from this nothing, and now it is impossible to have him disappear again.[38]

Similarly A's discourse, like a poet's metaphor, is not itself an image and yet evokes one. The comparison amounts to the paradoxical conclusion that his art both is and is not classical. It is not classical because the medium and the content—outside and inside—are not reflected into each other. Whereas Don Juan's sensuous desire was said to be music's absolute subject matter, a subject matter inherent in the medium itself, A's images are not present in his shadowgraphs. Yet they are precisely thereby classical, since the object represented is itself disharmonious, contains itself an inside-outside discord. Any true representation of Socrates is bound to be paradoxical in this same way. If irony is pure negativity, the lack of any substance, then it is a contradiction, Kierkegaard remarks, to say that irony is the substance of Socrates' existence. But this is as it ought to be. It is as difficult to "hold on to the picture" of Socrates in his irony as it is to depict an elf "in the cap that makes him invisible."[39] For strictly speaking sight offers us always a plenitude—there are no gaps in our visual field; any void is itself visible, has shape and color. But Kierkegaard's tree analogy suggests how, in a looser sense, negativity might appear. Socrates' speech is like those trees, he writes. "One hears his speech," he explains,

> in the same way one sees the trees; his words mean what they say, just as the trees are trees. There is not a single syllable that gives a hint of any other interpretation, just as there is not one single mark that suggests Napoleon, and yet the most important thing is right there, hidden in this empty space, this nothing.[40]

The trees are the outside, in this metaphor; the empty space that is also a silhouette is the inside. In the same way, Socrates' speech traces the outlines of a void. He says that the virtues are one and this proposition is meaningful, yet all it does is trace the outlines of the concept of virtue. It is a line around an unknown, an intellectual emptiness, labeled "virtue." When Socrates' definitions and theories and remarks evoke this void before us, this negativity, then we have a negative image, an image of irony.

Philosophy as Art

Although Adorno identifies Fichte as the "archenemy" of Kierkegaard's view of the relation between inside and outside,[41] the conventional wisdom holds that it's a sustained attack on Hegel. In his notes to *Either/Or*, Howard Hong quotes a passage from the *Science of Logic* to clarify what Kierkegaard is targeting when he insists that the inside is not the outside. The "activity of force," Hegel writes, "consists in *expressing itself*," that is,

> in sublating externality and determining it as that in which it is identical with itself. Therefore what force in truth expresses is that its relation to other is relation to itself, that its passivity consists in its very activity. [. . .] In other words, what force expresses is this, that its *externality is identical* with its *inwardness*.[42]

When an object falls to the ground, the force of gravity manifests itself by acting on that object, determining its spatial location. Yet this determination is not some external consequence of the force of gravity but, Hegel would say, identical with it. The passivity of the object that falls and the activity of the force that causes it are but aspects of the same thing.

This discussion of physics, however, has little apparent bearing on Kierkegaard's claims about inside and outside in his first two books where these categories pertain to ethics and psychology, and even less on something like Johannes de Silentio's argument that faith is an inwardness that cannot be expressed in language. In his discussion of *Fear and Trembling*, Jon Stewart suggests as an explanation for this mismatch that Kierkegaard's "polemical usage" of the terminology of inner and outer is not really an attack on Hegel but rather on the Danish Hegelian Johan Ludvig Heiberg.[43] But this conclusion is too hasty. Surely, to borrow Adorno's phrase, the entire pathos of Hegel's philosophy is behind an identification of the thing itself and appearance. Hong's choice of quotation is misguided. Much more relevant is Hegel's *Phenomenology of Spirit*—whose title alone expresses the project of externalizing the interior—or his aesthetics. In his lectures on art, Hegel writes that the center of art is "a unification," one that is "self-enclosed so as to be a free totality, a unification of the content with its entirely adequate shape."[44] In the classical era of art, a work of art is not a mere symbol whose significance lies outside of it. Symbolic art points beyond itself, but the object that constitutes a classical work is self-reflexive. The object "must in art produce its shape out of itself and have the principle of its externality in itself," Hegel says.[45] The meaning of the work is inherent in the medium itself. To shape the object is to actualize that latent meaning. In a classical work, spirit reflects on itself, becomes an object for itself, and in "this objectivity of itself," Hegel says, "it then has the form of *externality* which, as identical with its own inner being, is therefore on its side the meaning of its own self."[46] Kierkegaard might have said that in a perfect work of art, an idea "loves itself." Although literature—the only form that can finally do justice to persons—is a romantic rather than a classical art, according to Hegel, here too we find inside and outside reflected into one another. Poetry, Hegel says, is

> *figurative* because it brings before our eyes not the abstract essence but its concrete reality, not an accidental existent but an appearance such that in it we immediately recognize the essence through, and inseparably from, the external aspect and its individuality.[47]

The perfect work of art is concrete yet reveals an ideal essence. At the same time, this ideal "inside" expresses the meaning of the outside. Together they form an explanatory whole.

From the discussion earlier about making the audible visible, it should be clear that Adorno's claim about Kierkegaard's stance toward inside-outside discord is an oversimplification. At least in his first two books, Kierkegaard has a more complicated view of the relation between inner and outer. Granted, he insists that a person is something beside his speech, deed, and appearance. But he defines the task of philosophy generally and his own dissertation specifically as that of bringing outside and inside into convergence. His project in *Irony* is really that of conjuring forth an outward representation that reveals Socrates' inside. Far from being an attack on Hegel, it exemplifies art as Hegel understands it. Kierkegaard's dissertation is, like Hegel's magnum opus, a phenomenology of the spirit.

Lover's Knowledge

In *Either/Or*, too, inside-outside discord is a problem to be overcome—and not only for A's aesthetic projects. The fact that the voice can be a mere tap of the tongue without a home in the soul—the fact that deception is possible—is a source of grief for the Shadowgraphs; they yearn to be loved, but also to know the beloved as he is in truth. Dreading solipsism, philosophers and lovers alike seek truth and certainty of the external world. If like Florine in the Danish fairy tale, Gretchen could "find entry into an echo chamber," some cave in which, "A" says,

> she knew that every sigh, every lament would be heard by her lover, then she would not, like Florine, spend only three nights there—she would stay there day and night; but in Faust's palace there is no echo chamber, and he has no ear in her heart.[48]

Faust knows nothing of what moves inside Gretchen's soul. Only "A" knows the Shadowgraphs' secrets just as he knows Antigone's. What makes him perceptive enough to detect signs in faces which are invisible to others—what allows him to recollect these women's states of mind—is that "passion" of his which "searches hidden thoughts, conjures forth what is hidden by means of witchcraft and invocations."[49] This occult passion is "sympathetic anxiety"[50]—"sympathy with sorrow's secret."[51] For sorrow, recall, "sneaks about in the world so very secretively that only the person who has sympathy for it gains an intimation of it."[52]

Kierkegaard's method of inquiry in the dissertation is grounded in love, too, and his quest for the truth about Socrates is modeled first of all on the speech in the *Symposium* that has Socrates for its subject matter. In addition to the myth of Need and Plenty and the appeal to beauty as the object of love, Kierkegaard writes, the *Symposium* tries to offer what is missing in Socrates' negative conception of love "by illustrating love in the person of Socrates," in the last speech.[53] Alcibiades captures the essence of a certain kind of love—ironic seduction—and thereby also the truth about Socrates. In Alcibiades' view of him, as in Kierkegaard's, "irony is his essential aspect" and Socrates' amorous relationship with Alcibiades, "and what it tells us about the nature of love, is negative."[54] The fact that Kierkegaard accepts what Alcibiades has to say shows that he grants that Alcibiades' love of Socrates gives him an epistemic privilege. Whatever it is to understand a person, it must surely be something more than a propositional knowledge of facts. In *The Human Condition*, Arendt proposes that love is unconcerned with "what" the beloved is but possesses "an unequaled clarity of vision for the disclosure of *who*" he is.[55] This distinction between the "who" and the "what" of a person lines up with the distinction between *kende* and *vide* in Danish, where *kende* signifies acquaintance whereas *vide* is knowledge of facts. Kierkegaard's claim throughout the dissertation that irony is "a qualification of personality" suggests that his distinction between the "spirit" of irony and the historical facts of Socrates' existence can be mapped onto Arendt's dichotomy.[56] It is possible to know plenty of facts about what Socrates did and said (descriptions of his outside) without understanding his spirit, without understanding *who* he is (acquaintance with his inside). Alcibiades' speech in the *Symposium* is a model both for Kierkegaard's method and for his result. Like Alcibiades, Kierkegaard wants to present Socrates as the incarnation of a spirit, and for both young men, that spirit is irony.

We have seen in previous chapters how Socrates, Alcibiades, and Plato each exemplify in their approach to knowledge the view of love they put forth in the *Symposium*. For Socrates, love is a liberating lack and the seduction that liberates the beloved; for Alcibiades, it is lack as longing and despair—not liberation but alienation. For Plato, finally, love is the fullness of contemplating beauty. But this does not yet tell us about Kierkegaard's own idea of how philosophy should proceed. We can appreciate just how seriously Kierkegaard took Plato's idea that philosophy is a form of eros only when we consider his own metaphilosophical ethos in light of his interpretation of the Greeks.

In an exemplary academic manner, Kierkegaard begins his dissertation by laying out his methodology. He does so by invoking chivalry—a favorite Romantic idea of his, representing passion, longing, and striving. The "philosophical knight," Kierkegaard writes, must be "an eroticist" in his observation of a phenomenon.[57] This means that, on the one hand,

> he must not be indifferent to any feature, any factor. But on the other hand, he should also feel that he has the upper hand, yet use this only to help the phenomenon achieve its full revelation. Thus even if the observer brings the concept, it is crucial that the phenomenon remain inviolate and that the concept be seen as coming into existence through the phenomenon.[58]

The phenomenon, in this metaphor, is always, *qua* phenomenon, "of the feminine gender"; and if we expect it, "due to its womanly nature to submit to the stronger one," then the code of chivalry demands of the eroticist in his turn to be respectful of the phenomenon's integrity so that in applying a concept, he is not an invader and conqueror but a redeemer and servant.[59]

The phenomenon has a meaning, an essence, and in order to conceptualize that essence, the philosopher must disregard the phenomenon's accidental features or, as Kierkegaard puts it, resist being "infatuated by the charms of the particular"; not let himself be "distracted by the superabundance of the particular."[60] Just as in Kant's theory of inspiration it is nature that must "give the rule to art,"[61] so the phenomenon must according to Kierkegaard "give the rule" to philosophy. For Kant, art is not the artist's entirely free production, and a real genius cannot give an account of how he came up with his ideas.[62] He is the passive recipient of nature's suggestion. It is a similar receptiveness that allows the philosopher to grasp the phenomenon's essence and express it in a concept. When such a concept is in turn brought to bear on the phenomenon, it will appear to come into existence through the phenomenon, as an outside determined by its inside. Kierkegaard's methodological statement also implies the idealist view that in becoming intelligible, the phenomenon, too, achieves self-knowledge—just like the penitent when the father confessor articulates the gist of his confession. In loving the phenomenon—in looking at the phenomenon with desire—the philosopher brings out that wherein she can understand and love herself.

Despite the Hegelian ring of this, Tonny Aagaard Olesen detects in Kierkegaard's erotic metaphor the statement of an "anti-Hegelian hermeneutic," behind which "one finds an authentic Socratic eroticist and midwife."[63] Most probably Kierkegaard does have Hegel or Hegelians in mind when he complains about "modern philosophy" and its treatment of phenomena, in which one sometimes hears too much "the jingling of spurs and the voice of the master."[64] But the philosopher knight does more than a midwife. Without the concept he brings to bear, the phenomenon could not have given birth to her own essence. In an earlier draft to the introduction that melds this analogy with the confession metaphor, Kierkegaard wrote that history by itself is "sterile," yet "its embrace is fertile."[65] "In the arms of philosophy," he continues, "history rejuvenates itself unto divine youthfulness."[66] Philosophy is not maieutic so much as procreative. As in Diotima's myth, ideas are born upon the philosopher's erotic encounter with a beautiful sight.

It is easy to see why interpreters should attribute a purely Socratic methodology to Kierkegaard—we have been taught to think of Socrates as Kierkegaard's only philosophical hero. But Kierkegaard also confesses to a "youthful infatuation with Plato," and his metaphilosophy draws heavily on Plato's aesthetic epistemology.[67] The truth is an image the philosopher beholds or projects; the goal of philosophy, as Kierkegaard construes it in his dissertation, is a higher form of seeing. Like many others, his teacher Frederik Sibbern characterized art in this way and claimed that whereas Baumgarten had distinguished between sensory knowledge and abstract or philosophical knowledge, art has now been recognized as a form of knowledge on a par with philosophy.[68] In order to earn this status, the artist "must have an eye" for the "'inner' being of things" and their "essential nature."[69] Even as he may appear to add things to his representation by straying from his immediate impression of the object, the artist in fact only gives nature its due when he transfigures it in his work. The representation produced on the basis of such insight is neither purely mimetic nor entirely free. It results in "an ideal rebirth."[70] Kierkegaard's epistemology might be called art with a philosophical aspiration or philosophy by artistic means. He just prefers the metaphor of hearing to that of sight in describing the philosopher's access to the inner life of things.

Positive Tautology

Nevertheless, Kierkegaard's epistemology is certainly inspired by Socrates, too, and thereby differs from Plato's in important ways. Recall his claim that all Socrates' theses about the nature of love or the unity of virtue turn out to be purely formal. Socrates' definition of love boils down simply to "love is"; the unity of virtue turns out to be an empty tautology: "all virtues are varieties of virtue"—thus "virtue is virtue." The claim that virtue is one would have substance only if, as Kierkegaard would have it, that wherein the different virtues love one another became apparent. We must understand by means other than a repetition of the definiendum or a reflexive pronoun what it is that virtue loves when it loves itself. Yet such understanding would also, like a tautology, consist in a knowledge of identity. What Kierkegaard aims to offer in *Irony*, I want to suggest, is a *positive tautology*. Essences—the ground of things' identities—are the proper objects of philosophical knowledge. Kierkegaard's dissertation seeks to uncover Socrates' essence: what makes him identical to himself; what it is for him to be who he is, and not someone else.

Kierkegaard does give a definition of irony—"infinite absolute negativity"[71]—but a positive tautology is not a mere definition. Ultimately, the dissertation's conception of knowledge is not discursive. As we have seen, Kierkegaard conceives of epistemic fullness as a kind of intuition or image in which the essence of a phenomenon is revealed through a concept. The concept clarifies—*forklarer*—the phenomenon. The phenomenon, in turn, vindicates the concept. To contemplate Socrates' philosophical practice and his relation to his interlocutors, his lovers, and his society indeed gives substance to the concept of irony, defined as infinite absolute negativity—gives something for the imagination to grasp. Likewise the definition, by throwing certain aspects of Socrates into relief, sharpens our view of him. In keeping with nineteenth-century terminology, Kierkegaard writes in the introduction to the dissertation's second part that a concept's adequacy to the phenomenon is its "truth," but that philosophy must also achieve "actuality," which is when the concept is illuminated by the phenomenon. Looking back upon the first part of the dissertation, he writes that there "the concept always hovered in the background with a permanent urge to take shape in the phenomenon."[72] In the second part,

> the concept's phenomenal manifestation, as a constant possibility to take up residence among us, will accompany the progress of the investigation. These two factors are inseparable, because if the concept were not in the phenomenon, or rather, if the phenomenon were not understandable, actual, only by way of the concept, and if the phenomenon were not in the concept or, more correctly, the concept were not understandable, actual, only by way of the phenomenon, then all knowledge would be impossible, inasmuch as the first case would be wanting in truth, and the second case wanting in actuality.[73]

To see a concept and a phenomenon reflected into each other is to know a positive tautology—to understand the identity of the phenomenon, that wherein it loves itself.

In an early notebook entry, Kierkegaard had remarked upon Judaism that its monotheism is so abstract as not to allow any predication of God other than a tautological one: "God is God."[74] Fifteen years later, he elaborated on this idea. When Moses asks God to append a signature of sorts to his message—a name by which he can mention God to the people—the response has the form of a tautology. God called to Moses, saying "the cry of the Israelites has reached me,"—

> "and I have seen the way the Egyptians are oppressing them. So now, go. I am sending you to Pharaoh to bring my people the Israelites out of Egypt."

> But Moses said to God, "Who am I that I should go to Pharaoh and bring the Israelites out of Egypt?" And God said, "I will be with you. And this will be the sign to you that it is I who have sent you: When you have brought the people out of Egypt, you will worship God on this mountain." Moses said to God, "Suppose I go to the Israelites and say to them, 'The God of your fathers has sent me to you,' and they ask me, 'What is his name?' Then what shall I tell them?" God said to Moses, "*I am who I am*. This is what you are to say to the Israelites: '*I am* has sent me to you.'" God also said to Moses, "Say to the Israelites, 'The Lord, the God of your fathers—the God of Abraham, the God of Isaac and the God of Jacob—has sent me to you.' This is my name forever, the name you shall call me from generation to generation."[75]

In referring to this passage, Kierkegaard distinguishes between a high and a low form of tautology. The fact that "the highest principles for all thought cannot be proven but only tautologically rephrased," Kierkegaard writes, is analogous to the "inward infinity" that the divine statement conveys.[76] Here as everywhere, he adds, "the highest and the lowest have a similarity; for tautology is the lowest form of expression, it is gibberish—and then again it is the highest, so that by comparison everything other than a tautology would be gibberish."[77]

The distinction between low and high echoes that distinction of A's, between the law of the transitivity of identity and infinite judgments, which we saw in Chapter 1. What Socrates says of virtue is what the Jewish people say of God: that he is one. Neither is informative, and nor is God's "I am who I am." What Kierkegaard does not say in those reflections in his journal is that God's identity is revealed in the fact of the Israelites' return to their long-lost home. God doesn't close himself up egoistically in his "I = I." His promise to "be with you" is a promise to self-revelation through an act of love. As readers of the Bible, we must accept on authority that he did fulfill that promise. The text itself gives us no more insight into God's essence than does Plato's characterization of beauty-in-itself as that which is beheld at the top of the ladder of love. As with beauty, we can know God only by acquaintance. A description can at best tell us *what it is like* to be in touch with God, as Moses is on Mount Sinai. Acquaintance is necessarily first personal. It cannot be conveyed directly but only indirectly; we cannot capture it but only evoke it by relating its effect on us.

With the erotic metaphor that opens his dissertation, Kierkegaard promises to provide a true concept of irony that will also gain actuality when we see it in and with the phenomenon, Socrates. We have no direct access to that phenomenon, but must imagine it on the basis of Plato's descriptions. Yet this erotic-philosophical chivalry, this seduction of the phenomenon with the concept, is an advance upon Socrates' ironic questioning, which seduces not in order to reveal the true nature of phenomena but in order to show their inadequacy. In this way, Kierkegaard's conception of knowledge is a collaboration between the Socratic and the Platonic ways of knowing. Here I think we have compelling answers to the questions Hermann Diem and David Gouwens ask about whether Kierkegaard envisions a role for the imagination to play in speculative thought.[78] Diem looks too far when he locates the answer in *The Sickness unto Death*. There Anti-Climacus writes that the imagination is not just another mental capacity but a synthesizing or mediating capacity that can relate itself to other capacities: to feeling, knowing, and willing. As such, Anti-Climacus calls it "the capacity *instar omnium*." Imagination, he continues, "is infinitizing reflection, and therefore the elder Fichte quite correctly assumed that even in relation to knowledge the categories derive from the imagination."[79] Having concluded that Plato "destroys" the Socratic with his imagery, Diem writes that when Kierkegaard sets out to avoid such destruction, he "begins by refusing to isolate thought."[80] He envisions the imagination as a bridge between faculties. Anti-Climacus seems to think of imagination as a form of creativity rather than as the faculty of sensation. But we find both kinds of imagination—and the positive role for the imagination Gouwens despaired of finding in *Irony*—in the dissertation's own methodology. There is both an element of intuition and creativity in Kierkegaard's proposed strategy for getting to the truth about Socratic irony. But whereas Kierkegaard said that Plato's sphere is not thought but representation, his own imagination is complemented by thought. Abstract Socratic concepts and imagistic Platonic intuition are joined in Kierkegaard's epistemology, and here we have his model of speculative philosophy. A Kierkegaardian idea is clear in representing to us, aesthetically, a phenomenon's essence. But unlike a Platonic Form it is also distinct, because its conceptual component delineates its borders, tells us what it is *not*.

Socrates' definitions dwell in the realm of pure thought; Plato's myths and Forms are compelling images in which the beholder finds a perfectly clear transfiguration. Each in his own way, these two philosophers fail to establish a link between mind and world, the abstractions of thought and the concretion of existing phenomena. Not even when he adopts the Socratic method of dialogue does Plato, according to Kierkegaard, arrive at ideas through thought. It is because Kierkegaard shares the urgency of Alcibiades' desire to know something outside himself, a love of actuality, that his philosophy can hope to supersede those of Socrates and Plato. The philosophical knight's love of the phenomenon commits him to respecting her integrity. And as this love gives him insight into her essence, he takes it upon himself to help her reveal herself as she is in truth.

Although this epistemology is presented as a normative metaphilosophy, it only goes so far as a guide for the aspiring philosopher. Kierkegaard's methodological statement gives a diagnosis of a successful case but much of the process remains unaccounted for. What is it that allows someone to perceive a phenomenon's essence? How can the observer know which qualities are contingent and should be disregarded? How is the concept conceived—how is the essence of the phenomenon translated into a concept? We are given no criteria for how to get through these crucial turning points. The moment of insight and the process of conception are occult presences in the theory. This is the sense in which philosophy is not a science, but an art. The knowledge Kierkegaard vows to achieve in the dissertation is clear and distinct, both intuitable and conceptual. But his *theory* of knowledge is only intuitable. It lacks negativity, that by which the real thing is distinguished from troll changelings. Thus he believes in the possibility of a knowledge that transcends myth—the philosopher knight conceives a true and actual idea. But the account of how such knowledge is obtained is itself a myth.

5

The Irony of Christian Love

The Concept of Irony may have a precarious status in the scholarship, but everyone agrees that Socrates remained an important model for Kierkegaard. Socrates was the first "subjective thinker": he looked inward to answer the question "what is virtue?" But whereas to Plato, *a priori* thinking meant recollecting a long-forgotten idea, fully fledged but dormant in the soul, for Kierkegaard's Socrates the answer lay in the inwardness itself, the self-reflection that is ever separating the mind from its content. If virtue is wisdom and this wisdom is subjectivity, then it cannot be imparted from one person to another. And if subjectivity is the action of freeing oneself from external claims, detaching the intellect from ideas that try to impose themselves, then virtue is something entirely negative.

Yet Christianity is supposed to go further than Socrates, as Kierkegaard suggests already in *The Concept of Irony* when he locates a positive counterpoint to Socrates' negative notion of love in religion. Recall his remark that, although desire and longing are aspects of love, "love is also infinite love. When we say that God is love, we are saying that he is infinitely self-communicating; when we speak of abiding in love, we speak about participating in a fullness. This is what's substantial in love."[1] That comment would seem to anticipate *Works of Love* with its explication of the love commandment, "Thou shalt love thy neighbor as thyself," and its elaboration on the deeds in which love expresses itself. For neighborly love is but a rechanneling of God's love. And God's love consists in *Meddelelse*, meaning communication but also sharing. God is love because he shares himself with us infinitely; divine love consists in generosity. With the proclamation that God is love, the book would also seem to offer a positive theology.

Reading *Works of Love* in pursuit of a full idea of that infinite love, this chapter will put pressure on Kierkegaard's characterizations of neighborly love, its deeds and its aim, and thus reveal just how negative his theology and philosophy of love remain. Adorno and Knud Ejler Løgstrup criticized *Works of Love* for construing love negatively as denial of oneself, nature, and the neighbor's individuality, and as the separation rather than union of persons. Chapter 1's reconstruction of Kierkegaard's view of Socratic irony puts us in a position to elaborate these interpretations of *Works of Love*, applying to Kierkegaard the analysis and conceptual framework he used in *The Concept of Irony*.

Neighborly Love as an Ethics of Duty

From the book's title, it looks as if it sets out to rehabilitate the Catholic institution of good works, which the Protestant fathers had dismissed, propounding instead a doctrine of "grace through faith alone." In the first of fifteen "deliberations," Kierkegaard says that love can express itself—and be known—only through action. As a tree is known by its fruits, so too love is known by its works—or "deeds," as the Danish *Gjerninger* is more precisely translated.[2] Yet he quickly qualifies this, assuring us that the value of neighborly love is not instrumental. It is the *intention* to do good that matters. Even as he calls for loving deeds as outward expressions of faith, Kierkegaard maintains that those deeds are significant only with reference to the individual's inner state. Thus further ahead in the book, he explains that taking mercy on someone in need is an act of love even if it fails to actually help him:

> *Mercifulness has nothing to give.* Of course, if the merciful person has something to give then he is more than glad to give it. But we want to call attention not to this, but rather to the fact that one can be merciful without having the least bit to give. And this is of great importance, since *the ability* to be merciful certainly is a far greater completeness than having money and thereby being able to give.[3]

The talk about mercifulness and "the merciful person" might suggest that his ethics of Christian love is aretaic. There is really an undercurrent of virtue ethics in the book—we will return to this—but the overwhelming emphasis is on duty. In fact, this passage echoes the opening of *Groundwork of the Metaphysic of Morals*, where Kant states with much pathos that a good will is the only thing that's absolutely good, and that even if we are prevented by circumstance from achieving what we intend with our actions, those actions are still good as long as they issue from a good will.[4]

And just as for Kant the moral law must be obeyed out of duty, so too the neighbor must according to Kierkegaard be loved out of duty. The Christian must not love for the sake of being praised or loved in return—he must be ready to be hated for his love.[5] This might happen if a loving deed runs counter to the unsound desires of its beneficiary. With the same disinterest, the lover must "abide" in his love even toward those who have hurt or betrayed him. If true love consisted in feeling, this might not be possible. In fact, if like "the poet" we conceived of love as inclination, "then to command love would be a great mistake, completely unreasonable talk."[6] What is characteristic "of Christian love and its peculiarity, is that it contains this apparent contradiction: that to love is a duty."[7] Only when it is a duty "is love forever safeguarded against every change; forever liberated in blissful independence; forever happily secured against despair."[8] What we ordinarily call love—between friends, kin, or in couples—is essentially ephemeral, since it depends on external or otherwise contingent factors. Friends and lovers feel a need to vow eternal fidelity, Kierkegaard says. But they do not swear by God, but by love itself—that love which is a poetic invention:

> When this love swears, it gives itself the meaning of that by which it swears; it is love itself that casts its glow on that by which it swears, so that it not only does not swear by something higher, but actually swears by something that is lesser than itself.[9]

Attraction and affection are typically aroused by some quality of the beloved's, like his beauty, so that if he ceases to be beautiful then our love will cease as well. To the Christian lover, on the other hand, the beloved may as well be ugly. As our "neighbor," a person should be loved even if, to inclination, he is utterly unlovely.[10] In fact, Kierkegaard ventures, it is precisely "the ugly one" who is our neighbor, the one we do not love immediately but only out of duty.[11] Also tribal relations and kinship are disregarded by neighborly love. Thus the story of the Good Samaritan shows us what it is to relate to another person as neighbor to neighbor: whereas that man in distress lying by the roadside was ignored by one of his own people, the Samaritan, a supposed enemy, stopped to help him, acting thereby as the man's spiritual neighbor.[12] Whereas what most people call "love" implies elevating some person above others and at the expense of others,[13] for the true Christian every person is a fit object of love, since all people are the same once we disregard particular qualities and our personal relationships with them. This makes it natural that, just as Kant insisted we must respect ourselves no less than others, Christianity wants us also to love ourselves.[14] Kierkegaard takes the duty to self-love to be implied deep down when Jesus says, "Love thy neighbor *as thyself*." We are not free to treat ourselves any way we like, then: "When, because the world or another person faithlessly betrayed him, a human being abandons himself to despair, of what is he guilty [. . .] except not loving himself properly?"[15]

Love's Negative Labor

Still, the love commandment would seem to have a different orientation than Kant's supreme principle of morality. In Kant's discussion, the categorical imperative figures mainly as a negative criterion. A type of action that seems harmless in a particular case is nonetheless prohibited if it cannot be universalized. Thus in Kant's key examples, I may *not* make a false promise, may *not* take my own life.[16] Respect and reverence, the central moral feelings for Kant, likewise suggest distance, a stepping back and letting be. By contrast, we think of love as oriented *toward* the other: it cares, gives, reaches out, and embraces. But if respect involves restraint whereas love is an outpouring, and if the categorical imperative seems mainly prohibitive whereas love bears fruit, Kierkegaard's characterization of neighborly love is mostly negative, too. Christian love must *not* be based on inclination, must *not* be restricted to friends or family, must *not* be dependent on any contingent qualities of its object. Even when, like the Good Samaritan, we come to a stranger's aid, this must *not* be motivated by fellow feeling. There is a certain "natural good disposition, a certain kindly compassion and helpfulness," Kierkegaard writes, which "has some time to spare," and this "we gladly praise."[17] But "that it becomes tired over the course of time, or when things drag on [. . .], this is all too certain."[18] Compassion may perhaps accompany deeds of love, but it is not what makes them such deeds, it is not what *moves* the genuine Christian lover. We must look past all affect and inclination in the psyche, in search of something purer—a pure volition perhaps. Anyway, something in there that constitutes love's content and can be given a positive characterization.

Yet the negativity of the characterization reflects an essential negativity in the phenomenon of neighborly love itself. That such love is not an inclination also means that the lover must *suppress* his inclinations, putting bounds on his natural tendency to privilege the interests of his friends over those of strangers, for example. At least with regard to the self, love's deed is a negative one. In fact, Kierkegaard says quite explicitly, and repeatedly, that loving the neighbor involves self-denial, and the term "self-denial's love" is used as a synonym for Christian love, implying that such denial is its essential feature. "The point of contention between 'the poet' and Christianity," he writes, "can quite accurately be specified thus: *Romance and friendship are preference and preferential passion*; Christian love is self-denial's love."[19] Romantic and filial love is covert self-love.[20] As self-denial, neighborly love is the complete opposite of preferential love.

The negativity of Kierkegaard's concept of love has been a target of criticism, notably by Adorno. On his view, Kierkegaard doesn't go very far in pursuing his ostensible aim of "supplementing his negative theology with a positive one."[21] Kierkegaard never gives his concept of love a positive definition, says Adorno:

> Negatively, however, his concept of love is distinct enough. He regards love as a matter of pure inwardness. He starts from the Christian command "Thou shalt love." He interprets this command by emphasizing its abstract generality. Speaking exaggeratedly, in Kierkegaard's doctrine of Love the object of love is, in a way, irrelevant. [. . .] In love, the other person becomes a mere "stumbling block" to subjective inwardness. This [love] has no object in the proper sense, and the substantial quality of love is "object-less." In Kierkegaard's doctrine the "Christian" content of love, its justification in eternity, is determined only by the subjective qualities of the loving one, such as disinterestedness, unlimited confidence, unobtrusiveness, mercifulness, even if one is helpless oneself, self-denial and fidelity.[22]

Although the book is supposed to be about love's "fruit," the outward manifestation was soon said to be irrelevant. The loving deed is not some physical action that carries out an intention and has a result, but the inner movement of the will. On Adorno's analysis, then, neighborly love is not in fact outward-oriented. It takes place inside the person and does not relate him to another. Even when he does give to others, this qualifies as love only insofar as it involves self-denial; what matters to the Christian lover, therefore, is not some positive contribution he makes to the world, but the negative force he exerts on himself.

We are now ready to see the similarities between Kierkegaard's account of love and Socrates' speech in the *Symposium* and, more generally, to rephrase the preceding interpretation in the words Kierkegaard used about Socrates in his dissertation. Let us first note a commonality in the impetus of the two discourses. Kierkegaard's text sets out to dispel the poets' glorifying characterizations of love and shows that loving is actually difficult, that it runs counter to our inclination, that loving deeds are often not welcomed, and that the lover will be rewarded with hatred. This criticism of false rosy representations of love clearly recalls how Socrates begins by chiding the previous speakers for portraying Eros as beautiful without regard for truth: "In my foolishness," he says ironically,

> I thought you should tell the truth about whatever you praise, that this should be your basis, and that from this a speaker should select the most beautiful truths and arrange them most suitably. [...] But now it appears that this is not what it is to praise anything whatever; rather, it is to apply to the object the grandest and the most beautiful qualities, whether he actually has them or not.[23]

Having vowed to speak the truth about love, Socrates proceeds to detach the concept of love from the objects of love. Recall how Kierkegaard summarized the speech:

> Love is continually disengaged more and more from the contingent concretion in which it appeared in the previous speeches and is taken back to its *most abstract definitions*, wherein it appears not as this or that love, or as love for this or that, but as love for a something which it does not have, that is, as desire, longing.[24]

In his own account of love, Kierkegaard goes further in abstraction, since he doesn't simply make the point that all instances of love share in the same essence. Also the object of love is everywhere the same: everyone is loved *qua* neighbor, *qua* human being. So far, this is a standard rationalist way of proceeding. What is remarkable about Kierkegaard's account is what he found most remarkable about Socrates:

He starts out from the concrete and arrives at the most abstract and there, where the investigation should begin, he stops. The result he arrives at is actually the indeterminate determination of pure being: "Love *is*," because the addendum that it is longing, desire, is no determination, since it is merely a relation to a something, which is not given.[25]

The only amendment we need to make to this characterization to make it fit Kierkegaard's own account concerns the last part: the "addendum" in his case is that love is action, but this is no real determination since nothing is said about the nature of this action, the telos that defines it, *except that that telos need not be achieved*, and so does not constitute it after all. To sum up, then: despite the claim that love is known by its fruits, we are not allowed to understand love through its effects; but when we try to locate it inside the lover, we are told that love is not a feeling, an inclination, or a benevolent disposition. Finally our search for that source inside the individual from which love issues as an action turns out to have been misguided. Neighborly love is not a giving, an outpouring, an outward movement. It is suppression, a negative action of the self on the self—in short: self-denial.

If Socrates' seductive practice takes something away from the beloved, thus arousing a desire in him, Kierkegaard's love is the action of taking away, or blotting out some part of, *oneself*. But so long as the temporal self exists, new inclinations and selfish desires will arise. Self-denial cannot be accomplished once and for all, but must be a lifelong task, the continuous encroachment of the will upon the sensuous self, or as Adorno put it, "a breaking down of nature."[26] Kierkegaard's love is *ascetic*, not only in that it shuns earthly pleasures, but in the most basic sense that it consists in endless spiritual exercise. Against the background of Noreen Khawaja's interpretation of Kierkegaardian Pietism, this should not be surprising. When Kierkegaard formulated the question guiding his writing as "what does it mean to become a Christian?," the answer was implied, Khawaja says.[27] Christianity is about becoming, not being; only this becoming can never be accomplished. The life of faith is a life of striving and endless spiritual labor. This view of faith as a "constant conversion" Kierkegaard takes from the Pietist movement, Khawaja writes, in which "conversion is transformed from one moment in the process of justification into an encompassing devotional ideal."[28] If this is right, *Works of Love* would seem to be anything but a concession to Catholicism and its good works. The allusion to that Catholic notion is ironic. Yes, Christian love expresses itself in action, but this is an invisible action, ineffectual on anything other than the individual's own spirit.

In due time, we will consider objections to the claim that neighborly love is pure inwardness for Kierkegaard. But first, I want to point out how the lover's striving and continuous spiritual labor is reduplicated as the intellectual task Kierkegaard quietly sets for *Works of Love*'s reader by not giving a positive concept of love. "Wherefrom does love come," he asks;

> where does it have its origin and its source, where is that place in which it dwells, and from which it springs forth? Well, that place is hidden or lies in what's hidden. It is an innermost place in a person; from this place love's life begins, because "life begins in the heart." But you cannot see this place; however far you penetrate, the origin retreats in distance and hiddenness; even when you have penetrated to the very inside, the origin is yet further inside, just as the source of the well is further away right when you are closest to it.[29]

To try to grasp love intellectually is to look further and further into the soul, past desires, feelings, and inclinations, in search of something more ethereal than these. Yet that "heart" where love lies hidden ever eludes us. The innermost cannot be reached; love cannot be seen with the mind's eye, and so we cannot form an idea of it. It is a humbling exercise, since it deprives us of ever being certain whether a particular deed is a deed of love. Why bother, then? Perhaps because this continuous inward penetration, this exercise in abstract thinking, is itself the point, the only wisdom and virtue that can be achieved in earthly life.

Adorno had charged that neighborly love, consisting in inwardness, is indifferent to its object and even comes close to callousness.[30] This is the criticism that Løgstrup elaborates. When Kierkegaard says the lover must not seek reciprocation or some reward for his love, that is not just because love should be disinterested. It is also for the beloved's protection. If she felt indebted or became attached to the lover for his kindness and help, she would be transferring to him the kind of gratitude that she should really direct to God. Her relation to God would thereby be jeopardized.[31] Løgstrup does not exaggerate when he says that "the worst thing that could happen," on this view, "would be for our neighbor to realize that he or she was the object of love."[32] Instead, "everything depends on being misunderstood and hated."[33] This, it turns out, won't usually require much effort, since most of the time, the goodness of loving deeds is not immediately apparent to their recipients. Neighborly love demands the sacrifice of earthly love, of other people's appreciation.[34] The beneficiary's hatred is the mark of a loving deed, just as the execution of Jesus is a testament to his: "If Christ had not been love," Kierkegaard asks, "would he then have been crucified?"[35] In this, the Savior was not exceptional: *all* those who "love human beings will be hated in the world."[36] Kierkegaard's ethics of love, Løgstrup concludes, is really "a brilliantly thought out system of safeguards against being forced into a close relationship with other people."[37]

The criterion that loving deeds be performed for their own sake, without any ulterior motive of personal gain, is not difficult to accept, yet it is not what Løgstrup objects to. His point is that there is something perverse about forbidding love to be recognized as love by the neighbor. Rather than simply safeguarding love's disinterestedness and the neighbor's relation to God, Kierkegaard seems to fetishize the ingratitude and hatred that will be love's reward, reveling in the idea that martyrdom is every Christian's fate. Ironically, it seems then that love *does* afford pleasure after all: the negative pleasure of persevering through self-denial and relinquishment of social goods. It is what Kierkegaard termed cynical enjoyment in *The Concept of Irony*:

> Cynicism enjoys the absence, the lack; it is not unfamiliar with desire but seeks its satisfaction in not giving in to it, and instead of entering the desire, it turns back into itself at every moment and enjoys the lack of enjoyment—which enjoyment vividly recalls what ironic satisfaction is, in an intellectual regard.[38]

Self-love as a Guide to Neighbor Love

Jamie Ferreira's commentary on *Works of Love* is geared toward rebutting the damning criticism it has received from Adorno, Løgstrup, and others. Further ahead we will consider some of the book's positive moments, which those criticisms should also reckon with. But for now we will consider Ferreira's replies to the charge that Kierkegaard's neighborly love is forbiddingly abstract, negative, and antisocial.

Regarding the abstractness of Kierkegaard's characterization of love, Ferreira concedes that he rarely gives concrete examples in *Works of Love*.

For that reason, she says, the few examples he does offer should be maximally exploited.[39] Ferreira seizes in particular upon Kierkegaard's reference to the parable of the Good Samaritan—"surely an unambiguous illustration," she says, "of the kind of care for another that [Kierkegaard] believes is implied by the phrase 'as yourself,'" thus invalidating also the criticism that neighborly love is never given a positive characterization and consists in pure inwardness.[40] Ferreira takes loving the neighbor to mean quite simply helping people who are in need, and in the New Testament story, she says, "attending to the person's need means binding his wounds, getting him to a place where he can be cared for, and financially arranging for this care."[41] On Ferreira's interpretation, Kierkegaard's idea of the love commandment is as commonsensical and straightforward as Luther's gloss on it in "Lectures on Galatians." In fact we should assume, she says, "that Kierkegaard is in theological agreement with Luther except for those places he specifically notes otherwise."[42] Paraphrasing Luther, she says that loving one's neighbor as oneself "requires that we support, help, increase, protect, and preserve, in addition to abstaining from harm, and we are 'commanded to further' the welfare of the other because that is what we would wish for ourselves."[43]

Actually, when Kierkegaard first mentions the Good Samaritan, it is to illustrate the very same thing Jesus meant his parable to show: what it is to be a *neighbor* in the Christian sense. The closeness between loving neighbors is an ethical or spiritual one, not the closeness of kin, friends, or members of the same ethnic group.[44] Though we can assume he endorses the Samaritan, he does not say what principle he takes to be guiding his actions, or under what description the man's actions express neighborly love. Is the Samaritan heeding the other man's wishes, or treating him as he himself would like to be treated? Given Kierkegaard's assault on commonly held ethical "wisdoms," we can hardly presuppose that he would agree with some interpretation just because it seems commonsensical to us. As for the assumption that, unless he explicitly states otherwise, Kierkegaard agrees with Luther—and not just to the broad strokes of his theology but to every last passage in his writings—this is quite an assumption. Surely the extent to which the two are in agreement should be a conclusion drawn after a careful reading of the book, not an assumption brought in from the start.

And sure enough, directly following his reference to the parable, Kierkegaard complicates what it means to love one's neighbor "as oneself."

First he draws from that little qualification the inference that everyone ought to love themselves.[45] Then he adds that, of course, we should not love ourselves the way we *typically* do; when the commandment "is understood correctly," he explains, "it also says the opposite: *Thou shalt love Thyself in the right way*."[46] Ferreira is grateful for this further qualification, since it confirms Kierkegaard's rejection of a self-love that amounts to selfishness. But she fails to note that it undermines Luther's commonsense interpretation of the commandment. If the way we naturally love ourselves is not the way we ought to, then we cannot use our intuitions about what we would want for ourselves as a guide to how we ought to treat others. Far from clarifying the addendum "as thyself," the qualification "in the right way" cancels it out. For the difference between how we actually love ourselves and how we ought to love ourselves is potentially infinite—Kierkegaard himself admits that proper self-love is the opposite of our ordinary self-love. Ironically, the new qualification deprives us of the grasp we previously had on neighborly love by way of our acquaintance with self-love. As Kierkegaard himself writes in *The Concept of Irony*, it is typical of irony "to take away with one hand what it gives with the other."[47]

The Neighbor's Good

Rather than draw on experience and intuition—our concern for ourselves, our sense of what we would have wished for in the neighbor's place—we are brought back to the original, abstract conception of love. Loving *the right way* may plausibly be interpreted as doing what is good for the beloved, and indeed Kierkegaard does say that we should seek the neighbor's good. Of course, this is still a very abstract characterization, and so formal as to be almost tautological. There are many different views of what is good for people: pleasure, meaning, virtue, asceticism, and so on. Only much later does Kierkegaard come out and say what is the highest good for human beings. For now, he gives a negative qualification to the abstract claim, which has exactly the same form as the one we just saw (i.e., "in the right way"):

> If your beloved or friend asked you for something that you found upon due deliberation would be harmful to him, precisely because you loved him properly, then you will have something to answer for if you love by obeying the loved one's wish instead of denying it.[48]

Neighborly love is paternalistic, in other words; and Ferreira, again, lauds this tenet in Kierkegaard's ethics, illustrating it with an example of her own:

> Consider the test case in which we are faced with a demand from another that as far as we can conscientiously judge is contrary to the person's best interest—for example, an addict's pressing demands for more heroin. Does unconditional love for others mean fulfilling all their desires or needs? Kierkegaard has no trouble in his ethic concluding that he should not fulfill the addict's demand.[49]

It would be hard to come up with a more simplistic and less illuminating example than this one, which not only Kierkegaard but most readers will agree on without much reflection. Close relationships are fraught with far more complicated conflicts of this kind. If a woman asks her husband to drive her to the Pentecostal Church in which she has become deeply involved, can and should he refuse because he thinks she is losing her autonomy and being brainwashed by a sect? Or does she have a right to pursue any projects she wishes, a right that trumps everyone else's concerns about her, and in which pursuit her husband could reasonably be expected to provide at least minimal assistance?

Even if we accept paternalism, we won't be in a position to settle such dilemmas—not even Ferreira's case—until we have an idea of the good. What is the ultimate value we should seek for our neighbors and ourselves? We touched upon Kierkegaard's answer earlier, through Løgstrup's remark about the danger that threatens the neighbor if she becomes aware of another's loving deed toward her. Her gratitude must always be directed to God, not to other persons. In fact, it is the relationship she has with God through her gratitude to him that Kierkegaard considers the highest good. The good we should pursue on our neighbor's behalf is not physical well-being, happiness, autonomy, or communion with others. To love the neighbor is to assist her in loving God, or to push her toward such love for the first time.[50] The Good Samaritan's deeds can only count as loving insofar as they promote the wounded man's self-denying gratitude toward God; if relieving his pain and prolonging his life is laudable, it is because it enables him to go on loving God. That love, the wounded man should in turn express through self-denying love of neighbor, which means pushing *his* neighbor to a love of God. Ferreira had protested that the Good Samaritan "is not praised for having given spiritual instruction to the wounded man, for reminding him how much he was loved by God, or for providing him with spiritual reading for his stay in the ditch."[51] But nor did Kierkegaard—or Jesus—praise his deeds for relieving pain and distress. Only now do we know under what description the Samaritan's actions are laudable, by Kierkegaard's lights. In no way, then, does his reference to the Good Samaritan license Ferreira's commonsense interpretation. By invoking such an immediately compelling example, Kierkegaard seduces the reader into accepting the view of neighborly love he is about to articulate. But on that view, love is, ironically, something far more abstract, spiritual, and unattractive than it was on the down-to-earth view that made the example compelling in the first place.

Ferreira's replies all share in a common spirit. From her appeal to the Samaritan with his practical assistance, through the banal drug-addict example that makes paternalism so easy to swallow, to the assumption that Kierkegaard basically conforms to Protestant orthodoxy, she tones down all of what is radical in *Works of Love* and serves its account of neighborly love up to the reader as an immediately appealing, intuitively plausible ethics that really just reiterates what our nannies taught us. Anxious to make Kierkegaard palatable and fend off all criticism, she tames Kierkegaard the way Xenophon, according to *Irony*, tamed Socrates. In Xenophon's view, the Athenians were not operating with flawed moral principles when they charged and sentenced the subversive philosopher—they were mistaken about his being subversive. According to Kierkegaard, Xenophon defends Socrates

> in such a way that Socrates is made not just innocent, but altogether harmless, making us deeply perplexed as to what demon must have possessed the Athenians to make them see more in him than in any other good-natured, chatty and quirky dude.[52]

As Xenophon brings everything back to the empirical, cashing out "the good" as "the useful," so too Ferreira wants to redeem the ethics of self-denial—which demands sacrificing all earthly happiness and love, promises hatred as its reward, and regards close bonds between humans as threats to their faith—for a few conventional rules of thumb, illustrated by compelling examples. Her Kierkegaard is a peddler in platitudes: "Love of truth and of humanity," she says, "require us to go deeper than the sound bites and photo opportunities that Kierkegaard insightfully anticipates as our modern mode of communication and relation."[53] When she sums him up by saying that we must "refus[e] to call good what is evil, and refus[e] to go by the majority opinion just because it is the majority one,"⁵⁴ one wonders why Kierkegaard should even be worth reading.

Love as Practicing Dying

Kierkegaard appears to regard his articulation of love's aim as final, but it actually raises further questions: Why should we love God? Wherein does the goodness of this love lie? These are slightly different questions, but the answers ultimately converge. We should love God because God loves us, and indeed "loved us first."⁵⁵ He expressed this love by creating us and sending us his son to redeem our sins. Thus we owe him gratitude.

On this answer, too, we must put pressure: wherein lies the goodness of our earthly existence—what is it we have to be grateful for? Kierkegaard's answer cannot be that we will achieve great happiness in this life, since he has made clear true happiness is rarely achieved in this vale of tears populated by sinners. Perhaps then, the goodness of being alive resides in the fact that it allows us to bear witness to God's love for us. But this begs the question, since witnessing God's love is presumably good only if that love is good, yet the goodness of God's love is precisely what is in question. We could seize upon a remark in the book's conclusion, that loving people is the only thing worth living for.⁵⁶ This claim is deceptively attractive in seeming to locate the goodness of life in communion with other people. But we know that for Kierkegaard, loving others does not mean having relationships with them that bring us joy or comfort or meaning. Loving people can at best make life worth living because in loving the neighbor, we imitate God's love for us, and feel ourselves truly to be creatures made in his image. It is the closest we get in earthly life to partaking in God's glory. But this is again question-begging, for until we know what is good about love, we cannot understand the goodness of God, nor therefore why it is good to be like him. Kierkegaard's answers takes us around in a circle: the goodness of God is supposed to be manifested in his loving us, but the goodness of that love, in turn, lies in God's goodness.

To be sure, this circularity does not lie on the ontological level: it is not the case that the items in the circle rely on each other for their existence, so that it is impossible for either of them to have come into being. The circularity I am concerned with is the conceptual or explanatory one. God, love, and human existence are all supposed to be good—the account invests goodness with all the explanatory power. Yet the goodness of each is explained in terms of the goodness of another, and remains formal. We need an idea of at least one of these things—God, love, or human existence—with a content that is not derived from the others. Otherwise, all those answers given earlier are empty—as empty, indeed, as Socrates' thesis about the unity of virtue. The goodness that circulates through these ideas is just as "egoistically concluded in itself" as Socrates' idea of virtue was said to be in *Irony*. In Kierkegaard's treatment, too, goodness passes through its different manifestations (God, love, human life) "as a slow whisper, a shiver, without becoming audible—let alone articulated—in any of them."[57] Kierkegaard has given us nothing but the thinnest possible concept of the good. This—that goodness is to be grasped through one concept rather than its manifold spatiotemporal instantiations—can count as a meaningful conclusion in a negative argument against naïve empiricism, yes. But in an overall account of the good, it can only be an intermediate conclusion. Having decided that there is one concept of the good, the ethicist must now proceed to give it a determinate content, proposing an answer to the question of what the essence of all good things is, what feature it is in virtue of which they are rightly deemed "good." I said in Chapter 1 that what remained of Socrates' thesis about virtue's unity is the mere *form* of that concept: its normative and teleological form, the idea that there is something to which we must aspire. If the ethical theory of *Works of Love* cannot make apparent the goodness of love, all that will remain of the commandment, "Thou shalt love thy neighbor as thyself," is "Thou shalt." As Løgstrup also notes, it will be an ethics reduced to the bare bones of obedience.[58]

Stephen Evans tries to give substance to *Works of Love* by fleshing out the goodness of human existence. Kierkegaard's is "a humanistic ethic," he says, one "directed to human flourishing."[59] In Evans's very systematic reconstruction, *Works of Love* "unites an ethic of self-actualization and a divine command theory of moral obligation."[60] As God's creations, human beings possess a nature with an inherent telos. We realize this telos by following God's commands, and in so doing we become who we truly are, that is, who we were meant by God to be. That telos, more specifically, is love. Thus we become ourselves and achieve the purpose of our earthly existence by loving. This flourishing, Evans wants to claim, also leads to happiness:

> God's own reality as Creator and providential sustainer of the universe guarantees that the one who wills the Good in this way will be happy eternally. Even in time such a person can have a kind of happiness, in spite of the "temporary" ingratitude, lack of appreciation, poverty, contempt, suffering, and even premature death that this life typically offers the person truly committed to the Good. This is so because this person already possesses a relation to God, though this kind of happiness is not what is ordinarily thought of as happiness.[61]

As is evident in the last sentence, Evans is careful to distinguish between true and false happiness. The word *Lykke* occurs many times in *Works of Love*, almost exclusively in the context of the ephemeral and shallow happiness that accompanies non-Christian love. Kierkegaard here exploits the ambiguity of the Danish word, which means both "happiness" and "good fortune."[62] Earthly happiness is a matter of luck, whereas the Christian must seek an absolute good that does not depend on earthly contingencies, so that he can be sure to possess it forever.

I said that Evans "wants to claim" that loving makes us happy, because the character of true, eternal happiness remains obscure, on his account, and earthly happiness is only "a kind of" happiness. All Evans has told us about the latter is that it is *not* what we ordinarily take happiness to be; very much in Kierkegaard's spirit, he discourages us from trusting our intuitive idea of what happiness is. In fact, understanding "my own deepest happiness requires a transformation of the self," Evans writes; "it is only when I have learned to practice self-denial with respect to those goods that I currently naturally seek that I can be truly happy."[63] In sum, then: To flourish is to fulfill my God-given telos. This is done through a self-denial by which I cease to exist as I know myself and am reborn as a new person. This self-fulfillment through self-denial will give me a kind of happiness. But even this quasi-happiness is nothing like what I currently know happiness to be. Finally, God's love for me, and its goodness, consists in his creating me to this end. Again, this may be true, but as yet we don't know what it means. If Evans's account appears to inject content into the circle, it is thanks to good associations smuggled into it by the words "flourishing" and "happiness."

At any rate, the only real good that Kierkegaard and Evans promise us is the happiness of the eternal afterlife. Loving people and God may be the only thing worth living for, but that does not mean living itself is particularly good. Presumably, by what Kierkegaard calls "eternity's scale of measurement,"[64] everything in earthly life is infinitely insignificant. The best thing about life is that it will one day end, and give way to eternity. It is not far-fetched to conclude that what *Works of Love* ultimately wants to induce in us is a longing for death, and that to love one's neighbor is to begin to die, and push her, too, toward death. In a journal entry from around the time *The Concept of Irony* was completed, Kierkegaard makes the connection between love and death explicit. The congregation's relationship to Christ, he writes, is like that of a bride to a groom. To see the truth of the metaphor, "we must recall that all of life is a long engagement, the grave is the bridal chamber" where the love is consummated.[65] Or isn't that, he continues, "how we imagine that blessed moment when the believer, after all the delusions, all the misunderstandings, after having overcome adversity and temptation, finally sinks into his Savior's arms."[66] In the same spirit, he writes in *Works of Love* that all humans "are of one soil"; they share in "a kinship of death."[67] With such remarks, he could be addressing the Symparanekromenoi, who hold a vigil on summer solstice in anticipation of longer nights and, ultimately, the truly restful eternal night. The dreamy way Kierkegaard speaks of death is also a repetition of Socrates' sublimely unafraid speech in the *Phaedo*. Like the philosopher, the Christian lover longs to be taken out of the only world he knows, and brought to an afterlife of which he knows nothing. Kierkegaard promises us that the beyond is blissful, just as Socrates proclaims to his disciples that Hades is the philosopher's true home. But again like Socrates, Kierkegaard characterizes the afterlife only in terms of its differences from earthly life: as the negation of all that is familiar to us, including those things we regard as good. To direct all one's yearning toward a completely unknown object, to exercise constant self-denial and forgo all pleasures for the sake of that obscure end, isn't that quite ironic?

Positive Moments

In the chapter III.A *Kjerlighed er Lovens Fylde*, Kierkegaard seems to admit to the abstractness, the negativity, of his exposition on neighborly love. Hong's translation, "Love is the Fulfilling of the Law," may adhere to the standard translation of the phrase from Romans 13, but it makes for an underwhelming title in the context of Kierkegaard's book. If the law commands us to love, then obviously to love is to fulfill the law. Kierkegaard's Danish title, however, doesn't refer to a kind of action—fulfilling the law, as in obeying it. It binds together three nouns: "Love is the Law's Fullness." And indeed the chapter goes on to speak not just about interrelated actions, but about kinds of thing that complete each other, as aspects of one entity. The law, we are told, "resembles death."[68] It is "the opposite of life, and life is the fullness."[69] Life and death are complementary: death gives life its shape, delimits it; but it also depends on life, since nothing can die without first living. So too love and the law correspond to each other as positive to negative. The law "demands," "takes," and "hungers," Kierkegaard says.[70] For "despite its many determinations, the law remains something indeterminate, and love is the fullness" which the law itself cannot be; love is "completely determinate."[71] The commandment relates to love as a question to an answer, or as a concept to the phenomenon which it defines and which in turn gives it actuality. Moreover the commandment would seem to have a force of attraction, like vacuum, for just as a question automatically starts the mind working, moves us to find the answer, so too the commandment draws up love in us.

The analogy with question and answer is soon made explicit, and is accompanied by a mention of Socrates. That "sage of Antiquity" understood well the art of asking, Kierkegaard writes; he knew how to "trap the respondent in his ignorance."[72] But Christianity knows how to answer, and by this answer to bind the questioner to a task. "When someone asks 'what is love,' then Paul answers 'it is the law's fullness,' and this answer instantly bars any further question."[73] The response doesn't provide the intellectual fullness the question had sought; it looks at first like an evasion. Yet that is because Paul would be impatient with such a question, as though the inquiry were just a way of putting off the task of fulfilling the commandment. As Kierkegaard later remarks: "How many people haven't asked 'what is truth' and deep down hoped that it would be a long while before the truth came within his reach," hoped to stave off action with skepticism.[74] The response "love is the law's fullness" hands the theoretical negative in the question back to the questioner in the form of a practical negative: the task that he must fulfill. The implications, it seems, is that we all know how to love the neighbor, making conceptual explication redundant. Rather than try to define it, we must get on with the task of living love, actualizing it. The law has expressed its desire, and now its object must be supplied—posited—giving the law its desired fullness. Christ was the ultimate fullness, Kierkegaard writes; he was at once an explanation and the thing explained; the union of question and answer.[75] He was what the world needed, and by coming into the world, he showed the world what it was it needed.

To dismiss theory in favor of practice in this way—to identify *true* understanding with acting—calls into question Kierkegaard's own project in *Works of Love*, and this again he readily admits. In a way, he writes, "it does no good to speak to people about the highest, because what's needed is a revolution"—a tipping over, a turning around—"quite different from any that speech can prompt."[76] On one interpretation, this means that *Works of Love*'s explication of the commandment is negative, as empty as the law itself. But one may also, like Ferreira, take this discussion of the law and its fullness as a self-reflexive remark on the book's own structure—to wit, that in parallel with the formal line of argument (focused on the universal law), there is another, "material" strand running through the book, homing in on love in its concreteness.[77] Thus in the deliberation "Our Duty to Love the People We See," Kierkegaard explains what is involved in loving the particular persons we actually encounter in life, and the positive view he develops there is according to Ferreira an ethic of vision.[78] When loving the people we see is a duty, Kierkegaard writes, "*then the task is not to find the lovable object; but the task is: to find the already given or chosen object lovable, and being able to persist in finding him lovable, no matter how he changes.*"[79] Loving the one you see first requires *seeing* the one you see, presumably in that higher, metaphysical sense in which—as I argued in the previous chapter—the father confessor sees the penitent.

The idea that loving a particular person involves seeing her as she is is compelling enough, and would seem to take care of Adorno's objection that Kierkegaard's Christian lover is indifferent to the neighbor and blind to her particularities. But what prevents this ethic of vision from being positive rather than negative—material rather than formal, in Ferreira's preferred terminology—is the imperative mode in which seeing is couched. Kierkegaard does not so much describe what it is like to love a particular person as reformulate the law. "Thou shalt love" becomes "thou shalt see." Yet seeing is not an action but something that happens to one who looks; it is the success of looking. It depends on factors beyond the subject's control, such as his receptive capacity and, of course, the object seen. Looking can always be accomplished, but if seeing is a task, it is a potentially infinite one. No matter what effort we expend, we might fail. Nor can we ever be sure of having succeeded. Finding a lovable feature in the neighbor is not sufficient, because that "feature" might just be a mask. Perhaps it is a matter of seeing his pure humanity, then—abstracting all his contingent qualities from his essence. But in that case, Adorno would be vindicated: the lover is indifferent to the neighbor's individuality, and Ferreira's ethic of vision does not make Kierkegaard's account of neighborly love any more concrete.

I will have occasion to comment further on Ferreira's suggestion in a minute, but first let us look at some other fragments of concreteness in *Works of Love*. In these "positive moments" as I want to call them, love becomes intuitable through examples or some appeal to the reader's own experience. They offer an intellectual fullness, then, but they might also affect us in such a way as to prompt action, belying the claim that it does no good to talk about love. This is a possibility Kierkegaard suggests in a different deliberation, "Love Builds up." Consider what it takes to build a house, he says: we must first have a foundation, and the taller the house we want to build, the deeper in the ground must we lay its foundation.[80] Love's foundation lies deep in the person, and when he witnesses love, his own capacity for loving awakens and builds up:

> When we thus see a lone human, by praiseworthy modesty frugally get by with little, then we honor and praise him, we are joyed, we are assured by the good at this sight, but we don't really say that it's an upbuilding sight. But when we see how a housewife, who has many to care for, through modesty and a certain frugality lovingly knows how to bless the little things, ensuring there is enough for everyone, then we say that this is an upbuilding sight. The upbuilding lies in the fact that, as we see the modesty and frugality, which we honor, we also see the housewife's loving care.[81]

The sight of the mother is upbuilding to those who witness it, and that should include us, who read about it. It draws up our own resources of love, building love up from a foundation already present in us.

Thus the pedagogical function of *Works of Love*'s concrete examples should be practical rather than theoretical. In fact, what Kierkegaard claims is that witnessing love affects us the same way as being loved. For kindness can breed kindness; a calm, magnanimous response to aggression and pettiness can be disarming. Though

Kierkegaard doesn't refer to "turning the other cheek," his characterization of the upbuilding power of loving deeds evokes precisely that idea. By appealing to the other as a kind and generous person, no matter that he just acted disrespectfully, it is possible to make him precisely that—to bring out the better in him. The lover, Kierkegaard writes, "presupposes that there is love in the other person's heart, and precisely by this presupposition he builds up love in him—from the foundation and up, since he lovingly presupposes it as a foundation."[82]

But why is it only love that builds up, according to Kierkegaard—why should not the sight of frugality and perseverance be upbuilding too? We will understand this once we see that the mother's deed is positive in a way that the poor man's isn't. The "lone human" is confronted with scarcity and accommodates this by frugality. The world gives him little, and he survives without any supplements. The mother, on the other hand, sees the world's provisions in their abundance rather than their lack, sees the good in them and, in making a home for her family, brings this goodness out. The way she serves the food makes it feel like a treat; the way she mends hand-me-downs makes them pretty. Thus she manages to not only sustain her children's lives but to make those lives joyful. Her love is positive in that it adds something to life. Recall Kierkegaard's remark in *Irony* that when we say that God is love, we mean that he communicates himself to us, as in sharing himself with us. So does this woman, with her family.

The Good Samaritan, as Kierkegaard at one point reimagines him, is not as successful. He does not even manage to save the wounded man's life. That story shows love as a positive force in a different way. Kierkegaard asks the reader to imagine the figure in Jesus' parable as a man without means. If this poor Samaritan, he writes,

> came not riding but walking on the road from Jericho to Jerusalem, where he saw the unfortunate man lying; if he had nothing on him with which to bind the man's wounds; if he lifted him onto his shoulders and carried him to the nearest inn, whose host would have neither him nor the unfortunate one, as the Samaritan had not a single penny, and begged and pleaded with the coldhearted man to be merciful, since a man's life was at stake [. . .]. If rather than lose patience at this point, he carried the unfortunate one away, found a soft place to lay him down, sat by his side, did all he could to stop the blood flow, and yet the unfortunate one died in his arms—hadn't he nonetheless been as merciful, at least as merciful, as that [original] Good Samaritan?[83]

This poor Samaritan adds something to the world in that he acts; he has the power of initiative. What I want to call attention to, though, is how neighborly love seems to be part of his constitution. He is motivated by fellow feeling, and Kierkegaard contrasts him with the innkeeper in terms of character. As Kierkegaard narrates the story, the Samaritan acts out of a compassionate inclination, based on a loving disposition. The sight of the wounded man immediately calls up the Samaritan's love; his response is not mediated by a commandment.

The idea conjured up in these examples is of love as a virtue—not duty. Crucially, the mother and the reimagined Samaritan appear in Kierkegaard's narration in unison with their deeds. The poor Samaritan's outside reveals his inside: we *see* him through his actions. This would not be the case if Kierkegaard had presented him as acting out of duty: we would see only his obedience, and this obedience with its suppression of inclination would hide his dispositions. But the Samaritan's deeds are fruits by which we know the tree. If these ideas of love as virtue are aesthetic, it is also because they offer the kind of intelligibility Kierkegaard attributes to myths. The virtuous disposition *explains* the action. The action, in turn, reveals the meaning of the disposition. Hence the virtue ethicist's aesthetic pedagogy: rather than formulate principles for action, the teacher points to the virtuous man as a model, trusting the student to grasp his virtue by intuition, obviating the need for rules and definitions. In "Love Builds up," Kierkegaard outlines a version of this pedagogy. The sight of a virtuous person performing a loving deed will automatically draw up the beholder's own virtue, building up a love whose foundation is present in her already, since it is part of her nature.

It is tempting to seize upon these aesthetic ideas of love as rafts in a vast sea of abstraction. But if they appear to be counter-examples to the criticisms that neighborly love is something wholly inward for Kierkegaard, something that does not manifest itself in concrete acts, is unconcerned with the neighbor's physical needs and even indifferent to the neighbor as a particular person, that does not yet refute Adorno's and Løgstrup's critical interpretations. The poor mother draws on her inner resources in caring for her family; if there is self-denial in her love, it is hardly its dominant feature. The poor Samaritan helps another out of compassion, which would preclude his actions from counting as loving deeds according to Kierkegaard's negative criteria. However compelling these examples are, they do not exemplify love as Kierkegaard defines it.

We cannot dismiss these positive moments as spurious, but nor do they cancel the general claims Kierkegaard makes—and endlessly repeats—about love. They are to the negativity of Kierkegaard's concept of love what Plato's myths are to Socrates' purely formal arguments: a break during which the weary intellect lies down to rest, and in the world of dreams finds the object it has so far sought in vain. Kierkegaard's general treatment of love has consisted in an ironic reflection that peels off feeling, inclination, and compassion from love's motivation, on the one hand, and reciprocation, gratitude, and well-being from its result, on the other. He has severed love from its outward fruits altogether, leaving us to identify the loving deed as a purely inward one, thus also making the beloved redundant. Through this negative characterization, our minds were strained to their utmost trying to conceive what this love might be, given that it is not all those other things. The vanishingly thin space left open by these negative criteria was the spirit's negative exercise upon itself. We tried then to inquire what good self-denial's love achieves, and were given answers that begged further questions until we were back at the beginning. Now, suddenly, love is made intuitable through images that compel us not just because they are beautiful but because they feel real, resonating with our own experience. We are familiar with characters like those in Kierkegaard's pictures, quickly sketched though they are. But they are as different from his negative definition as Diotima's idea of Eros as a poor but resourceful person is from Socrates' concept of love as lack. Kierkegaard insisted that the contradiction between Plato's and Socrates' views is never finally *aufgehoben*— it cannot be canceled through some third view that synthesizes the two—and nor can we hope to reconcile the positive and negative in his own account of neighborly love.

A Rhetoric of Breaking Down

We do get a clue as to how Kierkegaard thinks the two are related when, at the end of the book, he discusses a line from John's letters: "My beloved ones, let us love one another."[84] In those words, written by one "whom love has made complete," Kierkegaard observes,

> you do not hear the rigidity of duty, the apostle does not say "you shall love one another," but nor do you hear the vehemence of poetic passion, of

inclination. There is something conclusive and blissful in these words, but also a sadness moved by life and softened by eternity. It is as if the apostle said, "Good Lord, what are all those things that have prevented you from loving, what is that grand gain you can make through self-love! The commandment is that you shall love—oh, but once you understand yourself and life, it will be as if that need not be commanded, because loving people is the only thing worth living for, and without this love you are not really living, and loving people is the only blissful comfort, whether here or beyond, and your love for people is the only true sign that you are a Christian."[85]

John's plea strikes a tone and a mood intermediate between the commandment and the poet's passion, Kierkegaard says.[86] The poet's appeal is insufficient, since the feelings he stirs up in us are fleeting. The commandment, compelling us from the outside, becomes redundant once we hear God's own voice from within and recognize that to love is to become ourselves. Yet John's words "are not the beginning of the discourse but the completion," Kierkegaard writes. Even at the end of these Christian deliberations, "[w]e do not venture to speak thus," as "love's apostle" spoke.[87] Instead Kierkegaard has spoken to us in the harsh voice of a disciplinarian. Only in those few positive moments has he allowed himself to address us as John does, with the faith that love will build up.

These remarks about John confirm our conclusion about the mother and the Samaritan: that the true nature of the good, that is, love, can be expressed only in terms of virtue, not duty. But sinners that we are, goodness is something we must continuously pursue, and be directed toward by the law. At any rate, *Works of Love* is written for those who do not possess or even understand the good. In a journal entry, Kierkegaard explains why the book consists of "deliberations" rather than "upbuilding discourses." An upbuilding discourse about love would assume that the reader knows what love is, and move him to put this knowledge to practice. "But that's certainly not the case [with those for whom *Works of Love* is written]. Therefore the deliberation first needs to bring them up from the cellar, call on them, turn them around, and turn their thinking upside down with the dialectic of truth."[88] The imagery here explains the significance of the term *Overveielse*. Like "to deliberate," *at overveie* literally means "to weigh (something) over" as in weighing the pros and cons of a certain course of action. When one reason or feeling or impression dominates, tipping the scale one way, it is said to be *overveiende*, to outweigh the other. But

Kierkegaard uses the term ironically, with a secret meaning in mind. It is not the scales of argument but the reader himself that he wants to tip over.

The rhetorical strategy of the book is then not to build the reader up but to shake her up and even break her down. Kierkegaard employs a number of rather aggressive tactics to this end. There is, first of all, the constant attack on the "ordinary" and "poetic" views of love. Of course, calling into question the common way of thinking is one of the main motivations of philosophical writing. But *Works of Love* underscores its rejection of common sense with ironic mockery of "people in general." In this passage, Kierkegaard speaks of the deterioration of the word "love" in common parlance:

> What the world ordinarily calls being "lovely" [*elskværdig*, lit. "loveworthy"], eternity will of course regard as something blameworthy and punishable. A so-called lovely man is a man who above all takes care not to take to heart eternity's or God's call to an essential and essentially strenuous existence. The lovely man knows all the excuses and distractions and ploys, all about negotiating and haggling and detracting.[89]

This man is ingratiating; his friendliness is manipulative. But attending only to his surface, people call him "lovely." This passage is a typical example of the caricature by which Kierkegaard presents love as ordinarily conceived as something base, utilitarian, and selfish.

The love the poets have in mind is banal, too, but they reach for the most dramatic superlatives in portraying it. The love whose praises the poets sing, Kierkegaard writes,

> is disguised self-love, and that explains the intoxicated saying: to love another person more than oneself. Romantic love is not yet the eternal, it is infinity's pleasant dizziness, its highest expression is the foolishness of enigmas; hence its attempt at an even more dizzying saying, "to love a person more than God." And this stupidity pleases the poet beyond measure, it has esprit to his ear, it inspires him to song.[90]

The truth about the infatuation poets euphemize as "love" makes their lofty pathos ridiculous. Kierkegaard doesn't mention any particular writers: the target here is poetry as such, which is essentially unsuited to speaking about love. Its very form, with its commitment to beauty over truth, is fraudulent. This is a claim more than an argument, but the mockery is so effective rhetorically that Kierkegaard can afford to dispense with substantiating it. The attack on art also has a populist slant. It is no "art" to praise love, Kierkegaard writes later—and the scare-quotes are his—but a deed, "because 'art' is related to the contingency of talent, deed is related to the universally human."[91] Love does not, like art, begrudge simple people a share in its glory.[92]

A reader who goes along with these derisive views of the common and the poetic will now find herself ill-equipped to counter Kierkegaard's further claims in any way. For most ideas about love that will occur to her can be scorned as all too mundane—and if not, then ridiculed as yet more poetic clichés. The dismissal of feelings and inclinations as a basis for love adds to this. If these are unreliable as sources of love, then we cannot use introspection and imagination in thinking about the nature of love. Intuition, inclination's epistemic cousin, is banned from the inquiry. With common sense, intuition, and any secular literature of love delegitimized, the obedient reader will not be able to trust her judgment as the concept of love Kierkegaard proceeds to construct runs afoul of what she has so far considered love to be. The effect is really that of a conspiracy theory: everything you have been made to believe is wrong, and if you should suspect my motives or intelligence, that is just what "they" want you to do. This conspiracy theory is made quite explicit when Kierkegaard identifies contemporary society's disdain for true Christian love as part of the same persecution Jesus suffered. Recall the claim that anyone who truly practices love of neighbor will be rewarded by the world's hatred, just as Christ was condemned and executed for his unrelenting love.[93] The premise that if you are hated, you must be doing something right, is shaky to say the least, but like every conspiracy theory, this one capitalizes on our deep-seeded anxiety about being duped. And why fuss about the dubious soundness of some modus ponens when simply accepting it will grant entry to the camp of rebels and martyrs?

The contempt with which the author expresses his criticism also serves to inhibit any questioning from the reader. It hangs over her as a constant threat: she is either with Kierkegaard or against him, and if the latter, then all that mockery and scorn is directed at her, too. As Adorno remarked, the book does not "tolerate any protest";[94] it is indignant about the very idea that anyone should dare question it. His claim to authority is despotic and, in the religious context, borders on blasphemy. Quite unlike Nietzsche's unapologetic, take-it-or-leave-it ire and offense, Kierkegaard's derision seems calculated to intimidate the reader. As such, it also prepares her to embrace him all the more gratefully when he then relents for a moment, claiming, for example, that he himself has yet to learn to love the neighbor.[95]

Then there are Kierkegaard's many apparent self-contradictions, some of them blatant. No sooner has the reader gotten a grasp on his idea of love than she is stumped as he back-tracks. Consider his sudden celebration of our need for love and companionship, in "Our Duty to Love the People We See":

> How *deeply* grounded it is in our Being, that human craving for love! The first remark, if we daresay, that was made about human nature—about the first human beings, and by the only one who could truly make it, God—expresses precisely this. Thus we read in holy Scripture: "God said, it is not good that the man should be alone." [. . .] Those who think more deeply about human nature have always recognized in it this longing for companionship.[96]

The reader must not have understood exactly what Kierkegaard meant when he railed against sensuousness and equated the desire for reciprocation in love with selfishness. She had better defer to Kierkegaard as an authority, since she is apparently not intelligent enough to grasp his subtle distinctions. There is a similar contradiction between Kierkegaard's idea that "love believes all things," which in his use seems equivalent to "love believes the best about all things," and his condemnation of looking away from the beloved's flaws and loving a glorified image of him. A different kind of contradiction—not logical but psychological—occurs when Kierkegaard admonishes those who would congratulate themselves for loving the neighbor with proper self-denial. In effect, he is chastising any reader who has been swept along with his own pathos of martyrdom.

These apparent contradictions may of course be riddles with solutions, as I noted in the introduction. The point here is to note that their immediate effect is to throw the reader off and deflate her self-confidence. A Kierkegaardian "deliberation" works not just to tear down some unfounded philosophical or theological edifice, but prepares the reader for accommodating its message by first breaking her down. Also in his subversive rhetoric, then, we see Kierkegaard regarding and treating the reader the way he took Socrates to relate to his interlocutors. The student must be shaken up and deprived of her hold on the world in order then to begin constructing her worldview afresh, without the previous delusions.

Yet there are some important differences between the situation of Kierkegaard's teaching and that of his ancient precursor. One of the things Kierkegaard admired so in Socrates was how he spoke with individuals face to face, meeting them at the intellectual place where he found them, and worked *with* them to disentangle their thoughts. Kierkegaard often spoke disdainfully of those who lecture an audience from behind a pulpit, rather than *converse* with one particular interlocutor:

> Today while Spang stepped onto the pulpit with all his aplomb and unction etc., and gesticulated all over the place, a maidservant sat just beneath the pulpit. She had sung the hymn quite calmly, but as soon as the sermon began, she began to cry. Now it's difficult to be brought to *tears* by Spang in general, but in the case of the beginning of this sermon in particular it was quite impossible, from which I infer that she had come to church *for the purpose* of crying. I was shaken: *on* the pulpit, all that pretention with mimicry and gestures; just *beneath* it, a maidservant who hears none of what he says or only occasionally picks up a word of it, and who regards God's house if not as a prayer-house, than as a weeping-house in which to weep herself clear of all the abuse she's suffered since she was last there. It should really be stipulated that every servant go out each Sunday and go to church every Sunday morning. Maidservants are the dearest kind of people to me, both in church and in Fredriksberg.[97]

Kierkegaard despises lecturing because it is one-way communication. But so is writing. If in his "engagement" with the congregation, Spang was no Socrates, Kierkegaard was even less so. A book may be part of a "national conversation" and respond to another book or to some prevalent view, but the author cannot control who will read it. He does not see the reader, let alone listen to what she has to say. He sends his products out with the wind to land where they will. When, in *The Point of View*, Kierkegaard discusses how the pseudonymous works are intended to lure the reader in by first pretending to share her aestheticism, he seems to trust that the character of a text itself will determine who reads it, as if by some fine-tuned force of attraction.[98] This is a nice idea, but quite implausible. *Works of Love* has no doubt been read by people other than the ones Kierkegaard intended. It should actually have been more attractive to the readers who needed it the least—insecure readers prone to excessive self-sacrifice, due to a weak sense of self-worth, or an overwhelming sense of guilt. What effect would the book's harsh preaching and castigation have on the crying maidservant? Granted, she was probably not an avid reader; but one can hope that if it were Kierkegaard preaching self-denial on that pulpit, she would have ignored him just as she ignored Spang.

One could conclude that Kierkegaard did not learn enough from Socrates, but that is not the point. Kierkegaard didn't learn anything from Socrates; he recollected through Socrates an intellectual mode that was already his own. As he noted himself in private, the reason Socrates had made such a deep impression on him was that "indirect communication was my nature."[99] Feeling this kinship, he naturally projected more of himself onto Socrates than was actually there, just as he thought Plato had.

"Forever Yours"

The journal entry outlining *Works of Love*'s intended effect on the reader tells us that Kierkegaard is not addressing his equals in that book. In that sense, the book is not earnest but calculating. That pretty line about how he is really trying to convince himself to love the neighbor—"O, dear listener, it is not *you*, whom I am addressing, it is me to whom eternity says: thou shalt"[100]—may be the most deceitful moment in the book. This is not to condemn the book but to state a fact that should inform our interpretation. Having already been reborn, grasped the significance of self-denial, perhaps even assimilated love as a virtue and thus transcended duty, Kierkegaard could allow himself to re-enter earthly life with its pleasures and desires. He had advanced in the dialectic, so that his enjoyment of art and his whole emotional life was not like the simple aesthete's. He was certain that his own friendships were not selfish, even though an outsider might have a hard time telling the difference between what *Works of Love* derided as poetic swooning and something like this epistolary declaration of love, which Kierkegaard made to a dear friend, and which is really an homage to friendship as such:

> You my friend, the only one whose intercession enabled me to endure the world, which seemed to me in so many ways unbearable; the only one who remained after I let doubt and distrust rummage like a raging storm and wash away and annihilate all else [. . .]
>
> You, my faithful brother, who hasn't shrunk from relieving me by occasionally bowing Your back, when mine was oppressed like Atlas by carrying that world which my own imagination let me believe I was able to carry [. . .]

Speak up, "that I might see You." ... These and similar texts of interjections, addresses of thanksgiving and inquiring petitions my head has conceived according to my heart's dictation and under the sail of my personality; but in vain have I awaited the promised postal delivery, that is, that continuity of mood, without which they could not reach Your hand and, by goodness, continue to Your heart. But in order that these letters to You as You are— which as Paul says, are written not with paper and ink but *inscribed in the heart*—might become something more or, if You will, as I would, something less; briefly: in order that the thought of You should not stagger unstably b/w an ecstatic *exacerberatio* [provocation] and the *emolities cerebri* [drowsiness] of a *Somnambüle* [sleepwalker], please receive these lines.

How different everything is from that time when I visited You so often, that time of great turnover, whose fruit was a *depositum* [deposit] in our *Fiskus* [treasury], an outstanding balance between us that we would still for some time recall with joy; a debt that separates only to the same degree that it unites [. . .]

17 July   Forever yours,
                                                                      S. K.[101]

In his letters from Berlin, three years later, Kierkegaard would tell Emil Bøsen he hoped their friendship would gain yet greater intimacy, intensity, and sympathy once they reunited upon his return to Copenhagen.[102] Repeatedly he proclaimed Emil to be his only confidante: "You are and remain the one person who has a seat and a vote in the council of my many and manifold thoughts."[103] Thus we need not look further than Kierkegaard's private writings to find a vivid representation of the invigorating power of preferential love. Among many other flourishes, he addressed Emil with the Greek *syzyge*—"my companion," "my yokemate"—Plato's word for the complementary relation between the two horses together pulling the carriage in the *Phaedrus*.[104] This notion is not identical to that of an "other self" from which Kierkegaard, with some purely linguistic acrobatics, jumps to the conclusion that friendship as ordinarily conceived and practiced is selfish. But it implies the related and more complex idea that a relationship between friends can be constitutive of each one's identity. Søren felt himself resonate in Emil; each young man achieved a self-realization in this communion that he could not achieve on his own. When like understands like, whether emotionally or intellectually, they are afforded a reprieve from the isolation that is otherwise a basic fact of our existence as individuals, as creatures with an outside that is not transparent to the inside.

It was likely on this friendship that Kierkegaard drew when he spoke of Plato's love for Socrates in his dissertation. Recall that lyrical description of their "love-secrets of knowledge"; how in the communication with a "likeminded," we find "a self-expression that is not constricted by the other's limitations but is expanded," since "thought understands itself and loves itself only when it is absorbed by the other's being"; how such friends or lovers become so dependent upon one another for their own reality and identity that it "becomes not only irrelevant but also impossible to determine what belongs to each, because each one always owns nothing but owns everything through the other." Socrates "flows through the whole fertile territory of the Platonic philosophy," Kierkegaard said; and Plato wanted to owe Socrates everything, wanted to remain in this debt.[105] When such friends promise to be "forever yours," this is not taking eternity's name in vain.

Afterword

Immediate Redemption

No other speaker than Socrates, says Alcibiades, ever

> upset me so deeply that my very own soul started protesting that my life—*my life!*—was no better than the most miserable slave's. And yet this is exactly how this Marsyas here at my side makes me feel all the time: he makes it seem that my life isn't worth living![1]

Alcibiades pursued social glory through a military career, and it is easy to see his despair as the necessary and deserved pain of a Philistine awakening to higher values. Too easy: because it is not only vices and illusions that appear as such by a probing Socratic inquiry. Any pursuit and attachment can be made to look irrational and even absurd if analyzed; perfectly good and innocent people are no more capable than tyrants of giving ultimate justifications for their values and actions. The Good Samaritan acted out of immediate fellow feeling, and if asked why he helped the man by the side of the road, he would say simply that he saw the man was wounded, and to him that would be as final and illuminating an answer as could possibly be given. But a philosopher would push on: what about wounded mice, does he help them, too? If not, if only human beings are worthy of help, what feature exactly makes them so special? It must be some feature shared universally by all human beings, meaning wounded people everywhere should be helped. But does the Samaritan help all the wounded people? Does he go out of his way to look for needy fellow humans? If not, Socrates might ask, doesn't that imply that what really makes a person worthy of help is the fact that the Samaritan encounters him? A remarkable power he has, the ironist would exclaim: that of conferring value on others by his sheer presence.

The Samaritan's very first answer, I said, would seem final to him, making further explanation redundant. He helped the man because he was wounded.

But the ensuing questions probe the presuppositions of that answer, and as the respondent articulates them, he may for the first time become fully aware of his ethical commitments. Philosophy prides itself on laying assumptions bare, and thereby arriving at persons' most fundamental beliefs and values. But interrogations like the one I have just sketched tend to overleap the point at which the respondent's values appear in their clearest form, the point that actually anchors their normative commitments. For the Good Samaritan, I think, the value on which everything turns is lodged in his idea of a human being. If that concept is analyzed further, for instance into "rational animal," the normativity will lose its foothold. To ordinary people, "human being" is a simple idea: it has no parts and cannot be clarified through any definition. It does not seem to require a definition to most of us: we know a human being when we see one, and we have an intuitive sense of what makes them special. The idea is also ethically primitive—"x is a human being" is a description on the precise level where the magic happens, that is, where the value and moral status of x becomes apparent. It is the point of ethical focus: if we zoom further in or out we will lose sight of it. In Alcibiades' case, we can suppose that "courage" and "heroism" are simple and ethically primitive ideas. Abstracting from them to find some common essence or defining them in other terms will not clarify them and therefore cannot help explain his commitment to them. If the philosopher actually wants to understand persons' values, he must try to grasp their primitive ideas, and grasp them in the simplicity in which it appears to them. He must stop reflecting and analyzing, and instead take up a task of an entirely different nature: the partly aesthetic task of conceiving an idea, intuiting the meaning a word has for his interlocutor.

In "The Present Age," Kierkegaard himself rails against excessive reflection. Our age has no passion, he complains, and neither religious nor political life puts any stock in eros, enthusiasm, and inwardness.[2] But the problem he sees with reflection isn't that it destroys meaning but that it staves off action, serves as an alibi for inertia and cowardice. Thus Kierkegaard's wager is not that action can recover immediacy. But we do find a suggestion along those lines in Judge Wilhelm's letters. Might not an Alcibiades brought to aporia by Socrates put an end to reflection by resolutely choosing himself and all his normatively charged intuitive ideas; choose himself as someone partaking in a culture, the heir to a particular tradition in which courage and heroism are virtues and obviously so, no further explication or justification required? Wilhelm's promise is that

Alcibiades would then achieve a properly ethical, responsible relation to his values, but without losing any of the aesthetic content. Anthony Rudd in fact thinks that Wilhelm's own ethics consists in a commitment to the virtues attached to social roles. "By accepting the role of husband or judge within a society," Rudd explains, "one accepts the standards of evaluation that go with those roles."[3] The significance the Judge ascribes to the wedding ceremony would also seem to speak in favor of interpreting him as a communitarian virtue ethicist. Prescribed by tradition, that ceremony "is not something the lovers themselves thought up in an opulent moment, something they could simply abandon later if they thought better of it."[4] And still, the meaning of marriage expressed by the ceremony and the wedding vows resonates with the lovers, as though this tradition allowed them to become themselves.

This communitarian strand, however, has a heavy counterpoint in Wilhelm's emphasis on choice. Choosing something given changes our relation to it, as the Judge himself points out. That relation is in fact changed as soon as we think of the given as something that *can* be chosen, affirmed, or denied; the moment we make it an object of reflection. The Judge vows that our whole immediate being can be chosen, but that is not so. What we can never choose is immediacy itself. Yet that state of being immersed in a worldview, so that it does not seem separate from us, is valuable by itself, quite aside from the value of the particular characteristics of that culture. Whereas in communitarianism, values are given to the individual by her culture, to the Judge ethical value first comes into being by the individual's act of choosing.[5]

The more purebred communitarian among Kierkegaard's fictional authors is "A." His essay on modern tragedy is *Zeitkritik*, as Henrich Fauteck notes, a critique of the present age.[6] Recall A's complaint that the predominant contemporary mindset misconstrues persons by not realizing that they have their truth only in their families and communities.[7] What makes the modern Antigone's pain so acute and lonely is that she reflects on her predicament and on what course of action she should take. The ancient Antigone, by contrast, had rested in immediacy. She knew what to do when her brother died because she had a clear idea of what it meant to be a sister, what it would be virtuous for a sister to do. Thus "A" is mourning the passing of the kind of world where values were not pursued through reflection but given, a world where negative freedom was highly restricted in order to give way to a positive freedom. Nothing now can revive that world, because there is no way back from reflection to immediacy. Someone awoken to individual freedom and responsibility cannot through an act of will immerse himself in a culture, adopting its worldview and mores unthinkingly. If "A" has lost his way in life, that is not due to some idiosyncratic character flaw of his. Over-reflection and ambivalence is the malaise of the age; and as Garff points out, A's despair is "the expression of a healthy reaction to 'the dissolution of the times.'"[8]

The anti-traditionalist, anti-cultural pull in Kierkegaard's philosophy is given succinct expression in the epilogue to *Fear and Trembling*. No matter what one generation can learn from another, writes de Silentio, "the essentially human no generation can learn from the previous one. In this regard every generation begins primitively, has the same task as every preceding generation."[9] In its dismissal of culture and tradition as sources of practical wisdom, the claim resounds both with the ethos Kierkegaard attributes to Socrates in *The Concept of Irony* and with his own criticism of institutionalized religion, voiced for example in *Works of Love*. But this point of view is distinctly modern; its individualism is a call to self-reflection, to ironic abstraction from conventions, received wisdoms, and the views of life embedded in cultural practices.

Johannes de Silentio's remark is thought-provoking, but in its stated, absolute form it is false. Every word in our language, every practice and every tradition down to the most ordinary ceremony of shaking hands and wishing health upon a person when we meet him reflect an interpretation of what it is to be a human being. To be born into a culture is to be heir to a world of meaning. What we figure out on our own about existence is vanishingly small by comparison. Even when we reject aspects of the culture passed down to us, we rely on that very culture as the background against which we define a new view of life. It is difficult even to imagine what it would be for one individual to build from scratch an edifice of meaning and value as vast and intricate as the one we are born into. That also means that A's characterization of modernity was exaggerated. There is still such a thing as culture; some values are still assimilated through immersion rather than arrived at through reflection. But the modern tendency is to question more and more of our cultural presuppositions, dismissing, for example, the cultural interpretation of sexual differences that is encoded in gender roles. Reflection is ever encroaching on immediacy, ever trading positive for negative freedom.

As Socratic irony is a war against immediacy, so too is Kierkegaardian faith. Both are ascetic, exercises in relinquishment of the world one is naturally inclined to regard as the real one. Along with *Works of Love*'s condemnation of aesthetic love, Kierkegaard disdained aesthetic religious expressions. God hates all ceremony, he wrote in his journal; he lets us speak to him directly, without frills.[10] Carl Hughes brings out this anti-aestheticism in his reading of the "Eucharistic Discourses," even as he sets out to show the opposite. These are texts meant to be read before the Friday morning communion in Vor Fru Kirke, the newly built church Kierkegaard attended all his life. Hughes contends that far from abandoning aesthetics, Kierkegaard repeatedly refers to the design and ornamentation of the church, whose architecture and statues of Christ and the apostles had received much attention.[11] Thus "the religiousness expressed in these texts," Hughes writes, "is neither anti-ecclesial nor wholly inward. Indeed, these sermons call attention to the aesthetics of their surroundings again and again."[12]

But those references are made as part of the Socratic-Kierkegaardian trick of meeting the interlocutor or reader where he is, and slowly pulling him away by negating the beliefs and values in which he is nested. Suspecting as he does that some in the congregation take an aesthetic interest in the church, Kierkegaard shepherds them through and out of this appreciation. In his journal he had berated those who came to Vor Fru Kirke to admire the art work:

> Do you really believe that the benediction that the pastor pronounces from the holy altar works just as powerfully on those who inquisitively walk around admiring the works of man as it does on those who are gathered here in stillness to devote their attention to God?[13]

Any worshipper might become irritated at those who visit the church as though it were a museum. But to Kierkegaard's mind, church tourism was just the most overt expression of aesthetic heresy. Faith should be disentangled not only from aesthetic pleasure but also from matter, sensuousness, culture, and convention. Thus in one "Discourse" he commends the congregants for coming to take communion on a Friday rather than Sunday. Without being commanded by God or unthinkingly following tradition, they came to church out of a personal urge.[14] In another, he begins by describing the atmosphere created in the church by the statues and ornaments:

> How still everything is in God's house, how safe. To him who enters, it seems as though by a single step he had come to a remote place, infinitely removed

> from all the noise and cries and loud-talking, from the terrors of existence, from the storm of life [. . .]. And wherever you turn your gaze in there, everything makes you safe and calm. The glorious building's high walls, standing so firm, guard this safe haven so reliably [. . .]. Look how the man who hewed these images in stone took his time [. . .], as an artist he needed the deep calm that peace offers, and therefore that which he brought forth evokes this same calm.[15]

But no sooner has he called our attention to the mood and the careful craft of artists than he turns against it in an ironic jolt. "How calming, how soothing—oh and what danger lies in this safety?"[16] We ought to go to church in order to be awoken to reality in all its horror, and yet we find that some churches are full of things that would soothe us and put us to rest.[17] The works of man in God's house are deceitful and do the congregants a disservice; the very fact that the artists demanded peace and quiet to do their precious work already makes their products false, Kierkegaard implies. Thus he mentions the aesthetics only to condemn them, and insists that we not look at the statues and golden embroidery on the pulpit, that we turn away from the space that surrounds us. Kierkegaard thus ushers the congregants inward by denying significance to external, material, and cultural expressions of religion. This process of abstraction culminates in his instruction to his listeners to disregard the outward act of taking communion in order to connect with Christ inwardly. At the altar, he says, "what matters is hearing *His* voice"; if you do not hear his voice, "then you went to the altar in vain."[18]

Hughes applauds this, reiterating the larger Protestant metaphysics of which the denial of transubstantiation is part: "Nothing objective, visible, or graspable—from statues to preaching to bread and wine—can render the living Christ present. Communion with him is a personal relationship that eludes all objectivity."[19] But it's one thing to hold this view as a piece of theology, and quite another to proclaim it in church, as part of preparing the congregants for communion. In that setting, the statements will reflect the listeners out of their immediate experience and prompt them to think of the ritual as something separate from the *actual* communion with God and thus also as redundant. For even though Kierkegaard seems to grant that the two are supposed to coincide, to call attention to the distinction between the physical act and the spiritual communion is to force a wedge into what used to be one whole experience. Hughes suggests that Kierkegaard's "Eucharistic Discourses" make of the church a theater in which a desire for God is "staged."[20] Yet this assigns an importance to religious "theatricals" that Kierkegaard—and Hughes too—ultimately denies. The texts' "staging of desire" is really a process of abstraction from all the "playacting" and "props" that surrounds the worshippers. Insofar as Kierkegaard's speeches arouse a desire for God, it is in the same way Socrates arouses a desire for knowledge: by robbing us of the connection we previously thought we had with God, thus forcing us to embark on our search for that connection anew.

It is as anthropologists, from a sober outsider's point of view, that we may speak of religious aesthetics as "props." When myrrh is burned and spreads into the church during communion, the priests appeal to our sense of smell to convey the significance of the sacrament. Together with candle-light, the fragrance creates a particular atmosphere and induces a solemn and reverent mood in the congregation. At the most basic level, this change in the quality of the air conveys that something extraordinary is happening. The tone of the chanting adds its bit to the meaning of the words, inducing in the worshippers a trance-like state.

Much fuss has been made over the question of whether the priest's words really make Christ present in the wafers and wine—Catholics affirm and Protestants deny it. But what matters for the ritual is not whether those who receive the sacrament consciously believe they are imbibing their Savior. The practice is properly aesthetic insofar as the congregants are not made to reflect upon the doctrinal question. The integrity of their experience should not to be disturbed by reflection on how the physical act relates to the spiritual communion, or the mechanics of transubstantiation. When the priest pronounces upon the wafer and wine, "body and blood of Christ," the recipient should not be prompted to ask if he means that literally or metaphorically. She should take its meaning in *immediately*, without making such distinctions. She is engaged in practice, not theory, and the question whether the wafer and wine *are* or only *symbolize* the body and blood of Christ, need not arise. The ritual is *meaningful*, and we lose this meaning if we reflect on it and try to detach the aesthetic from the religious. This meaning is simple and religiously primitive in a way that is analogous to the simplicity and ethical primitiveness of the idea "human being."

The "works of man" that want to mediate our connection with God aroused Kierkegaard's suspicion of deceit just as art and culture often did, more generally. But he was ready to abandon himself to religious feeling when it was prompted by nature. In the midst of a string of bitter journal entries from the mid-1840s preoccupied with the human folly that jumped out at him wherever he turned, he remarks that every natural phenomenon has a calming effect—the more so,

> the more and the longer one looks upon or listens to it. Every work of artistry eggs our restlessness on. The rule for fireworks is that each one shall burn for five minutes, the shorter the better. But the whoosh of the wind and the alternating song of the waves, and the whistling of the grass etc. gains something the more we listen to it.[21]

This response to natural beauty is evident already in the oldest of Kierkegaard's written records. At the height of summer in 1835, he took to describing at length the scenery he explored on day trips from Gilleleje. "When you see this landscape in afternoon lighting," he remarked regarding the woods and lake around the Gurre Castle ruins—

> when the sun still stands high enough to give the friendly landscape its requisite sharp outlines, like a melancholy voice that's accentuated enough not to become a lisp, then our whole environment seems to whisper to us: it is good to be here.[22]

In nature, he wrote a couple of weeks later, we are

> free from life's stuffy air, the spirit is freer, and the soul opens itself willingly to every noble impression. Here the human being comes out as nature's lord, but he also senses that something higher appears, something he must bow to; he feels it necessary to devote himself to that power, which rules the whole.[23]

This religious enchantment also propelled Kierkegaard forward intellectually. After recording these experiences, he made in his journal an accounting of his many academic interests, debating with himself what study he should devote himself to: natural science? Theology?—everything seemed interesting. On the 1st of August, he proclaimed with all the pathos of youthful ambition, and the exhilaration of facing an open future, that what all these deliberations must come down to "is to understand my purpose, to see what divinity really wants *me to do; I must find a truth that is a truth for me, find that idea for which I want to live and die.*"[24] As we follow the train of thought which his experiences prompted, we get an illustration of how natural beauty can be inspiring or, to use Kierkegaard's preferred term, "upbuilding." But other kinds of experience can do this too, depending on the individual's temperament: a concert, a religious ritual, fireworks. As it draws out our love of life and builds up our faith in the world, it arouses a desire to create something, be someone.

Enchantment is but an acute experience of meaning. As a propelling force, it is negative, but the philosopher need not agree to a metaphysical realism that would posit some external, even transcendent, object on behalf of this experience, in order to ascribe a positive aspect to it. Enchantment is positive in its very phenomenology; it is an experience that contains the fullness of life. In its grip we feel alive, feel that it is good to be here, in this world. It is indeed the strange bastard offspring of Penia and Poros, lack and plenty.

Notes

Introduction

1. Chantal Anne's book on love in Kierkegaard's thought is a notable exception which recognizes that *The Concept of Irony*'s discussion of the *Symposium* should be read in the context of other references to love in the dissertation. But she quickly moves ahead to later works in search of a truer love. See Chantal Anne, *L'amour dans la pensée de Søren Kierkegaard* (Paris: Éditions L'Harmattan, 1993).
2. SKS 16, 15 incl. fn. / KW 22, 29 incl. fn.
3. M. Jamie Ferreira, *Kierkegaard* (Malden: Blackwell, 2009), 14.
4. William McDonald, "Love in Kierkegaard's Symposia," *Minerva* 7 (2003): 60–93.
5. Sylvia Walsh, *Kierkegaard: Thinking Christianly in an Existential Mode* (New York: Oxford University Press, 2009), 27.
6. SKS 2, 39 / KW 3, 30.
7. Joakim Garff, "The Eyes of Argus," in *Kierkegaard: A Reader*, ed. Jonathan Rée and Jane Chamberlain (Oxford: Blackwell, 1998).
8. SKS 7, 570 / KW 12.1, 626.
9. SKS 7, 571 / KW 12.1, 627.
10. SKS 2, 21 / KW 3, 14.
11. Joakim Garff, *"Den søvnløse": Kierkegaard læst æstetisk/biografisk* (Copenhagen: Reitzel, 1995), 80.
12. Ibid., 95.
13. SKS 3, 30–1 / KW 4, 21–2.
14. SKS 2, 210 / KW 4, 237.
15. Joakim Garff, *Kierkegaard: A Biography*, trans. Bruce Kirmmse (Princeton: Princeton University Press, 2005), 212.
16. George Pattison, *Kierkegaard and the Quest for Unambiguous Life* (Oxford: Oxford University Press, 2013), 62.
17. Ferreira, *Kierkegaard*, 20.
18. NB 17:33 (1850).
19. See Hong's Historical Introduction (KW 2, vii).
20. SKS 27, 167 / SKP 244 (1837).

21 Isak Winkel Holm, *Tanken i billedet* (Copenhagen: Gyldendal, 1998), 125–6.
22 SKS 2, 45 / KW 3, 35.
23 SKS 1, 117 / KW 2, 56.
24 KW 2, ix, Hong's translation in his Historical Introduction.
25 SKS 1, 355 / KW 2, 327.

Chapter 1

1 SKS 2, 64 / KW 3, 56.
2 SKS 2, 209 / KW 3, 214–15.
3 Plato, *Symposium*, trans. Alexander Nehamas and Paul Woodruff, in *Plato: Complete Works*, ed. John Cooper (Indianapolis: Hackett Publishing, 1997), 217e–18a.
4 SKS 2, 171 / KW 3, 174.
5 SKS 2, 171 / KW 3, 173.
6 Plato, *Symposium*, 222b.
7 SKS 2, 101 / KW 3, 97.
8 SKS 2, 97 / KW 3, 93.
9 SKS 2, 98 / KW 3, 94.
10 SKS 2, 106 / KW 3, 102.
11 SKS 2, 100 / KW 3, 96.
12 SKS 2, 134 / KW 3, 132.
13 SKS 2, 99–100 / KW 3, 95.
14 SKS 2, 65 / KW 3, 58.
15 In Hegel's view, the immediate is abstract because indeterminate. A thing is concrete in proportion as it is determined by various qualities and mediated by, for example, space and time. Although "sense-certainty immediately appears as the *richest* kind of knowledge, indeed a knowledge of infinite wealth," Hegel writes, this certainty "proves itself to be the most abstract and poorest *truth*. All that it says about what it knows is just that it *is*; and its truth contains nothing but the sheer *being* of the thing" (Georg W. F. Hegel, *Phenomenology of Spirit*, trans. A. V. Miller [Oxford: Clarendon Press, 1977], 58). When "A" speaks of music as concrete immediacy, he seems to be using "concrete" in the everyday sense of physical, perceptible.
16 SKS 2, 64 / KW 3, 56.
17 SKS 2, 71 / KW 3, 64.
18 SKS 2, 71 / KW 3, 64.

19 SKS 2, 88 / KW 3, 108.
20 SKS 2, 106 / KW 3, 102.
21 SKS 2, 102 / KW 3, 99.
22 SKS 2, 97 / KW 3, 92. One might ask why "A" should pick an opera as the perfect piece of music, when operas are also works of literature. "A" has little to say about this, except a sudden remark that language is a richer medium than music and that to make everything musical would be retrogressive rather than progressive. "This is why," he continues, "I have never had any sympathy for the sublimated music that thinks it does not need words" (SKS 2, 52 / KW 3, 69–70). Crucially for *Either/Or*, the representation of sensuality through persons allows the opera to have the tragic aspect that "A" explores in "Shadowgraphs," that is, a collision between different forces or principles, embodied in characters.
23 SKS 2, 123 / KW 3, 121.
24 SKS 2, 124 / KW 3, 122.
25 SKS 2, 102 / KW 3, 99.
26 SKS 2, 194 / KW 3, 198.
27 SKS 9, 102–3 / KW 3, 108.
28 SKS 9, 102 / KW 3, 108.
29 SKS 2, 88 / KW 3, 99.
30 SKS 1, 293fn. / KW 2, 329fn.
31 Plato, *Symposium*, 215bc.
32 Ibid., 215cd.
33 SKS 1, 244 / KW 2, 198.
34 SKS 1, 228 / KW 2, 181.
35 SKS 1, 294 / KW 2, 256.
36 SKS 1, 294–95 / KW 2, 256.
37 SKS 1, 295 / KW 2, 256.
38 Plato, *Theaetetus*, trans. M. J. Levett and Myles Burnyeat, in *Plato: Complete Works*, 151bc.
39 SKS 1, 287 / KW 2, 248.
40 SKS 1, 65 / KW 2, 6.
41 SKS 1, 286 / KW 2, 247.
42 SKS 1, 286 / KW 2, 247–48.
43 SKS 1, 218 / KW 2, 170. Kierkegaard refers to Friedrich Schleiermacher, "Über den Werth des Sokrates als Philosophen," in *Abhandlungen der Königlichen Academie der Wissenschaften* (Berlin, 1814–15), 51–68.
44 Heinrich Theodor Rötscher, *Aristophanes und sein Zeitalter* (Berlin, 1827), 253, quoted at SKS 1, 221–22 / KW 2, 174.

45 SKS 1, 221–22 / KW 2, 174.
46 E.g. SKS 1, 197–98 / KW 2, 147.
47 SKS 1, 99 / KW 2, 37.
48 SKS 1, 102 / KW 2, 41. The term "abstraction" is associated almost exclusively, in Kierkegaard studies, with the significance it has in *Concluding Unscientific Postscript*, where to think abstractly is to be detached from one's own existence; it is a failure of inwardness. "To ask abstractly about actuality," Climacus writes, "and to answer abstractly is not nearly as difficult as to ask and answer what it means that this definite something is an actuality. Abstraction disregards this definite something, but the difficulty lies in joining this definite something and the ideality of thinking by willing to think it" (SKS 7, 174–5 / SKS 12.1, 301–2). In *The Concept of Irony*, by contrast, abstraction is an exercise in subjectivity and freedom, though it is certainly understood in opposition to "actuality."
49 SKS 1, 96 / KW 2, 35.
50 SKS 1, 344 / KW 2, 106.
51 SKS 1, 174fn. / KW 2, 122fn.
52 SKS 1, 97 / KW 2, 36.
53 Plato, *Republic* I, trans. G. M. A. Grube and C. D. C. Reeve, in *Plato: Complete Works*, 345e–346c.
54 Ibid., 346e.
55 SKS 1, 170fn. / KW 2, 118fn.
56 SKS 1, 118fn. / KW 2, 58fn.
57 SKS 1, 118 / KW 2, 57.
58 Plato, *Protagoras*, trans. Stanley Lombardo and Karen Bell, in *Plato: Complete Works*, 349b.
59 Ibid., 349d.
60 Ibid., 333ab.
61 SKS 1, 121 / KW 2, 61.
62 SKS 1, 119 / KW 2, 58.
63 SKS 1, 119 / KW 2, 59.
64 SKS 1, 263fn. / KW 2, 220fn.
65 SKS 2, 47 / KW 3, 38.
66 Georg W. F. Hegel, *Science of Logic*, trans. A. V. Miller (New York: Humanities Press, 1969), 643.
67 Ibid.
68 Ibid.
69 Plato, *Phaedo*, trans. G. M. A. Grube, in *Plato: Complete Works*, 65c.
70 SKS 1, 128 / KW 2, 68.

71 SKS 1, 128 / KW 2, 68.
72 Plato, *Phaedo*, 74de.
73 "To posit" is etymologically related to "positive," and in Kierkegaard's notes from Schelling's lectures, we read that positive philosophy "proceeds from *dem geradezu Seienen* [the that which simply is]. In negative philosophy, it is the thought preceding *Seyn* that everything revolves around; in positive philosophy, *Seyn* precedes thought" (KW 2, 370, Hong's translation in his notes). Schelling understands positive and negative as mapping onto the dichotomy of existence—*that* something is—and essence—*what* it is. This is certainly in the background for Kierkegaard, yet his dichotomy of negative and positive in his discussion of Socrates is not straightforwardly a discussion of essence and existence. He does not merely claim that Socrates only gives definitions without regard for the question whether anything instantiates those definitions. Socrates' negativity keeps him in the realm of the purely formal and logical and Kierkegaard speaks not only of things but of ideas as (capable of being) positive.
74 SKS 1, 120 / KW 2, 60.
75 See Georg W. F. Hegel, *Lectures on the History of Philosophy*, vol. I, trans. E. S. Haldane (Lincoln: University of Nebraska Press, 1995), 400.
76 SKS 1, 107 / KW 2, 46.
77 Plato, *Cratylus*, trans. C. D. C. Reeve, in *Plato: Complete Works*, 398d. Thanks to Frisbee Sheffield for helping me with the Greek and locating the reference.
78 Plato, *Symposium*, 200a–1c.
79 SKS 1, 106 / KW 2, 45.
80 SKS 1, 106–107 / KW 2, 45 (emphasis in original).
81 SKS 1, 112 / KW 2, 51.
82 SKS 1, 107 / KW 2, 46.
83 SKS 1, 107 / KW 2, 46.
84 SKS 1, 107 / KW 2, 46.
85 Jacob Howland, *Kierkegaard and Socrates: A Study in Philosophy and Faith* (Cambridge: Cambridge University Press, 2006), 59.
86 SKS 7, 91 / KW 12.1, 92.
87 Howland, *Kierkegaard and Socrates*, 59.
88 Ibid., 73.
89 SKS 1, 217–18 / KW 2, 169.
90 Plato, *Phaedo*, 74de.
91 Jonathan Lear, *A Case for Irony* (Cambridge: Harvard University Press, 2011), 9–12.

92 René Descartes, *Meditations on First Philosophy*, trans. John Cottingham (Cambridge: Cambridge University Press, 1996), 31.
93 SKS 1, 218 / KW 2, 169 (emphasis in original).
94 SKS 1, 260 / KW 2, 216.
95 Christine Habbard, "Kierkegaard's Concept of Irony and the Philosophical Issue of the Beginning," *Kierkegaard Studies Yearbook* (Berlin: De Gruyter, 2009), 272. See Hegel, *Science of Logic*, 67.
96 Habbard, "Kierkegaard's Concept of Irony," 273.
97 Ibid., 274.
98 Ibid.
99 SKS 1, 259 / KW 2, 214.
100 Habbard, "Kierkegaard's Concept of Irony," 277.
101 John Lippitt, *Humour and Irony in Kierkegaard's Thought* (New York: St. Martin's Press, 2000), 136–7.
102 Martin Andic, "Clouds of Irony," in *International Kierkegaard Commentary: The Concept of Irony*, ed. Robert Perkins (Macon: Mercer University Press, 2001), 190.
103 Ibid.
104 Cf. Hegel, *Lectures on the History of Philosophy*, vol. I, 400.
105 Lippitt, *Humour and Irony*, 137.
106 Louis Mackey, *Points of View: Readings of Kierkegaard* (Tallahassee: Florida State University Press, 1986), 19
107 Ibid., 20.
108 Hegel, *Lectures on the History of Philosophy*, vol. I, 384.
109 Georg W. F. Hegel, *Lectures on the History of Philosophy*, vol. II, trans. E. S Haldane and F. H. Simson (Lincoln: University of Nebraska Press, 1995), 13.
110 Ibid.
111 Ibid.
112 SKS 1, 298 / KW 2, 260.
113 SKS 1, 244 / KW 2, 198.
114 SKS 1, 245 / KW 2, 199.
115 Mackey, *Points of View*, 21.
116 Ibid.
117 Hegel, *Lectures on the History of Philosophy*, vol. I, 385.
118 SKS 1, 267 / KW 2, 223–24.
119 Georg W. F. Hegel, *Philosophy of Right*, trans. T. M. Knox (Oxford: Clarendon Press, 1942), 92.
120 Ibid.

121 Plato, *Protagoras*, 358d.
122 SKS 1, 110 / KW 2, 49.
123 SKS 1, 223 / KW 2, 176.
124 SKS 1, 235 / KW 2, 188.
125 SKS 1, 225 / KW 2, 178.
126 SKS 1, 235 / KW 2, 188 (emphases in original).

Chapter 2

1 SKS 2, 148 / KW 3, 149.
2 SKS 1, 238 / KW 2, 191.
3 SKS 1, 225 / KW 2, 178.
4 SKS 1, 241 / KW 2, 194.
5 SKS 1, 225 / KW 2, 177.
6 SKS 1, 232-33 / KW 2, 185 (emphases in original).
7 SKS 1, 234 / KW 2, 187.
8 SKS 1, 89 / KW 2, 27.
9 SKS 2, 141 / KW 3, 142.
10 SKS 2, 141 / KW 3, 142.
11 Friedrich Nietzsche, *The Birth of Tragedy*, in *Basic Writings*, trans. Walter Kaufmann (New York: Modern Library, 1992), 91.
12 Ibid., 94–5.
13 SKS 2, 158 / KW 3, 160. Not advocating any particular way of fashioning one's life, any particular value, Socrates is not evil but precedes good and evil. It is an echo of *The Concept of Irony* we hear when Judge Wilhelm proclaims that judgments of good and evil come into play only after the individual has chosen himself and thus tied himself to an ethical system or outlook (SKS 3, 165 / KW 4, 169).
14 SKS 2, 158 / KW 3, 160.
15 Bernard Williams, *Shame and Necessity* (Berkeley: University of California Press, 2008), 70 (my emphases).
16 SKS 2, 155 / KW 3, 156.
17 SKS 2, 147 / KW 3, 148.
18 SKS 2, 148 / KW 3, 149.
19 SKS 2, 144 / KW 3, 145.
20 SKS 2, 144 / KW 3, 145.
21 SKS 2, 143 / KW 3, 143–4.

22 SKS 2, 145 / KW 3, 145–6.
23 SKS 2, 152 / KW 3, 153–4.
24 SKS 2, 152–53 / KW 3, 154.
25 SKS 2, 153 / KW 3, 154.
26 SKS 2, 159 / KW 3, 160.
27 SKS 2, 159 / KW 3, 160.
28 SKS 2, 159 / KW 3, 161.
29 SKS 2, 157 / KW 3, 158–9.
30 SKS 2, 159 / KW 3, 161.
31 SKS 1, 312 / KW 2, 276.
32 I'm putting aside the "tragic collision" in A's play between Antigone's filial and romantic love. Her relationship with her father may not be sufficient for a dramatic play, according to "A," but it involves tragic guilt all the same.
33 SKS 2, 150 / KW 3, 151.
34 SKS 2, 150 / KW 3, 151.
35 See Arthur Schopenhauer, *The World as Will and Representation,* vol. II, trans. E. F. J. Payne (New York: Dover, 1958), 434; 579.
36 Sophocles, *Philoctetes* in *The Complete Plays*, trans. Richard Claverhouse Jebb (Toronto: Bantam Books, 1967), 193.
37 SKS 2, 174 / KW 3, 177.
38 SKS 2, 187 / KW 3, 190.
39 Plato, *Republic* VII, 523ad.
40 SKS 2, 176 / KW 3, 178.
41 SKS 2, 169 / KW 3, 171.
42 SKS 2, 169 / KW 3, 171–2.
43 SKS 2, 175 / KW 3, 178.
44 SKS 2, 176 / KW 3, 178.
45 SKS 2, 178–79 / KW 3, 181.
46 SKS 2, 176 / KW 3, 179.
47 SKS 2, 184 / KW 3, 187–8.
48 SKS 2, 177 / KW 3, 179.
49 SKS 2, 177 / KW 3, 179.
50 SKS 2, 168 / KW 3, 170.
51 SKS 2, 182 / KW 3, 185.
52 SKS 2, 182 / KW 3, 185.
53 SKS 2, 185 / KW 3, 188.
54 SKS 2, 185 / KW 3, 188.
55 SKS 2, 185 / KW 3, 188.

56 Plato, *Symposium*, 218a.
57 Ibid., 215c.
58 Ibid., 215ce.
59 Ibid., 217a.
60 Ibid., 222b.
61 Ibid., 219d.
62 SKS 1, 237 / KW 2, 191.
63 Plato, *Symposium*, 216c.
64 Ibid., 222a.
65 Ibid.
66 Ibid., 216a.
67 SKS 1, 236 / KW 2, 189.
68 Plato, *Meno*, 80ab.
69 Descartes, *Meditations*, 15.
70 Ibid., 16.
71 SKS 2, 206 / KW 3, 211.
72 SKS 2, 205 / KW 3, 210.
73 SKS 2, 205 / KW 3, 210.
74 SKS 2, 177 / KW 3, 180.
75 SKS 2, 187 / KW 3, 191.
76 SKS 11, 165fn. / KW 19, 50fn.
77 SKS 11, 135 / KW 19, 20.
78 SKS 11, 135 / KW 19, 20.
79 SKS 11, 129 / KW 19, 13.
80 SKS 11, 135 / KW 19, 20.
81 Jean-Paul Sartre, *Being and Nothingness*, trans. Hazel Barnes (New York: Washington Square Press, 1956), 475–8.
82 Sharon Krishek, *Kierkegaard on Faith and Love* (Cambridge: Cambridge University Press, 2009), 11.
83 Ibid.
84 Ibid.
85 SKS 2, 200 / KW 3, 205.
86 SKS 11, 129; 168 / KW 19, 13; 53.
87 SKS 4, 136 / KW 6, 41.
88 SKS 4, 136 / KW 6, 41.
89 SKS 4, 138 / KW 6, 44.
90 SKS 4, 139 / KW 6, 44.
91 SKS 4, 139 / KW 6, 44.

92   SKS 4, 139 / KW 6, 45.
93   SKS 4, 141 / KW 3, 46.
94   George Pattison, *Kierkegaard: The Aesthetic and the Religious* (Norwich: SCM Press, 1999), 137.
95   Ibid.
96   SKS 7, 282 / KW 12, 198; SKS 11, 135 / KW 19, 20.
97   Plato, *Meno*, 80cd.
98   SKS 1, 295 / KW 2, 257.
99   JJ:54 (1843).
100 EE:122 (1839).
101 See JJ:11 (1842).
102 NB 15:6 (1849).
103 Céline Léon, "(A) Woman's Place within the Ethical," in Céline Léon and Sylvia Walsh (eds.), *Feminist Interpretations of Søren Kierkegaard* (University Park: The Pennsylvania State University Press, 1997), 106, 113.
104 NB 15:10 (1849).
105 SKS 2, 130 / KW 3, 128.

Chapter 3

1   SKS 1, 93 / KW 2, 31–2.
2   SKS 1, 154 / KW 2, 101.
3   SKS 1, 157 / KW 2, 103–4.
4   Plato, *Meno*, 81c.
5   Ibid., 81ab.
6   Ibid., 81d.
7   SKS 1, 107 / KW 2, 45–6.
8   Plato, *Symposium*, 201d.
9   SKS 1, 160 / KW 2, 108.
10   Plato, *Symposium*, 203d.
11   SKS 1, 159 / KW 2, 106.
12   SKS 1, 159–60 / KW 2, 106.
13   SKS 1, 151 / KW 2, 97.
14   Hegel, *Lectures on the History of Philosophy*, vol. II, 20.
15   SKS 1, 158 / KW 2, 104.
16   SKS 1, 155fn. / KW 2, 102fn.
17   SKS 1, 151 / KW 2, 97.

18 SKS 1, 157fn. / KW 2, 103fn. *Forestilling* derives from the German *Vorstellung*: something being (figuratively) "put before" a person for him to see. In its reflexive verb form, "*at forestille sig noget*" is to imagine something, or to be able to picture a situation described by someone.
19 SKS 1, 192–93 / KW 2, 104.
20 SKS 1, 193 / KW 2, 105.
21 Plato, *Symposium*, 211cd.
22 Ibid., 210d.
23 SKS 1, 160 / KW 2, 107 (emphasis in original).
24 SKS 1, 160–1 / KW 2, 107.
25 SKP 195 (1836) Kirmmse's translation (amended), from Jørgen Bukdahl, *Søren Kierkegaard and the Common Man*, trans. Bruce Kirmmse (Grand Rapids: W. B. Eerdmans Publishing, 2001), 9.
26 EE:11 (1939).
27 SKS 1, 157 / KW 2, 104; Bukdahl, *Kierkegaard and the Common Man*, 13.
28 Henrik Steffens, *Inledning til philosophiske Forelæsninger i København 1803* (Copenhagen: Gyldendahl, 1905), 21 (Pattison's translation, *The Aesthetic and the Religious*, 6).
29 Pattison, *The Aesthetic and the Religious*, 63.
30 Kierkegaard uses this term of Hegel's in *The Concept of Irony*. See SKS 1, 155 / KW 2, 101; Georg W. F. Hegel, *The Philosophy of History*, trans. J. Sibree (Toronto: Dover, 1956), 141.
31 DD:80 (1837), Pattison's translation (amended), *The Aesthetic and the Religious*, 51.
32 Pattison, *The Aesthetic and the Religious*, 62, 52.
33 SKS 1, 154 / KW 2, 101 (emphasis in original).
34 Bukdahl, *Kierkegaard and the Common Man*, 9.
35 Holm, *Tanken i billedet*, 132 (the root of *Anskuelse*—*at skue*—means either "to look" or "to behold").
36 Ibid., 125–6.
37 SKS 7, 188 / KW 12.1, 205.
38 SKS 7, 188fn. / KW 12.1, 206fn.
39 Gordon Marino, *Kierkegaard and the Present Age* (Milwaukee: Marquette University Press, 2001), 19.
40 SKS 2, 51 / KW 3, 42.
41 SKS 2, 41 / KW 3, 32.
42 SKS 2, 41 / KW 3, 32.
43 SKS 2, 286 / KW 3, 295–6.

44 SKS 2, 294 / KW 3, 304.
45 SKS 2, 295 / KW 3, 305.
46 SKS 2, 323 / KW 3, 334.
47 SKS 6, 22 / KW 11, 14–15.
48 SKS 6, 22 / KW 11, 14–15.
49 SKS 6, 22 / KW 11, 14.
50 SKS 1, 152 / KW 2, 98.
51 Holm, *Tanken i billedet*, 129.
52 SKS 3, 207 / KW 4, 216.
53 SKS 3, 207 / KW 4, 216.
54 Alastair MacIntyre, *After Virtue* (Notre Dame: University of Notre Dame Press, 2007), 215–16.
55 John Davenport, *Narrative Identity, Autonomy and Morality: From Frankfurt and MacIntyre to Kierkegaard* (New York: Routledge, 2012), 102–3.
56 Ibid.
57 John Lippitt, "Getting the Story Straight: Kierkegaard, MacIntyre and Some Problems with Narrative," *Inquiry* 50, no. 1 (February 2007): 43.
58 JJ:167 (1843).
59 SKS 6, 17 / KW 11, 9.
60 SKS 6, 18 / KW 11, 10.
61 SKS 1, 97 / KW 2, 36.
62 SKS 1, 97 / KW 2, 36.
63 SKS 1, 155 / KW 2, 103.
64 SKS 1, 108 / KW 2, 47.
65 Alexander Baumgarten, *Reflections on Poetry*, trans. Karl Aschenbrenner (Los Angeles: University of California Press, 1954).
66 SKS 1, 96 / KW 2, 34.
67 SKS 1, 96 / KW 2, 34.
68 Hegel, *Science of Logic*, 439.
69 Hannah Arendt, *The Life of the Mind* (New York: Harcourt, 1978), 167.
70 Ibid., 185.
71 SKS 1, 96 / KW 2, 34.
72 SKS 1, 96 / KW 2, 34.
73 SKS 1, 94 / KW 2, 33 (incl. fn.). The Danish is *tale* (speak) and *samtale* (converse).
74 SKS 1, 97 / KW 2, 35.
75 SKS 1, 113–14 / KW 2, 53.
76 SKS 1, 94 / KW 2, 33.
77 SKS 1, 92 / KW 2, 30.

78 SKS 1, 178 / KW 2, 126.
79 SKS 1, 236 / KW 2, 189.
80 SKS 1, 178 / KW 2, 126.
81 SKS 1, 178 / KW 2, 126.
82 SKS 1, 203 / KW 2, 153.
83 SKS 1, 174 / KW 2, 122.
84 SKS 1, 174 / KW 2, 123.
85 SKS 1, 175 / KW 2, 122 (emphases in original).
86 SKS 1, 90 / KW 2, 28–9 (emphasis in original).
87 SKS 1, 90 / KW 2, 29.
88 SKS 1, 91 / KW 2, 29.
89 SKS 1, 91fn. / KW 2, 29fn.
90 SKS 1, 92 / KW 2, 30.
91 SKS 1, 91–92 / KW 2, 29–30.

Chapter 4

1 Theodor Adorno, *Kierkegaard: Construction of the Aesthetic*, trans. Robert Hullot-Kenter (St. Paul: University of Minnesota Press, 1989), 29.
2 SKS 2, 11 / KW 3, 3.
3 SKS 4, 202 / KW 6, 118.
4 SKS 1, 286 / KW 2, 247.
5 SKS 1, 295 / KW 2, 257.
6 SKS 1, 74 / KW 2, 12.
7 SKS 1, 244 / KW 2, 198.
8 SKS 1, 74 / KW 2, 12.
9 SKS 1, 260 / KW 2, 214–15.
10 SKS 1, 172 / KW 2, 120.
11 SKS 1, 172 / KW 2, 120.
12 SKS 1, 172 / KW 2, 121.
13 Paul Muench, "Socratic Irony, Plato's *Apology* and Kierkegaard's *On the Concept of Irony*," in *Kierkegaard Studies Yearbook*, ed. Niels Jørgen Cappelørn, K. Brian Söderquist, and Hermann Deuser (Berlin: De Gruyter, 2009), 71.
14 SKS 1, 206 / KW 2, 156.
15 SKS 1, 177 / KW 2, 126.
16 SKS 1, 72 / KW 2, 10.
17 SKS 2, 11 / KW 3, 3.
18 SKS 2, 11 / KW 3, 3.

19 Hegel, *Lectures on Fine Art*, vol. II, 890.
20 Ibid.
21 SKS 2, 74 / KW 3, 67.
22 SKS 2, 47 / KW 3, 64.
23 SKS 1, 74 / KW 2, 12.
24 SKS 1, 80 / KW 2, 18.
25 Ibid. The mention of situation, key in Hegel's analysis of drama, is what signals that Kierkegaard is comparing the dialogue to drama, where a *Replik* is any line spoken by an actor onstage. *Replik* also means "rejoinder," as Hong renders it, but that translation makes little sense in the context.
26 SKS 1, 81–2 / KW 2, 21.
27 SKS 1, 82 / KW 2, 21.
28 SKS 1, 87 / KW 2, 25.
29 SKS 1, 85 / KW 2, 23.
30 Plato, *Symposium*, 215b.
31 SKS 1, 76fn. / KW 2, 14fn.
32 SKS 2, 167 / KW 3, 169.
33 SKS 2, 167 / KW 3, 169.
34 SKS 2, 167 / KW 3, 169.
35 SKS 2, 167 / KW 3, 169.
36 SKS 2, 172 / KW 3, 174.
37 SKS 2, 170–1 / KW 3, 173.
38 SKS 1, 80–1 / KW 2, 19.
39 SKS 1, 74 / KW 2, 12.
40 SKS 1, 81 / KW 2, 19.
41 Adorno, *Construction of the Aesthetic*, 29.
42 Hegel, *Science of Logic*, 523 (emphases in original).
43 Jon Stewart, *Kierkegaard's Relations to Hegel Reconsidered* (Cambridge: Cambridge University Press, 2003), 326–7.
44 Hegel, *Lectures on Fine Art*, vol. I, 427.
45 Ibid., 431.
46 Ibid., 427.
47 Hegel, *Lectures on Fine Art*, vol. II, 1002 (emphasis in original).
48 SKS 2, 209 / KW 3, 214.
49 SKS 2, 173 / KW 3, 176.
50 SKS 2, 173 / KW 3, 176.
51 SKS 2, 171 / KW 3, 175.
52 SKS 2, 152 / KW 3, 174.

53 SKS 1, 102 / KW 2, 47.
54 SKS 1, 110 / KW 2, 49.
55 Hannah Arendt, *The Human Condition* (Chicago: The University of Chicago Press, 1958), 242.
56 E.g. SKS 1, 198 / KW 2, 147.
57 SKS 1, 71 / KW 2, 9.
58 SKS 1, 71 / KW 2, 9.
59 SKS 1, 71 / KW 2, 9.
60 SKS 1, 73 / KW 2, 10–11.
61 Immanuel Kant, *Critique of Judgment*, trans. Werner Pluhar (Indianapolis: Hackett, 1987), 174.
62 Ibid., 175.
63 Tonny Aagaard Olesen, "Kierkegaard's Socratic Hermeneutic in *The Concept of Irony*," in *International Kierkegaard Commentary: The Concept of Irony*, 112. Sylvia Walsh makes the same point in "Ironic Love: An Amorist Interpretation of Socratic Eros" (ibid., 124–25).
64 SKS 1, 71 / KW 2, 9.
65 SKP III B:12, Hong's translation in "Supplement," KW 2, 443.
66 Ibid.
67 SKS 1, 89 / KW 2, 27.
68 Frederik Christian Sibbern, *Om Poesie og Konst*, vol. I (Copenhagen, 1834), 4.
69 Ibid., 18, Pattison's translation in his *The Aesthetic and the Religious*, 8.
70 Ibid.
71 SKS 1, 299 / KW 2, 261.
72 SKS 1, 281 / KW 2, 241.
73 SKS 1, 281 / KW 2, 241-2. In *Concluding Unscientific Postscript*, Johannes Climacus will be concerned with actuality in a different sense of the term, just as he will change Kierkegaard's meaning of "abstraction." "Whether truth is defined more empirically as thought's agreement with being [*Væren*] or more idealistically as being's agreement with thought," Climacus writes, "the point in each case is to be very careful to note what is understood by being and also carefully note whether the knowing human spirit is not lured out into the indeterminate, fantastically becoming something such as no *existing* human being has ever been or can be—a phantom with which the individual deals with on occasion, though without ever explicating to himself [. . .] what significance being [in that fantasy] has for him, whether the entire endeavor out there is not dissolved into a tautology" (SKS 7, 173-4 / KW 2, 189). The "actuality" at stake is not the actuality of the object of knowledge, but the actuality of the thinker in his active engagement with the world.

74 DD:1 (1837).
75 Exod. 3:9-15 (New International Version).
76 NB 25:56 (1852).
77 Ibid.
78 David Gouwens, *Kierkegaard's Dialectic of the Imagination* (New York: Peter Lang, 1988), 79–81; Hermann Diem, *Kierkegaard's Dialectic of Existence*, trans. Harold Knight (New York: Frederick Ungar Publishing, 1965), 23.
79 SKS 11, 147 / KW 19, 31.
80 Diem, *Kierkegaard's Dialectic of Existence*, 23.

Chapter 5

1 SKS 1, 107 / KW 2, 45–6.
2 SKS 9, 15 / KW 16, 7.
3 SKS 9, 314 / KW 16, 317 (emphases in original).
4 Immanuel Kant, *Groundwork of the Metaphysic of Morals*, trans. H. J. Paton (New York: Harper Perennial, 2009), 61.
5 SKS 9, 113 / KW 16, 109.
6 SKS 9, 57 / KW 16, 50.
7 SKS 9, 31 / KW 16, 24.
8 SKS 9, 36 / KW 16, 29.
9 SKS 9, 37 / KW 16, 29.
10 SKS 9, 367 / KW 16, 373.
11 SKS 9, 367 / KW 16, 373.
12 SKS 9, 30 / KW 16, 22; Lk. 10:25f.
13 SKS 9, 27 / KW 16, 19.
14 SKS 9, 30 / KW 16, 23.
15 SKS 9, 31 / KW 16, 23.
16 Kant, *Groundwork*, 18, 47. There is also the positive duty to cultivate one's talents and thereby contribute something of value to the world (39).
17 SKS 9, 306 / KW 16, 309.
18 SKS 9, 306 / KW 16, 309.
19 SKS 9, 59 / KW 16, 52.
20 SKS 9, 60 / KW 16, 53.
21 Theodor Adorno, "On Kierkegaard's Doctrine of Love," *Studies in Philosophy and Social Science* 8, no. 3 (1939): 414.
22 Ibid., 415.

23 Plato, *Symposium*, 198de.
24 SKS 1, 106–7 / KW 2, 45 (emphasis in original).
25 SKS 1, 107 / KW 2, 46.
26 Adorno, "Kierkegaard's Doctrine of Love," 416.
27 Noreen Khawaja, *The Religion of Existence: Asceticism in Philosophy from Kierkegaard to Sartre* (Chicago: University of Chicago Press, 2016), 78.
28 Ibid.
29 SKS 9, 16–17 / KW 16, 8–9.
30 Adorno, "Kierkegaard's Doctrine of Love," 416.
31 SKS 9, 118 / KW 16, 114.
32 Knud Ejler Løgstrup, *The Ethical Demand*, trans. Hans Fink et al. (Notre Dame: The University of Notre Dame Press, 1997), 221.
33 Ibid., 227.
34 SKS 9, 118 / KW 16, 114.
35 SKS 9, 124 / KW 16, 121.
36 SKS 9, 130 / KW 16, 128.
37 Løgstrup, *The Ethical Demand*, 232.
38 SKS 1, 229–30 / KW 2, 182.
39 M. Jamie Ferreira, *Love's Grateful Striving* (New York: Oxford University Press, 2001), 34.
40 Ibid.
41 Ibid.
42 Ferreira, *Love's Grateful Striving*, 19.
43 Ibid., 33.
44 SKS 9, 30 / KW 16, 22.
45 SKS 9, 26 / KW 16, 18.
46 SKS 9, 30 / KW 16, 22.
47 SKS 1, 110 / KW 2, 49.
48 SKS 9, 27–8 / KW 16, 19–20.
49 Ferreira, *Love's Grateful Striving*, 131.
50 SKS 9, 133 / KW 16, 130.
51 Ferreira, *Love's Grateful Striving*, 34.
52 SKS 1, 77 / KW 2, 15–16.
53 Ferreira, *Love's Grateful Striving*, 238.
54 Ibid., 239.
55 SKS 9, 332 / KW 16, 336.
56 SKS 9, 368 / KW 16, 375.
57 SKS 1, 119 / KW 2, 58.

58 Løgstrup, *The Ethical Demand*, 244.
59 C. Stephen Evans, *Kierkegaard's Ethic of Love* (Oxford: Oxford University Press, 2004), 135.
60 Ibid., 112.
61 Ibid., 143.
62 SKS 9, 38–9 / KW 16, 31.
63 Evans, *Kierkegaard's Ethic of Love*, 146.
64 SKS 9, 362 / KW 16, 369.
65 HH:24 (1840–1).
66 Ibid.
67 SKS 9, 339 / KW 16, 346.
68 SKS 9, 110 / KW 16, 106.
69 SKS 9, 110 / KW 16, 106.
70 SKS 9, 109–10 / KW 16, 105.
71 SKS 9, 108 / KW 16, 104.
72 SKS 9, 101 / KW 16, 96.
73 SKS 9, 100 / KW 16, 96.
74 SKS 9, 101 / KW 16, 96. That comment is made about the Pharisee's question, "who is my neighbor?" to which Jesus responds with the Good Samaritan parable (Lk. 10:29).
75 SKS 9, 105 / KW 16, 101.
76 SKS 9, 107 / KW 16, 102.
77 Ferreira, *Love's Grateful Striving*, 100f.
78 Ibid., 105.
79 SKS 9, 160 / KW 16, 159 (emphasis in original).
80 SKS 9, 214 / KW 16, 211.
81 SKS 9, 216 / KW 16, 213.
82 SKS 9, 219 / KW 16, 216.
83 SKS 9, 314 / KW 16, 317.
84 1 Jn 4:7 (I translate Kierkegaard's Danish rather than cite any English Bible edition.)
85 SKS 9, 368 / KW 16, 375.
86 SKS 9, 368 / KW 16, 375.
87 SKS 9, 369 / KW 16, 276.
88 NB2:176 (1847).
89 SKS 9, 363 / KW 16, 370.
90 SKS 9, 27 / KW 16, 19.
91 SKS 9, 353 / KW 16, 359.

92 SKS 9, 354 / KW 16, 360.
93 SKS 9, 124, 130 / KW 16, 121, 128.
94 Adorno, "Kierkegaard's Doctrine of Love," 415.
95 SKS 9, 95 / KW 16, 90.
96 SKS 9, 155 / KW 16, 154 (emphasis in original); see Gen. 2:18.
97 JJ:210 (1844) (emphases in original).
98 SKS 16, 27 / KW 22, 35.
99 NB 14:30 (1849).
100 SKS 9, 95 / KW 16, 90.
101 SKS 28, 139 (July 17, 1838). The phrases "an outstanding balance" and "a debt" both translate *Mellemværdende*—"between-value," as in the difference between the amount paid and the sum owed.
102 SKS 28, 149 (November 16, 1841).
103 SKS 28, 155 / KW 25, 116 (January 1, 1842).
104 See Plato, *Phaedrus*, trans. John M. Cooper in *Collected Works*, 254a (*syzyge* is the vocative form). Thanks to Christos Hadjioannou for help with the Greek and locating the reference.
105 SKS 1, 91–2 / KW 2, 29–30.

Afterword

1 Plato, *Symposium*, 215e–16a.
2 SKS 8, 72 / KW 14, 74.
3 Anthony Rudd, *Kierkegaard and the Limits of the Ethical* (Oxford: Clarendon, 1988), 72.
4 SKS 3, 92 / KW 4, 89.
5 SKS 3, 165 / KW 4, 167.
6 Heinrich Fauteck, "Kierkegaards Antigone," *Skandinavistik* 4 (1974): 94.
7 SKS 2, 144 / KW 3, 145.
8 Garff, *Den søvnløse*, 96.
9 SKS 4, 208 / KW 6, 121.
10 JJ:516 (1844).
11 Carl S. Hughes, *Kierkegaard and the Staging of Desire: Rhetoric and Performance in a Theology of Eros* (New York: Fordham University Press, 2014), 80.
12 Ibid., 81.
13 EE:160 (Hong's translation modified by Hughes).
14 SKS 10, 288 / KW 17, 270.

15 SKS 10, 175 / KW 17, 163.
16 SKS 10, 176 / KW 17, 163.
17 SKS 10, 177 / KW 17, 165.
18 SKS 10, 289 / KW 17, 271.
19 Hughes, *Kierkegaard and the Staging of Desire*, 96.
20 Ibid., 13.
21 JJ:501 (1846).
22 AA:2 (1835).
23 AA:6 (1835).
24 AA:12 (1835) (emphases in original).

Bibliography

Adorno, Theodor. "On Kierkegaard's Doctrine of Love," *Studies in Philosophy and Social Science* 8, no. 3 (1939): 413–29.
Adorno, Theodor. *Kierkegaard: Construction of the Aesthetic*, trans. Robert Hullot-Kenter. St. Paul: University of Minnesota Press, 1989.
Andic, Martin. "Clouds of Irony," in Robert Perkins (ed.), *International Kierkegaard Commentary: The Concept of Irony*.
Anne, Chantal. *L'amour dans la pensée de Søren Kierkegaard*. Paris: Éditions L'Harmattan, 1993.
Arendt, Hannah. *The Human Condition*. Chicago: The University of Chicago Press, 1958.
Arendt, Hannah. *The Life of the Mind*. New York: Harcourt, 1978.
Baumgarten, Alexander G. *Reflections on Poetry*, trans. Karl Aschenbrenner and William Holther. Berkeley: University of California Press, 1954.
Baur, Ferdinand Christian. *Das Christliche des Platonismus oder Sokrates und Christus*. Tübingen, 1837.
Bukdahl, Jørgen. *Kierkegaard and the Common Man*, trans. Bruce Kirmmse. Cambridge: Wm. Eerdmans Publishing, 2001.
Davenport, John. *Narrative Identity, Autonomy and Morality: From Frankfurt and MacIntyre to Kierkegaard*. New York: Routledge, 2012.
Descartes, René. *Meditations on First Philosophy*, trans. John Cottingham. Cambridge: Cambridge University Press, 1996.
Diem, Hermann. *Kierkegaard's Dialectic of Existence*, trans. Harold Knight. New York: Frederick Ungar Publishing, 1965.
Evans, C. Stephen. *Kierkegaard's Ethic of Love*. Oxford: Oxford University Press, 2004.
Fauteck, Heinrich. "Kierkegaards Antigone," *Skandinavistik* 4 (1974): 81–100.
Ferreira, M. Jamie. *Love's Grateful Striving*. New York: Oxford University Press, 2001.
Ferreira, M. Jamie. *Kierkegaard*. Malden: Blackwell, 2009.
Garff, Joakim. *Den søvnløse: Kierkegaard læst æstetisk/biografisk*. Copenhagen: Reitzel, 1995.
Garff, Joakim. "The Eyes of Argus," in Jonathan Rée and Jane Chamberlain (eds.), *Kierkegaard: A Reader*. Oxford: Blackwell, 1998.
Garff, Joakim. *Kierkegaard: A Biography*, trans. Bruce Kirmmse. Princeton: Princeton University Press, 2005.

Gouwens, David. *Kierkegaard's Dialectic of the Imagination*. New York: Peter Lang Publishing, 1988.

Habbard, Christine. "Kierkegaard's Concept of Irony and the Philosophical Issue of Beginning," in Niels Jørgen Cappelørn, K. Brian Söderquist, and Hermann Deuser (eds.), *Kierkegaard Studies Yearbook*. Berlin: De Gruyter, 2009, pp. 269–84.

Hegel, Georg W. F. *Philosophy of Right*, trans. T. M. Knox. Oxford: Clarendon Press, 1942.

Hegel, Georg W. F. *The Philosophy of History*, trans. J. Sibree. Toronto: Dover, 1956.

Hegel, Georg W. F. *Science of Logic*, trans. A. V. Miller. Amherst: Humanity Books, 1969.

Hegel, Georg W. F. *Phenomenology of the Spirit*, trans. A. V. Miller. New York: Oxford University Press, 1977.

Hegel, Georg W. F. *Lectures on the History of Philosophy*, II vols., trans. E. S. Haldane and Frances H. Simson. Lincoln: University of Nebraska Press, 1995.

Hegel, Georg W. F. *Lectures on Fine Art*, II vols., trans. T. M. Knox. New York: Oxford University Press, 1998.

Holm, Isak Winkel. *Tanken i billedet*. Copenhagen: Gyldendal, 1998.

Howland, Jacob. *Kierkegaard and Socrates: A Study in Philosophy and Faith*. Cambridge: Cambridge University Press, 2006.

Hughes, Carl S. *Kierkegaard and the Staging of Desire: Performance and Rhetoric in a Theology of Eros*. New York: Fordham University Press, 2014.

Kant, Immanuel. *Critique of Judgment*, trans. Werner Pluhar. Indianapolis: Hackett, 1987.

Kant, Immanuel. *Groundwork of the Metaphysic of Morals*, trans. H. J. Paton. New York: Harper Perennial, 2009.

Khawaja, Noreen. *The Religion of Existence: Asceticism in Philosophy from Kierkegaard to Sartre*. Chicago: University of Chicago Press, 2016.

Kierkegaard, Søren. *Kierkegaard's Writings*, 26 vols., trans. Howard Hong et al. Princeton: Princeton University Press, 1978–2000.

Kierkegaard, Søren. *Søren Kierkegaards Papirer*. Copenhagen: Gyldendal, 1909–1948.

Kierkegaard, Søren. *Søren Kierkegaards Skrifter*, 28 vols. Copenhagen: Gads Forlag, 1997–2013.

Krishek, Sharon. *Kierkegaard on Faith and Love*. Cambridge: Cambridge University Press, 2009.

Lear, Jonathan. *A Case for Irony*. Cambridge: Harvard University Press, 2011.

Léon, Céline. "(A) Woman's Place within the Ethical," in Céline Léon and Sylvia Walsh (eds.), *Feminist Interpretations of Søren Kierkegaard*. University Park: Pennsylvania State University Press, 1997.

Lippitt, John. *Humour and Irony in Kierkegaard's Thought*. New York: St. Martin's Press, 2000.

Lippitt, John. "Getting the Story Straight: Kierkegaard, MacIntyre and Some Problems with Narrative," *Inquiry* 50, no. 1 (February 2007): 34–69.

Løgstrup, Knud Ejler. *The Ethical Demand*, trans. Hans Fink et al. Notre Dame: The University of Notre Dame Press, 1997.

Lübcke, Poul. "Kierkegaard, Aesthetics and the Crises of Metaphysics," in Birgit Bertung (ed.), *Kierkegaard: Poet of Existence*. Copenhagen: Reitzel, 1989.

Luther, Martin. *Martin Luther's Basic Theological Writings*, edited by T. F. Lull and W. R. Russell. Minneapolis: Fortress Press, 2012.

MacIntyre, Alastair. *After Virtue*. Notre Dame: University of Notre Dame Press, 2007.

Mackey, Louis. *Points of View: Readings of Kierkegaard*. Tallahassee: Florida State University Press, 1986.

Marino, Gordon. *Kierkegaard and the Present Age*. Milwaukee: Marquette University Press, 2001.

McDonald, William. "Love in Kierkegaard's *Symposia*," *Minerva* 7 (2003): 60–93.

Muench, Paul. "Socratic Irony, Plato's *Apology* and Kierkegaard's *On the Concept of Irony*," in Niels Jørgen Cappelørn, K. Brian Söderquist, and Hermann Deuser (eds.), *Kierkegaard Studies Yearbook*. Berlin: De Gruyter (2009). pp. 71–125.

Nietzsche, Friedrich. *The Birth of Tragedy*, in *Basic Writings*, trans. Walter Kaufmann. New York: Modern Library, 1992.

Olesen, Tonny Aagaard. "Kierkgaard's Socratic Hermeneutic in *The Concept of Irony*," in Robert Perkins (ed.), *International Kierkegaard Commentary: The Concept of Irony*. Macon: Mercer University Press, 2001.

Pattison, George. *Kierkegaard: The Aesthetic and the Religious*. Norwich: SCM Press, 1999.

Pattison, George. *Kierkegaard and the Quest for Unambiguous Life*. Oxford: Oxford University Press, 2013.

Plato. *Complete Works*, edited by John Cooper. Indianapolis: Hackett Publishing, 1997.

Rötscher, Heinrich Theodor. *Aristophanes und sein Zeitalter*. Berlin, 1827.

Rudd, Anthony. *Kierkegaard and the Limits of the Ethical*. Oxford: Clarendon, 1988.

Sartre, Jean-Paul. *Being and Nothingness*, trans. Hazel Barnes. New York: Washington Square Press, 1956.

Schleiermacher, Friedrich. "Über den Werth des Sokrates als Philosophen," in *Abhandlungen der Königlichen Academie der Wissenschaften*. Berlin, 1814–15.

Schopenhauer, Arthur. *The World as Will and Representation*, II vols., trans. E. F. J. Payne. New York: Dover, 1958.

Sibbern, Frederik Christian. *Om Poesie og Konst*, vol. I. Copenhagen, 1834.

Sophocles. *The Complete Plays*, trans. Sir Richard Claverhouse Jebb. New York: Bantam, 1982.

Steffens, Henrik. *Inledning til philosophiske Forelæsninger i København 1803.* Copenhagen: Gyldendal, 1905.

Stewart, Jon. *Kierkegaard's Relations to Hegel Reconsidered.* Cambridge: Cambridge University Press, 2003.

Walsh, Sylvia. *Kierkegaard: Thinking Christianly in an Existential Mode.* New York: Oxford University Press, 2009.

Walsh, Sylvia. "Ironic Love: An Amorist Interpretation of Socratic Eros," in Robert Perkins (ed.), *International Kierkegaard Commentary: The Concept of Irony,* Macon: Mercer University Press, 2001.

Williams, Bernard. *Shame and Necessity.* Berkeley: University of California Press, 2008.

Index

"A" (fictional author)
   communitarian   141
   cultural critic   141
   Judge Wilhelm knows privately   6
Abraham   64, 89
abstract(ion); *see also* irony (Socratic)
   Don Juan's seduction as exercise in   22
   objective thinker and   67, 152
   sensuousness is   24, 150
actuality/reality (*Virkelighed*)
   vs. abstraction   152
   Alcibiades wants to know   106
   irony dismisses, liberates from, separates ideality from   29, 35, 39, 43, 47, 67, 86
   the objective thinker forgets his own   163
   occasion for recollection   78–9
   as relation between concept and phenomenon   103–4, 124
   "why"-questions imply contingency of   56
Adam and Eve   19–20, 74, 133
Adorno, Theodor
   on inside-outside discord   89, 97
   on *Works of Love*   108, 111, 113, 125–6, 128, 132
aesthetic ideas ("images")   80, 83, 90, 92, 94–6, 102–3, 105, 128–9
aesthetic life, the
   disparities within   54–5
   oversimplified   7, 82
   Shadowgraphs live between ethical and   56
Alcibiades
   has been "bitten" by philosophy   20–1
   loses his values   139–41
   love for Socrates   45, 59–61, 68–9
   model for Kierkegaard   68, 100, 106
   philosophical approach   67, 100
   view of Socrates   26, 60, 94, 99–100

Antigone
   ancient   50–1, 54, 141
   Kierkegaard's identification with   68
   modern   48, 53–5, 141
anxiety   53–4, 77, 99
aporia   26, 29, 61–2, 67, 72, 140
Arendt, Hannah   84, 99
Aristophanes; *see* Socrates
art   92–3, 97–8, 102; *see also* music
asceticism; *see* faith

Baumgarten, Alexander   83, 102
beauty
   Kierkegaard suspicious of   112, 132
   as love's object   74–6
   as manifestation of intelligibility   80
   neighbor love disregards   109
   Plato's idea of   83
   as plenitude   76
   spiritual significance of natural   146–7

Catholicism   108, 113, 145
choosing oneself   54, 81, 140–1
Christ; *see* Jesus
communitarianism   141
compassion   52, 110, 128–9; *see also* sympathy as source of knowledge
concepts
   allow phenomena to realize and know themselves   29, 101
   as clear and distinct ideas   106
   do not by themselves yield knowledge   67
   must capture essences   101, 103
   not derived from experience   61, 67
   philosopher gives birth to   100
   Socrates' empty   29, 31, 73, 83, 96, 102

deception/deceptive
   aesthetic seduction by its
      nature   21, 25–6
   Alcibiades charges Socrates
      with   21, 46
   cause for reflective sorrow   57
   in love   19, 57–8, 62, 98–9
   maieutic method inherently   28
   and philosophy   21, 46, 61–2
   religious art is   144
   resignation secures against   65
deontology   108–10
depression   17, 49; *see also* melancholy
   Kierkegaard's   69
Descartes, René   39, 61–2
desire   19–25, 37–8, 46, 74
despair
   commanded love secures against   109
   vs. irony   100
   part of spiritual development   17, 139
   as sin   17, 110
   as symptom of cultural
      dissolution   142
   in unrequited love   59–69
dialogue, dialectic
   ethical significance in Plato   85–8
   negative trajectory of Socratic   30
   Platonic *vs.* Hegelian   84–5
   Socratic *vs.* Hegelian   30, 84
   Socratic *vs.* Platonic   82–3
Diotima; *see* Eros (divinity)
divination; *see* intuition, divination,
      premonition (*Ahnelse*)
Don Juan   22–8, 54, 57, 62, 77, 96
Donna Elvira   22–3, 25, 56–7, 60, 62
   Kierkegaard's identification with   68
doubt   39, 55, 57–8, 61–2, 124
   contrast with irony   67–8
doxastic voluntarism   36, 59
duty; *see* deontology; neighbor love

Eros (divinity)   37, 38, 46, 73–6
ethical
   commitments, becoming aware
      of one's   140
   primitives   140
   sensuousness is   25, 57
   significance of dialogue   86
   value depends on choosing   141
Evans, Stephen   121–3

faith
   as labor (asceticism)   113–14, 143
   as longing for death   123
fate
   Antigone's is reverberation of
      father's   51
   events in myth driven by   74
   if individual creates his own   50
   modernity doesn't believe in   49, 52
   Oedipus' life determined by   50
   resignation to, allows rest   52–3
   we cannot design our own   52
Faust; *see* Margaret, Gretchen (*Faust*)
feminine/femininity
   as abstract universal   22–4
   despair   62–4, 67, 69
   devotion   63, 69
   phenomena as   100–1
   relation to sensuality is ethical   25–6
   and substantiality   53
   virtues   68–9
feminist critique of Kierkegaard   69
Ferreira, Jamie   115–20, 125–6
friendship   135–7

Garff, Joakim   5–7, 142
God; *see also* theology
   acquaintance with   103–4
   goodness of   120–1
   "I am who I am"   103–4
   as love   73, 107
Good Samaritan   109–10, 116,
      118–19, 139
   Kierkegaard's reimagined   127–8
guilt; *see also* sin
   ambiguous, tragic   48, 50, 52–3
   Antigone shares in father's   53–4
   cannot be transferred of   51

Habbard, Christine   40–1
happiness, eternal *vs.* earthly   122–3
hearing
   apprehends subjective inwardness,
      spirit   90, 92–4
   philosopher's dearest sense   92
   yields mental image   92, 96
Hegel, Georg
   abstraction   24, 78
   art   93, 97–8
   beginning from nothing   40, 42

dialectic 30, 83–4, 101
ethics 43–5
freedom 43–4
history of philosophy 42–3
infinite judgments 33
Kierkegaard's critique of 22, 42, 97–8
myth 74
Plato 42, 74
Socrates 36, 41–4
Hegelians, Danish 97, 101
history; *see also* Don Juan; Hegel, Georg; myth; Socrates
personal 52, 80–2
and philosophy 92, 101
Holm, Isak Winkel 14, 78, 80
Howland, Jacob 38
Hughes, Carl 143–5

identity (personal)
as interpersonal 85–8, 135–7
as narrative 80–2
imagination 66, 71–2, 75–7, 95, 103, 105
immediacy—immediate; *see also* reflection; sensuousness
philosophy fights 139–41
and religion 141–5
value of 141
inside ("the inner"), knowledge of; *see* hearing; sympathy as source of knowledge
inside-outside discord
art transcends 24, 74
deception as 58
in irony 89–90
philosophy must transcend 92–102
in reflective sorrow 54–5
inspiration 80, 101, 147
intuition
divination, premonition (*Ahnelse*) 77, 105
view, mental representation (*Anskuelse*) 77, 94, 103
inward(ness)
"Eucharistic Discourses" usher congregants 144
irony drives Socrates 29
neighbor love as 111, 114, 129
Socrates' discourse points 94
sorrow as 95
as virtue for Socrates 107

voice conveys/hearing apprehends 58, 92
irony (Socratic)
as abstraction 29–39
as assertion of freedom 28, 36, 40–5
became for Plato "a negative power in the service of a positive idea" 87
and Cynicism 115
destroys established order 47–8
effect on students 39, 45–6, 60–1, 67
and evil 44–5, 155
as foundation of ethics 28, 38–45
and ignorance 29
is completely negative 39–42, 44
is not dissimulation 27
"is the beginning" 40
Kierkegaard's use of 14–16
in "Eucharistic Discourses" 143–4
in *Works of Love* 112–13, 115, 117, 123, 129, 131, 133, 135
and knowledge 36, 40, 67–8
is not theoretical 29
as solipsism 67
universal applicability of 27

Jesus
commands self-love 110
compared to Socrates 87
congregation as bride of 123
"everything is new in Christ" 16
known by his love 2
was both question and answer 125
was killed for his love 115, 132
Johannes the Seducer 78–81
vs. Antigone 55
like knight of infinite resignation 66
vs. Plato 86
straw-man 7
John 129–30
Judge Wilhelm
has not read A's papers 6–7
Kierkegaard protects aesthetes from 6–7, 17
oversimplifies aesthetic life 7
vs. Socrates 41
as virtue ethicist 80
Kant, Immanuel
aesthetics 101
ethics 108–10

Kierkegaard, Søren
　engagement to Regine　68–9
　friendship with Emil Bøsen　135–7
　Gilleleje trip　146
　hypocritical contempt for
　　lecturing　133–4
　looks down on his
　　readers　12–13, 135
　relation to father　16–17, 69
　use of pseudonyms and indirect
　　communication　4–7, 12
　view of women　68–9
　writings of:
　　The Concept of Irony (see
　　　individual themes)
　　Concluding Unscientific
　　　Postscript　4–5, 38, 41, 67, 78
　　Either/Or (see individual themes)
　　"Eucharistic Discourses"　143–4
　　Fear and Trembling　64–6,
　　　89, 97, 142
　　Philosophical Fragments　38–9
　　The Point of View of My Work as an
　　　Author　4–5, 13, 134
　　"The Present Age"　140
　　The Sickness unto
　　　Death　63–4, 105
　　Stages on Life's Way　66, 79
　　Works of Love　107–33
knight of faith and infinite
　　resignation　64–6
knowledge
　by acquaintance　20, 35, 76,
　　100, 104, 117
　of essences　78–9, 80, 92, 98, 101–6
　faith in possibility of　38–9, 49, 71
　of persons　99–100
Krishek, Sharon　64, 66

Lear, Jonathan　39
Lippitt, John　41, 81
Løgstrup, Knud Ejler　114–15, 121,
　　128
love; see also desire; marriage; neighbor
　　love; self-love; unrequited
　　(unhappy) love
　as communion　73, 86–8, 136
　filial　53–4
　has interest in beloved's freedom　63
　as longing　37–9, 45–6, 62, 86, 133
　significance of reciprocity in　63–6,
　　114, 133
Luther, Martin　116

Mackey, Louis　42–3
maieutic; see also dialogue, dialectic
　deceptive　27–8
　necessary for Plato　85
　not Kierkegaard's method　101
　Socrates explains　27–8
Margaret, Gretchen (Faust)　20, 56,
　　62, 64, 99
Marie Beaumarchais
　　(Clavigo)　20, 56–9, 62
marriage　79, 141
meaning
　in art　79, 97–8
　culture as world of　140–2, 145
　enchantment as experience of　147
　and explanation　74
　expressed as narrative　81
　philosopher must find
　　phenomenon's　101
　of Socrates' existence　90, 92, 94
melancholy　17, 77, 146; see also
　　depression
midwifery; see maieutic
morality; see also deontology; virtue ethics
　foundation of　38–45
music　23–6, 92–3
myth; see also Hegel, Georg
　explanatory power of　128–9
　Kierkegaard's relation to　14, 76–8,
　　80, 90, 106
　in Plato　72–5, 80

narrative　24, 71, 74–5, 81–2
negative freedom
　anxiety haunts　53
　as burden　52
　doesn't yield knowledge or ethics　40–1
　foundation of modernity　47, 51
　as the good　43–4
　irony as assertion of　27–8
　philosopher must relinquish　67
　Socrates' disciples don't enjoy　45
negativity; see irony (Socratic)
neighbor love
　brings happiness　122–3
　callous, detached　114–15

channels God's love   107, 120
characterized only
  negatively   110–11, 113
as compassion   110, 128
as continual striving   113
as ethics of duty   108–10, 125
as ethics of virtue   128, 130, 135
goodness of   120–3
helps neighbor love God   118
and inclination   109, 111, 131, 133
as inwardness   111, 113–14
is not rewarded   115, 132
is upbuilding   126–8
"known by its fruits"   108,
  111, 113, 128
as "the law's fullness"   124
lies hidden   114
modeled on self-love   110, 116–17
need not be effective   108, 111, 113
as negative labor   112
"the only thing worth living
  for"   120, 123, 130
paternalistic   117–18
vs. "poetic" love   109, 111, 129–31
positive examples of   126–9
as practicing dying   123
as "seeing"   125–6
as self-actualization   121–2
as self-denial   112–13
Nietzsche, Friedrich   49–50, 132

Oedipus   49–50

Pattison, George   7, 66, 77–8
Paul   124, 136
pedagogy
  aesthetics in   74–5, 126, 128
  ethical   128
  as function of Platonic myths   74
  Kierkegaard's   12–17, 77
  Socratic   41
Pelagianism   50
Philoctetes   20, 55–7
philosophy; see also knowledge; reflection
  as art, aesthetic task   37, 98, 102,
    140
  as "father confessor"   92
  lays assumptions bare   140
  not a science   106
  as procreative   101

speculative   43, 45, 74, 77–8,
  83, 86–7, 105
Plato; see also Hegel, Georg; myth;
  recollection; Socrates
aesthetic thinker   75
artistic creativity found a task in
  philosophy   75
beauty at center of philosophy of   76
Forms   75–6, 83, 90
and Kierkegaard's
  aesthetes   78, 80, 86
love for Socrates   85–8
not a dialectical thinker   83–4
philosophy driven by
  personal love   86
projecting himself onto
  Socrates   72–3
wanted to owe everything to
  Socrates   87
writings of:
  Apology   38, 48, 91
  Cratylus   37
  Meno   61, 67, 72–3
  Phaedo   34–6, 39, 123
  Protagoras   32–4, 39, 44
  Republic   31–2, 47, 57, 85
  Symposium   20–1, 26, 37–9,
    60–1, 73–6, 83, 94, 99–100,
    112–13, 139
  Theaetetus   27
positive freedom
  culture affords   141–2
  enjoyed when one says what
    one means   28
  traded for negative freedom in
    modernity   142
premonition; see divination, premonition
  (Ahnelse); intuition
Protestantism
  "constant conversion" (Pietism)   113
  question of Kierkegaard's conformity
    to   116, 119
  on transubstantiation   144–5

recollection
  in aesthetic life   66, 78–82
  as Kierkegaard's philosophical
    method   90–5
  Plato's idea of   35–6, 72–3
  vs. repetition   81

Socrates' idea of 35–6
sympathy as 99
reflection
   aims at truth, sufficient reason 55–6
   and anxiety 53–4
   cannot yield judgment 59
   vs. contemplative pleasure 72
   destroys meaning 140, 145
   destroys myth 75
   destroys religious rituals 144–5
   destroys value 139–42
   Don Juan incapable of 25
   estranges from world 56
   is endless 56, 58
   key in modern tragedy 53
   leads to individualism 54, 142
   modern Antigone caught between passion and 53
   and Modernity 47, 142
   no return from 56, 141–2
   prompted by deception 57
   prompted by misfortune 55–6
   prompts regret 52
   as recollection of ideals 39, 47–8
   staves off action 59, 140
   turns sorrow into pain 53
   would free Antigone from guilt if infinite 53
reflective aesthete 79, 82
regret 52, 54, 56
religion; *see also* faith; theology
   ceremonies and aesthetics in 143–5
repentance
   Antigone's regret is not 54
   as appropriating one's history 81–2
repetition 81
resignation 65–6
Romantic irony 71, 78
Romanticism 71, 76–8, 100

Sartre, Jean-Paul 63, 65
self-love 110–11, 116–17, 130–1
   as metaphor for identity and teleology 32, 75, 88, 98, 102–3
sense-perception
   deceptive 26, 34, 57–8, 92
   Plato's epistemology modeled on 75
sensuousness
   is abstract 24
   is amoral 25
   belongs in ethical realm for women 25–6, 57
   is contagious 25
   is deceptive 26
   is faithless 23
   music expresses 24
Shadowgraphs; *see also* Donna Elvira; Margaret, Gretchen (*Faust*); Marie Beaumarchais (*Clavigo*)
   cannot be portrayed in painting 56, 95
   can only be represented indirectly 95
   study themselves 21
Sibbern, Frederik 102
sight (metaphorical)
   as apprehension of "the neighbor" 125–6
   disregarded by father confessor/philosopher 92
   gives access to Platonic Forms 75
   perceives only "the outer" 92
   truth is apprehended by a higher form of 102
sin 17, 19, 50, 77, 110
skepticism; *see* doubt
Socrates; *see also* irony (Socratic)
   Aristophanes' 72
   as historical person vs. spirit 27, 90–6, 100
   ignorant 8–9, 28–9, 45
   Johannes Climacus' 38, 41, 78
   vs. Judge Wilhelm 41
   vs. Plato 31, 35, 42, 72–5, 82–3, 105
   Plato's 71, 86–8, 91
   seducer 26, 46
   Xenophon's 72, 94, 119
solipsism 66–7, 80, 99
sorrow 17, 67, 78
   reflective 19–21, 52–8, 60, 95, 99
speculation; *see* philosophy
Steffens, Henrik 76–7
subjectivity 28, 44, 56, 107
substantiality 47–8, 50–3
Symparanekromenoi 20–1, 95, 123
sympathy as source of knowledge 20–1, 99

tautology
   as "actuality" of a concept 103
   is both highest and lowest form of thought 33

The Concept of Irony offers 102
  as knowledge of essences 102
  "positive" *vs.* "negative" 102–4
  Socrates' unity of virtue
    thesis is 32–3
  Socratic question and
    answer form a 36
theology
  negative 16, 111, 120–1
  vs. religious practice 145
tradition 47, 140–3
tragedy 47–56
  modern 52–4
  vs. morality 49
  vs. problem of evil 55–6
  Socrates destroyed ancient 47–51

unrequited (unhappy) love 25, 56–8, 60, 62–4

philosophy as 46
upbuilding
  beauty as 147
  discourses, as genre of writing 130
  doctrine of recollection as 35
  love as 126–8
  tautology as 33

Victor Eremita 89, 91–3, 95
virtue
  as knowledge 13, 33–7, 49
  unity of 32, 102, 104
  unteachable 12, 36
virtue ethics 108, 128, 130, 140–1

women; *see* feminine/femininity; Kierkegaard, Søren

Xenophon; *see* Socrates

www.ingramcontent.com/pod-product-compliance
Lightning Source LLC
Chambersburg PA
CBHW070541300426
44111CB00013B/2196